Funded by
MISSION COLLEGE
Carl D. Perkins Vocational and Technical Education Act Grant

"What a gem! Enough that it's a thorough, practical manual for optimizing relationships and work environments, based on new and solid research in human behavior—but it's **a surprising, witty, well-written, and wonderfully engaging read.** I had countless 'aha!'s about how we can effectively get things done. Bravo, Ron Friedman."

—David Allen, author of *Getting Things Done*

"**A contemporary classic.** Dr. Friedman's new book offers a highly original guide to creating exceptional workplaces based on cross-field academic research and superb examples from real companies. You won't find these insights elsewhere. From office design to employee motivation to conflict resolution, *The Best Place to Work* is the best book to have on your shelf *now.*"

—Marshall Goldsmith, author of
What Got You Here Won't Get You There

"We've lost our way. In this **stunning** book, Ron Friedman helps us get back on track, exploring not only what work is for, but how we can leap forward and become more human, more alive and more effective."

—Seth Godin, author of *The Icarus Deception*

"In *The Best Place to Work*, Ron Friedman examines the factors that take a company from ordinary to extraordinary. The stories in this book—which range from cruise ship casinos to hostage negotiations—are fascinating in their own right, but they also pack **powerful, research-based lessons for better leadership in the workplace.** Friedman's findings are often **surprisingly counterintuitive, yet always convincing.**"

—Daniel H. Pink, author of *Drive* and *To Sell Is Human*

continued . . .

"*The Best Place to Work* is an engaging journey through the latest science of improving the quality of life in organizations. Psychologist Ron Friedman examines how to unleash creativity, boost motivation, and offer rewards and recognition that bring people together rather than driving them apart." —Adam Grant, Wharton professor and author of *Give and Take*

"I love this book! It's smart, fun to read, interesting, clear, and practical. We're all owners of our workplaces, and this is our owner's manual. Following Ron's advice is easy and will pay huge dividends for you and the people with whom you work." —Peter Bregman, author of *18 Minutes*

"An eye-opening, highly readable, and practical guide to improving the way we work. No matter what you do for a living, this book will change the way you see your workplace." —Professor Richard Wiseman, author of *59 Seconds*

"In *The Best Place to Work*, Ron Friedman brings together decades of psychological research into a package that offers organizations concrete advice to improve the well-being of workers and the quality of work. Much of the advice is eye-opening. I'm sure the results of taking the advice will be too." —Barry Schwartz, author of *The Paradox of Choice* and *Practical Wisdom*

"This fascinating book shows how to create workspaces that foster creativity, collaboration, and high productivity. It's a joy to read, filled with practical advice for leaders, engaging real-world stories, and grounded in scientific research." —Keith Sawyer, Morgan Distinguished Professor in Educational Innovations (UNC–Chapel Hill) and author of *Zig Zag*

"Friedman's book fills you with optimism about the future of work. If enough managers pay attention to the science he is promoting, then a lot of people are going to roll out of bed on Mondays truly eager to get to the other side of their commutes." —David McRaney, author of *You Are Not So Smart*

"When it comes to motivation and engagement, the problem is rarely that the work itself is terrible—it's that the way we are working is. In *The Best Place to Work*, Ron Friedman **tells you everything—and I mean everything—you need to know to bring out the best in your employees.** This powerful (and entertaining!) book is a guide to understanding how subtle, often unconscious influences in the workplace affect happiness, creativity, productivity and loyalty—and how you can use these insights to create real and lasting impact, on your team and in your organization. Everyone should be reading this book."

—Heidi Grant Halvorson, PhD, associate director of Columbia Business School's Motivation Science *Center* and author of 9 *Things Successful People Do Differently*

"If you want to attract and keep exceptional employees, your culture is the key. In this **entertaining** book, Ron Friedman **offers a practical game plan** for building a workplace that thrives."

—Todd Henry, author of *Die Empty*

"There's an astonishing gap between what science knows about human behavior and what companies think they know. In this **fascinating** book, Ron Friedman outlines the science behind thriving at work and offers practical advice for managers who are committed to making a real difference in the workplace." —David Burkus, author of *The Myths of Creativity*

"What a great relief to read a business book that is not just about how to be a better leader but about what makes work more fun, exciting and productive. By focusing on what managers at all levels of an organization can do, this book provides a rich inventory of practical, research-based ideas for making work engaging. A **most valuable and entertaining read full of powerful insights** that should be read by every manager and employee."

—Edgar H. Schein, professor emeritus at MIT Sloan School of Management, author of *Organizational Culture and Leadership,* and coauthor, with John Van Maanen, of *Career Anchors*

continued . . .

"Ron Friedman's *Best Place to Work* presents the latest scientific findings in a highly entertaining but rigorous way. **An excellent example of great science writing for practical application in the real world.** If you want to make the workplace better, this book is the best place to start."

—Dean Keith Simonton, PhD, distinguished professor of psychology, University of California, Davis

"*The Best Place to Work* **flows seamlessly** and is filled with practical, accessible ways of seeing not only oneself in depth, but also the complex mosaics of workplace environments with pitfalls and opportunities galore. The principles that undergird a fulfilling and healthy life, with room for authentic, creative play, are infused into practical, real-life vignettes throughout its pages. Bringing the science of human innovativeness and productivity into focus, and combining these science-based truths with a life well lived, are what can be gleaned from its chapters."

—Stuart Brown, MD, author of *Play* and founder and president of the National Institute for Play

"Ron Friedman **bridges the gap between cutting-edge science and the reality of the modern workplace in a way that is clear, sensible, and effective.** Friedman does more than offer recommendations— he provides empirically supported tools for turning most any office into a lively, engaging workplace. Written in a user-friendly style that will grab your attention, this book is **a must-read** for anyone who has wondered why workplaces can't be successful and welcoming at the same time."

—Harry Reis, PhD, University of Rochester professor of psychology, past president of the Society for Personality and Social Psychology, and winner of the International Association for Relationship Research's Distinguished Career award

THE
BEST PLACE
TO WORK

The Art and Science of
Creating an Extraordinary Workplace

Ron Friedman, PhD

A PERIGEE BOOK

A PERIGEE BOOK
Published by the Penguin Group
Penguin Group (USA) LLC
375 Hudson Street, New York, New York 10014

USA • Canada • UK • Ireland • Australia • New Zealand • India • South Africa • China

penguin.com

A Penguin Random House Company

THE BEST PLACE TO WORK

ISBN: 978-0-399-16559-7

An application to catalog this book has been submitted to the Library of Congress.

First edition: December 2014

PRINTED IN THE UNITED STATES OF AMERICA

10   9   8   7   6   5

Text design by Kristin del Rosario

Most Perigee books are available at special quantity discounts for bulk purchases
for sales promotions, premiums, fund-raising, or educational use.
Special books, or book excerpts, can also be created to fit specific needs.
For details, write: Special.Markets@us.penguingroup.com.

For my grandfather,
who taught me that in the end
the only thing worth being remembered for
is kindness

CONTENTS

A Tale of Two Menus

Near the heart of Silicon Valley, just a few miles south of the San Francisco Bay, sits an enchanting Indian restaurant called Baadal. It is run by Irfan Dama, an animated chef of forty-one, who designs three-course meals that alternate daily. Baadal is his first restaurant. Yet by all accounts, it is a colossal success. Within just days of opening, reservations were nearly impossible to secure.

Unlike more traditional Indian restaurants, Chef Dama's menus aim to demystify meals that often intimidate novice diners, by listing every ingredient included in a dish. The restaurant's decor also provides a range of dining experiences, from quiet booths surrounded by sheer curtains to open-space tables to a rousing Bollywood-themed room intended for group celebrations.

There's one other thing that's different about Irfan Dama's restaurant: It doesn't charge customers a penny. In fact, anyone who's had the good fortune of sampling Baadal's world-class cuisine has done so for free.

Baadal is owned by Google. It is one of the thirty gourmet restaurants that cater to employees at the company's Mountain View headquarters, known as the Googleplex.

At Google, eating is serious business. Every meal brings with it the opportunity to try over two hundred artisan-crafted dishes. Among the more recent offerings: roast quail, steak tartare, lobster bisque, black cod with parsley pesto and bread crumbs, and porcini-encrusted grass-fed beef. For lighter eaters, there is a salad bar, a noodle bar, a cheese and charcuterie bar, crudité platters, and seasonal sous vide vegetables. Between meals, Googlers are invited to visit one of the many microkitchens sprinkled throughout the campus, each open 24/7 and stocking organic fruit, yogurts, candy, nuts, and drinks. The goal at Google is for employees to be within three minutes of a food source at all times.

The vast and complementary food selection is one reason Google was ranked by *Fortune* magazine as the world's best place to work. But as far as Googleplex amenities go, it's only the tip of the iceberg.

Employees at the company are treated to massages, haircuts, eyebrow-shaping services, foreign language courses, and doctor visits, all on site and free of charge. They have access to three wellness centers, a bowling alley, basketball courts, a roller-hockey rink, ping-pong tables, arcade games, foosball tables, a rock-climbing wall, a putting green, and volleyball courts complete with actual sand. There's an indoor tree house, manicured gardens, apiaries for recreational beekeeping, a replica of Richard Branson's private spaceship, and the life-size skeleton of a *Tyrannosaurus rex*. Not to be forgotten: the heated toilet seats.

Google is far from the only organization investing heavily in the comfort of its employees. SAS, a business-analytics software company that earned more than $3 billion in 2012, provides its employees with access to tennis courts, saunas, a billiards hall, heated swimming pools, and work-life counseling, which includes confidential professional advice on financial planning, elder care, and family issues. At Facebook, employees can ride company-provided bicycles to the campus barber, drop off their dry cleaning, grab a latte, raid the free candy shop, and, conveniently, visit the on-site dentist.

And it's not just companies in high tech. Wegmans, a northeastern U.S. grocery chain, has consistently appeared near the top of *Fortune* magazine's list of 100 Best Companies to Work For over the past fifteen years. During that same time period, annual sales have nearly tripled. While many retail operations have tried growing earnings by reducing labor costs, Wegmans has steered in the opposite direction, offering its supermarket employees (many of whom are still in high school and simply glad to have a job) wellness programs, pretax spending accounts, 401(k) plans, life insurance, and education scholarships.

What's the rationale behind all this lavish spending? For many companies on *Fortune*'s list, the basic calculus is simple: *Happy employees mean bigger profits.*

The more invested and enthusiastic people are about their work, the more successful their organization is on a variety of metrics. Studies indicate that happy employees are more productive, more creative, and provide better client service. They're less likely to quit or call in sick. What's more, they act as brand ambassadors outside the office, spreading positive impressions of their company and attracting star performers to their team.

The bottom line for many of the world's most profitable organizations is this: Investing in workplace happiness doesn't cost their company money—it ensures they stay on top.

It's a perspective backed by some compelling data. Research conducted by the Great Place to Work Institute—the organization that compiles an annual list of leading workplaces in conjunction with *Fortune* magazine—reveals an eye-opening statistic: The stocks of companies on the Best Companies to Work For list outperform the market as a whole by a stunning factor of *2 to 1.*

Investors are catching on. Around the time the Googleplex opened its doors in 2004, San Francisco–based Parnassus Investments launched a mutual fund comprised exclusively of companies with outstanding workplaces, like the ones on *Fortune*'s list. Since the fund's inception, it's recorded a 9.63 percent annualized return. In comparison, the overall S&P index during that same time period was a considerably more modest 5.58 percent.

The evidence is clear: Creating an extraordinary workplace can pay significant dividends.

So how do you do it?

Google, SAS, Facebook, and Wegmans certainly set a high bar. But what if you don't have the budget of a multinational corporation? What if you're struggling to find room for a bigger copier, let alone the space for an on-site wellness center? What if the closest thing your office has to a gourmet restaurant is the vending machine at the end of the hall?

What then?

This book happened by accident.

It came about after I left academics, where I'd spent years studying human motivation in the lab and teaching psychology at colleges and universities. Shortly after earning a doctorate in social psychology and settling into a teaching position, I found myself restless.

I'd planned on spending my life as a college professor. But the moment I stepped into the role, I began itching for a new challenge. I wanted to do something practical. Something applied. And so I entered the business world, where I was hired to measure public opinion as a pollster.

Not long after I arrived, I noticed something unexpected. As a social psychologist specializing in human motivation, I'd read countless studies on the factors that promote productivity, creativity, and engagement. Yet to my surprise, very few of these findings were being put to use. Much of what I observed—from the way organizations hire to the way leaders motivate to the layout and design of most office spaces—appeared blind to a wealth of research on how we can build a better workplace.

Over the past decade, advances in brain imaging, data-gathering methods, and behavioral science experiments have produced powerful insights into the conditions that help us work more effectively. We now know how to build a room that boosts creativity, how to turn workplace colleagues into close friends, and how to make any job more meaningful. We know that decorating your office can make you more productive, that going for a walk can lead to better decisions, and that embracing failure can actually help you succeed.

Yet most of these findings have remained trapped in library stacks, collecting dust on university shelves.

In some ways, the knowledge gap between the worlds of business and psychology makes complete sense. Until recently, organizations have had limited need for the advice of psychologists. The traditional workplace, which evolved from the days of the factory floor, had been operating adequately.

But then something momentous happened: The economy shifted. And suddenly the workplace model we'd relied on for generations was no longer as effective.

Back in the days of the industrial economy, building a successful workplace meant finding efficiencies through eliminating errors, standardizing performance, and squeezing more out of workers. How employees *felt* while doing their job was of secondary interest, because it had limited impact on their performance. The main thing was that the work got done.

Today things are different. Our work is infinitely more complex. We rarely need employees to simply do routine, repetitive tasks—we also need them to collaborate, plan, and innovate. Building a thriving organization in the current economy demands a great deal more than efficiency. It requires an environment that harnesses intelligence, creativity, and interpersonal skill.

Businesses today need psychologists. In a world where productivity hinges on the quality of an employee's *thinking*, psychological factors are no longer secondary. They're at the very core of what determines success.

Which brings me back to how I unintentionally came upon the idea for this book: After academia I assumed my writing days were over. But as I experienced the business world firsthand, both in the role of employee and manager, and as I interacted with hundreds of clients, getting an unvarnished view of how their organizations operate, one theme kept resurfacing again and again: *There is a massive divide between the latest science and the modern workplace.*

This book is an attempt to bridge that gap.

In the chapters that follow, I am going to tell you about revolutionary findings in the fields of motivation, creativity, behavioral economics, neuroscience, and management, and show you how you can use them to create a better workplace. Each chapter will address a different aspect of the workplace, offering illuminating and often counterintuitive best practices for making you and your company more effective.

You'll learn how to motivate employees without relying on bonuses, how to choose between job applicants, and how to elevate pride in your organization. You'll discover how to reach better spending decisions, how to defuse workplace disagreements, and how to make yourself more persuasive.

Along the way, we'll meet some extraordinary individuals and hear their fascinating stories, each providing a unique lens for understanding workplace excellence. I'm going to take you behind the scenes of a hostage negotiation and demonstrate how verbal techniques used by the FBI can make you a better leader. I'll introduce you to the man who created the cubicle and explain why his vision for the modern workplace makes perfect sense. I'll show you what every organization can learn from the structure of video games, the design of a Las Vegas casino, and the hiring practices of a symphony orchestra.

We'll cover lots of ground in a short time frame. The work you're about to read fuses thousands of scientific studies in a way that I hope you'll find engaging and relatively jargon-free. I have attempted to write the sort of book I'd want to read on a business trip. For me that means three things: fast-paced, entertaining, and actionable.

I designed this book with two audiences in mind. The first and perhaps most obvious are managers, owners, and CEOs—those with the ability to apply many of the research recommendations and immediately transform their team's workplace experience.

But this book is not merely a playbook for those at the top of the corporate ladder. It is also written for emerging leaders who want data-driven insights for improving their own productivity and lifting their team's performance. Regardless of where you sit on your company's org chart, if you are interested in reaching smarter workplace decisions, having better colleague relationships, and making yourself indispensable to your company, this book can help.

There are many business books that provide broad principles and few practical recommendations. This is not one of them. Throughout every chapter, you will find specific, evidence-based changes you can apply at your workplace, regardless of your industry. In addition, at the conclusion of each chapter, you will find action items that build upon the findings, offering three more applications geared toward managers and emerging leaders, respectively.

An unavoidable downside of writing about workplaces *in general* and offering lots of specific recommendations is that not all of them will be applicable to everyone. Every organization is different. What works for Google may not be ideal for Wegmans, and vice versa. In that vein, some of the suggestions in this book may be perfect for your company, while others may appear less relevant. My intention here is not to offer a one-size-fits-all approach for building a great workplace (because that would be impossible) but to provide you with a menu of proven ingredients, so that you can choose what feels right within the context of your organization.

By the time you reach the conclusion of this book, I hope to have convinced you of a simple fact: that psychological insight can transform any organization into a great workplace.

The secret to happy workplaces isn't spending more money. It's about creating the conditions that allow employees to do their best work.

And how exactly do you do that? Turn the page. The answers, I believe, are here.

PART ONE

Designing an Extraordinary Workplace Experience

ONE

Success Is Overrated

Why Great Workplaces Reward Failure

Silas Johnson never expected to become famous.

At twenty-nine, he was simply grateful to be playing baseball. Just a few years earlier, he'd been slaving away on the family farm, working alongside his dad from the moment the sun hit his lids until the muscles in his back ached. On a good week he and his dad might find a few minutes to escape for a quick game of catch near the old windmill. His days were as predictable as they were long.

That all changed the morning Si spotted an ad in the Ottawa *Republican-Times*. The Rock Island Islanders were holding open tryouts.

Why not? he thought. It was worth a shot.

When he got there, he found himself competing with eighty-one other men—enough to fill the entire roster several times over. Si knew he was a long shot. Yet, miraculously, he was the only player offered a permanent spot.

Now, as a starting pitcher for the Cincinnati Reds, he would tell anyone who would listen: He was just relieved to have found an easier way of earning *twenty dollars a month*.

The year was 1935. The date: May 26. Si Johnson was preparing to take the mound at Crosley Field. And though he had no way of knowing it, he was about to have the single most memorable game of his professional career.

It started out much like any other day at the ballpark. Johnson put on his uniform, tied his cleats, and adjusted his cap, just as he did whenever it was his turn to pitch. As he stepped onto the field, there were over 24,000 in attendance, an unusually large crowd by Cincinnati standards. Johnson could hear them roaring, loud even before he'd thrown his first pitch.

He knew they weren't there to see him, or his team. They had come to watch a player on the opposing side. A left fielder. The one standing in the on-deck circle, swinging away, preparing for his turn, third in the lineup.

It didn't take Johnson long to get to him. By the time the left fielder stepped up to the plate, the Cincinnati fans were chanting his name. It wasn't anything out of the ordinary. By now he was used to being the main attraction wherever he played.

But on that Sunday, the cheering didn't last very long. Not once Johnson started pitching.

Truth be told, Johnson was far from an elite athlete. Over the course of his career, he collected far more losses than wins and averaged a paltry three strikeouts per outing. In today's highlight reel–driven game, it's hard to even see him as a starting pitcher.

So when Johnson struck out the renowned left fielder in that first inning, it raised more than a few eyebrows. And when he did it again a few innings later, and then a third time that very same game, it made him something of a celebrity. So much so, in fact, that he was still receiving fifty letters a week requesting his autograph the year he died, nearly half a century later.

Johnson was idolized for his performance that afternoon. But to those in the stands, the game was notable for a different reason. They'd witnessed the left fielder enter the record books. He'd achieved the ultimate mark of failure—the last distinction any hitter would ever want associated with his name: *He had struck out more times than anyone in baseball history.*

And the remarkable thing was this: No one cared. In fact, hardly anyone even noticed. It's because the strikeout mark wasn't the only record the left fielder had broken that week. Less than twenty-four hours earlier, he'd belted his 714th home run, setting an all-time high and sealing his fate as a Hall of Famer.

Failure or not, he was a living legend. And his name was Babe Ruth.

THE MERITS OF BEING REJECTED BY 129 WOMEN

Just three years earlier, on a quiet bench in the New York Botanical Garden in the Bronx, a shy but determined young man was battling his own record-setting futility.

Later in life he would develop a groundbreaking new method of therapy, publish more than twelve hundred articles and eighty books, and receive more votes than Sigmund Freud in the category of history's most influential psychotherapist. But at this moment, Albert Ellis was just a nineteen-year-old boy. A nineteen-year-old boy in search of a date.

There was one small hitch: He was terrified of women.

For as long as Ellis could remember, he had been uneasy around members of the opposite sex. In part, he blamed his childhood. He had grown up a sickly boy, the victim of kidney disease and tonsillitis. Much of his youth was spent inside hospitals, where he endured countless treatments, often for months at a time. He had been isolated from other kids his age, which would have been hard enough. Except his parents rarely visited. His father was regularly away on business and his mother had never been one to exhibit affection.

Intimacy was simply not an experience familiar to Albert Ellis.

And as he entered his teens, Ellis found himself longing for a connection—with a girl. He wanted so badly to speak to one, and yet he felt paralyzed at the thought of actually following though.

To deal with his phobia, he kept to himself. Ellis read voraciously and rarely spoke. On days when he was feeling adventurous, he would take long walks in the park by his home, where from afar he might secretly steal a glance at a passing girl.

"I would sit on a bench on the Bronx River Parkway," Ellis recalled, "a few feet from a seemingly suitable woman seated on another bench. I would look at her and often she would look back at me, and I could sense that some of these women were interested. But no matter how much I told myself that the time was right to approach, I soon copped out and walked away, cursing myself for my abysmal cowardice."

For a time the situation seemed hopeless. Ellis desperately longed for a relationship. And yet his mind was preventing him from taking a risk. "I heard and saw nothing but 'evil' and 'horrible' rejection, so I kept my big mouth shut."

And then one day he came up with a plan.

The month was July. There were exactly thirty days left before Ellis was due back at college, the perfect length of time for a brief experiment. For the remainder of the month, Ellis decided, he would continue visiting the botanical garden every day. But this time there would be no more long-distance flirting or clumsy escapes. Instead, he would casually seat himself next to every woman who happened to be visiting the park alone. And then, within one minute or less, he would force himself to speak.

What did Ellis hope to gain from this masochistic endeavor? Back then he wasn't entirely sure. But he did have a theory.

By avoiding failure at all costs he was impeding his growth. Ironically, it was his overwhelming fear of being rejected that was keeping him stuck in place. The only way to overcome his anxiety and achieve his goal, he reasoned, was to face his fears head on.

How? By giving himself permission to fail.

And fail he did. Repeatedly.

Over the course of the next several weeks, Ellis proceeded to awkwardly, nervously, haplessly solicit every solitary woman he encountered at the New York Botanical Garden. All told, he approached 130 women. Thirty fled the moment they saw him coming, before he could even open his mouth. Of the remaining 100, his results were only slightly better. A full 99 respectfully declined his request for a date.

As for the one woman who agreed to go out with young Albert Ellis? Sadly, she never showed up.

On the surface, Ellis's experiment would appear to be an unmitigated disaster. Except there's more to the story than what happened that month. As Ellis soon discovered, that July at the botanical garden completely transformed his life.

"I found, empirically, that nothing terrible happened," he later wrote. "No one vomited and ran away. No one called a cop. In fact, I had one hundred pleasant conversations, and began to get quite good at talking to strange women in strange places."

That's putting it mildly. To say Albert Ellis got "quite good" at speaking with women is a little like saying Babe Ruth was "quite good" at swinging a bat.

The next time Ellis performed his park bench experiment (and yes, he voluntarily approached *another* hundred women) he succeeded at lining up three dates—an impressive achievement for a man who had previously dreaded the thought of approaching the opposite sex. He was well on his way to becoming, as he would later term himself, "one of the best picker-uppers of women in the United States."

It's hardly an exaggeration. Ellis proceeded to marry three women, spent over a decade living with a fourth, and authored numerous bestselling relationship guides, with titles that include *The Art and Science of Love, Sex and the Single Man*, and somewhat ambitiously, *The Encyclopedia of Sexual Behavior.*

What Ellis came to realize in the process of conquering his fear is an important truth about the mathematics of risk-taking: *When your attempt rate is high, each individual failure becomes a lot less significant.*

Donald Trump doesn't enter a room with supermodel Melania Trump on his arm, followed by a long line of heckling women who have rejected his overtures. We see only Melania Trump. Few people know or care about your missteps—romantic or otherwise. Ultimately, it's your successes that stand out.

For Ellis, it no longer mattered that he was being rejected by a majority of women. He was approaching so many of them that by the end of each month his date count was still higher than most men. What's more, he was growing more comfortable speaking with women by the day and refining his approach with every conversation.

In short, he was improving.

There's an insight here with implications that extend far beyond the world of dating. Accepting failure doesn't just make risk-taking easier. In a surprising number of instances, it's the only reliable path to success.

THE DEFINING FEATURE OF RENOWNED ARTISTS, STAR ATHLETES, AND SUCCESSFUL ORGANIZATIONS

Dean Keith Simonton is a social psychologist with a fascinating specialty.

While most researchers in the field are content dissecting the life of the average undergraduate, Simonton investigates a different population. Among his subjects are the likes of William Shakespeare, Ludwig van Beethoven, and Leonardo da Vinci.

Simonton studies genius. Creative genius, more specifically, asking questions like: *Where does it come from? How does it develop? What can we do to foster it in our own lives?*

By examining the lives of highly creative individuals, including their backgrounds, educational upbringings, and productivity,

Simonton is able to offer a number of interesting observations on the ways successful artists differ from others in their fields.

So what's different about geniuses?

For one thing, Simonton argues, creative geniuses tend to hold a **broader array of interests** than their average contemporary. While working to find a solution in one domain, they'll dabble in unrelated fields, exploring the worlds of art, music, and literature. It might look as if they are slacking off, but it's often these extraneous experiences that fuel their ability to find unexpected connections.

Simonton also believes that, compared to others in their fields, creative geniuses receive only a **moderate level of education**. Too little formal study and they lack enough knowledge to make a valuable contribution. Too many years in the classroom and their thinking becomes tethered to the status quo.

But perhaps the most interesting finding in Simonton's research is his observation that creative geniuses don't simply offer more *creative* solutions. They **offer more solutions**, period.

What do Shakespeare, Dickens, Tolstoy, Picasso, Monet, Bach, Mozart, Wagner, Schubert, Brahms, and Dostoyevsky all have in common? They all produced far more than their contemporaries.

Importantly, not every one of their creations was a masterpiece. Today, in fact, they are remembered for a mere fraction of their complete body of work. Creative geniuses simply do not generate masterpieces on a regular basis. Yet the *quality* that distinguishes them would be impossible without the *quantity* of attempts.

Simonton likens the success of creative ideas to a genetic pool. If you're reading the words on this page, you're obviously alive and well, thanks to the genes that program your body. But will your genes still be around a century from now? That depends on a variety of factors, among them the number of children you produce. The more offspring you introduce into the world, the greater the chances of your genes being passed on to succeeding generations.

In Simonton's view, a similar principle applies to creative ideas. The more solutions you generate, the more likely you are to stumble upon a winning combination that lives on, because it is considered both novel and useful.

It's worth noting that quantity alone, of course, is never enough. If I were to quit my job and dedicate the rest of my life to painting landscapes, the likelihood of my work being inducted into the Metropolitan Museum of Art would still be incredibly slim. Yet "slim" is a vast improvement over my current odds. Because in the absence of quantity, my chances are nil.

The interesting implication of Simonton's research is this: Creative geniuses don't just attempt more solutions—they also miss quite often.

We're often told that Thomas Edison failed hundreds of times before successfully inventing the lightbulb. But not all of Edison's failures were salvaged by a happy ending. Edison also invested nearly two decades (*decades!*) trying to find ways of extracting iron from sand, as a means of reducing the cost of the metal. He ultimately abandoned the effort and reluctantly sold his company, losing a fortune in the process.

Edison is hardly the only famous inventor to have failed on a colossal scale. Before the iPhone and iPad revolutionized the world of personal computing, Steve Jobs accrued a remarkably long list of failures that includes the Apple I, the Apple II, the Lisa, the Newton personal digital assistant, and NeXT hardware.

A similar observation can be made for star athletes. When Babe Ruth set the record for most career home runs *and* most career strikeouts in a single week, he knew the two measures were inextricably linked. "If I just tried for them dinky singles," Ruth told reporters, "I could've batted around .600."

Ruth's hold on the career strikeout mark lasted nearly three decades before his record finally fell. And who eventually claimed the embarrassing distinction? For a while it was sixteen-time All-Star

Mickey Mantle. Then along came an outfielder who shattered the previous mark: five-time World Series winner Reggie Jackson.

Not a bad club to belong to.

And it's not just baseball where failure seems to accompany greatness. In basketball, Kobe Bryant has missed more shots than any
player in history. In football, the record for most career interceptions
by a quarterback is held by eleven-time Pro Bowler and Super Bowl
champion Brett Favre.

As Daniel Coyle points out in *The Little Book of Talent*, successful
athletes don't just fail during games. They go out of their way to seek
out failure during practice. Hockey great Wayne Gretzky, for example, would often fall flat on the ice during skating exercises. It's
not that he'd forgotten how to skate. He was deliberately pushing his
boundaries, experimenting with the limits of his ability.

When practice is effortless, Coyle argues, learning stops. It's by
walking the precipice between your current abilities and the skills
just beyond your reach that growth happens. Master performers don't
get to where they are by playing at the same level day after day.
They do so by risking failure and using the feedback to master new
skills.

The willingness to grow through failure is an approach that's not
limited to individuals; a surprising number of leading organizations
tend to do the same. Take Google. We all know about its game-changing
products, including its search engine, Gmail, and Google Maps.

But what about Google X, the homepage customization tool that
lasted all of one day? Or Froogle, a price comparison tool whose name
confused so many users it had to be dropped? How many of us remember Google Reader, Google Web Accelerator, Google Answers,
Google Video Player, or Google Buzz?

As far as missteps go, it's not an inconsequential amount.

"Our policy is we try things," said then Google CEO Eric Schmidt,
when announcing in 2010 that the company was pulling the plug on

Google Wave. "We celebrate our failures. This is a company where it is absolutely OK to try something that is very hard, have it not be successful, take the learning and apply it to something new." Cofounder Larry Page echoed the sentiment. "Even if you fail at your ambitious thing, it's very hard to fail completely. *That's* the thing that people don't get."

And in a way, that's what makes them so prolific. It's the successful innovators' dirty little secret: They fail more than the rest of us.

SPANX AND THE SECRET OF SUCCESS

In 1998, twenty-seven-year-old Sara Blakely revolutionized women's underwear using a pair of scissors.

She was standing in front of her closet, trying to choose an outfit for a party later that night, when she came across a pair of crème-colored pants that she desperately wanted to wear. But there was a problem. The pants were tight and didn't fit her body perfectly. She needed something she could wear underneath to firm up her physique.

Finding a solution wasn't going to be easy.

"The options [for women] were not that great," she said, recounting the event to an audience at *Inc.* magazine's 2011 Women's Summit. "We had the traditional shapers that were so thick and left lines or bulges on the thigh. And then we had the underwear which leaves a panty line. And then came along the thong, which still confuses me because all that did was put underwear exactly where we had been trying to get it out of."

Form-fitting pantyhose were one possibility. But Blakely didn't want the nylon ruining the look of her sandals. And that's when inspiration struck. With her pantyhose in one hand, Blakely reached for the scissors and made two quick snips, creating the first pair of what are now known to shapewear aficionados everywhere as Spanx.

Blakely came home that night with the self-satisfied air of an inventor. "I remember thinking, this should exist for women."

Today Blakely is a billionaire. Her company sells more than two hundred body-shaping products that range from Skinny Britches thigh shapers to Undie-tectable panties to full-body Shape-Suits. If you're interested in buying some Spanx for yourself, you won't need to travel far. They are sold in over ten thousand locations, from high-end retailers including Saks Fifth Avenue and Neiman Marcus to big-box stores like Target and Walmart. And that's not counting the other thirty countries in which they sell. There's even Spanx for men, which, for obvious marketing reasons, have been shrewdly rebranded Zoned Performance.

Between that inspired evening in the closet and her current status as the owner of a multimillion-dollar powerhouse, Blakely overcame a series of remarkable obstacles, including zero experience in the hosiery industry, not having taken a single business course, and a bankroll that was limited to $5,000.

Asked where she found the courage to surmount such staggering odds, Blakely says a big part of the credit belongs to her father. Or, more specifically, to the one question he would ask his children every night at dinner.

Some parents are content asking their children, "Did you have a good day?" or "What did you learn at school?" Not at the Blakely household. The question Sara and her brother had to answer night after night was this: "What did you *fail* at today?"

When there was no failure to report, Blakely's father would express disappointment.

"What he did was redefine failure for my brother and me," Blakely told CNN's Anderson Cooper. "Instead of failure being the outcome, failure became *not trying*. And it forced me at a young age to want to push myself so much further out of my comfort zone."

Blakely was taught to interpret failure not as a sign of personal weakness but as an integral part of the learning process. It's this mindset that prepared her to endure the risk involved in starting her own business. When coming up short is viewed as the path to learning, when we accept that failure is simply feedback on what we need to work on next, risk-taking becomes a lot easier.

Her father's question taught her an important lesson: *If you're not failing, you're not growing.*

What's odd is that in many ways it's the precise opposite of the view espoused in most classrooms. From an early age, children are taught that success means having the right answers. That struggling is a bad sign, the sort of thing you do when you're not quite "getting it," or the work is too hard. Throughout much of their education, students are encouraged to finish assignments quickly. Those who don't are sent off to tutors.

After twelve years of indoctrination, it's no wonder that so many of us view failure the way we do: as something to avoid at all cost. We're implicitly taught that struggling means others will view us poorly, when in reality it's only by stretching ourselves that we develop new skills.

Some educators have begun recognizing the way this fear of failure is impeding their students' long-term growth. Edward Burger, for one, is doing something about it. For more than a decade the Williams College mathematics professor has literally been rewarding students for failing in his class.

"Instead of just touting the importance of failing," Burger wrote in a 2012 *Inside Higher Ed* essay, "I now tell my students that if they want to earn an A, they must fail regularly throughout the course of the semester—because 5 percent of their grade is based on their 'quality of failure.'"

Burger believes this approach encourages students to take risks. His goal is to reverse the unintended consequences of a school system consumed by testing. What was originally introduced as a feedback tool to foster better learning has had the opposite effect. When we reduce performance to As or Bs, pass or fail, good or bad, we make the learning opportunities that failure provides hard to appreciate.

At the end of each semester, students in Burger's class are asked to write an essay examining a mistake they made. In it, they describe why they initially thought their approach might work and how their mistake helped them uncover a new way of understanding the problem.

Failure, per se, is not enough. The important thing is to mine the failure for insight that can improve your next attempt.

To be fair, at just 5 percent of a student's grade, Burger's unusual grading scheme hardly constitutes an academic revolution. But research suggests that his approach of rewarding intelligent failure may have more of an impact on his students than we might initially suspect, especially when it comes to promoting a thinking style that's conducive to innovation. The reason, as we'll soon discover, is that when the possibility of failure looms as a major threat, our mind does some funny things.

Think creativity is an innate ability? Think again.

HOW TO SPARK CREATIVITY

You know that aha! feeling you get when you solve a difficult problem with a clever insight? Let's see if we can re-create that experience now. We're going to play a little game to test your creativity.

I'm going to list three seemingly unrelated words. Your job is to come up with a fourth—one that conceptually *connects* the first three words in a group.

Here's an example:

SWISS   CAKE   COTTAGE   _____

The answer is cheese: (Swiss) cheese; cheese (cake); (cottage) cheese.

Now let's see how well you do on some of these.

PAINT	DOLL	CAT	_____
FALLING	ACTOR	DUST	_____
STICK	LIGHT	BIRTHDAY	_____

These are just a few items from the Remote Associates Test (also known by the somewhat unfortunate acronym RAT), a tool psychologists use to measure creative insight. To find the right answers—in this case, house, star, and candle—you need to discover a link between ostensibly unrelated concepts, the same activity at the heart of many creative endeavors.

Now suppose we raise the stakes. Instead of doing the RAT for fun, I'm going to start paying you based on how well you do. You're going to see ten RAT items. For each item you get right, I'll give you a crisp five-dollar bill. OK, ready?

But wait. Before we start, let's pause here for a second.

Take a moment to examine the way you feel. Are you eager? Focused? Engaged? If so, you're likely experiencing what psychologists term an "approach motivational state." When people are in an approach mind-set, their focus is on achieving positive outcomes, because they see the potential for gain.

Contrast that with the feeling you get when we change the terms of the exercise slightly. Instead of paying you after every correct response, I'll just give you the full fifty dollars right at the start. Not bad, right? But here's the catch. This time around, for every mistake you make, I'm going to take away five dollars.

Notice the shift in the way you feel. If you're like most people, your attention is no longer centered on the potential gain. Instead you've become sensitized to the possibility of loss. You've entered what's called an "avoidance motivational state."

Every task we engage in can involve an approach or avoidance mind-set. Take a relatively low-stakes activity, like visiting a gym. Some of us exercise in order to gain a fitter body or impress a romantic partner (approaching a positive outcome), while the rest of us may do so in order to stop gaining weight or stave off high cholesterol (avoiding a negative outcome). In each case our action is exactly the same. But the difference in our psychological framing can strongly influence our experience, affecting everything from the emotions we feel stepping onto a treadmill to our likelihood of returning the next day.

Our motivational mind-set is particularly critical when we're engaged in creative activities. Research shows that when we're energized by the possibility of gain, we adopt a flexible cognitive style that allows us to easily switch between mental categories. We take a broader view, seeing the forest instead of the trees, while exploring a wider array of possibilities. In sum, when we're energized by approach motivation, we instinctively use the very mental techniques that make us more creative.

It's a different story when avoidance motivation enters the picture.

The moment evading a negative outcome becomes the focus, our attention narrows and our thinking becomes more rigid. We have a hard time seeing the big picture and resist the mental exploration necessary for finding a solution. All of a sudden, insights become a lot more elusive.

In part, the reason is physiological. That's the conclusion of a 2009 study conducted at the University of Buffalo, where psychologist Mark Seery took that RAT experiment we discussed and actually ran it.

In the study, Seery split participants into two groups: one in which every correct solution on the RAT was *rewarded* with a cash payment and one in which every incorrect solution was *penalized* with a loss of the same amount. Before starting, Seery connected his participants to a series of monitoring devices that measured their physiological reaction while taking the test.

Initially both groups reacted the same way. Nearly everyone showed elevated heart rates when the task was first presented, which was a good sign. It meant they found the task engaging.

But then something funny happened. Participants in the loss group started registering some unusual cardiovascular activity. The amount of blood being pumped out of their hearts dropped and their arteries constricted. Their bodies were reacting as if they were under attack.

As Stanford neuroscientist Robert Sapolsky points out, years of evolutionary history has shaped our biological response to seemingly hazardous situations. When our mind senses danger, our body flicks a switch, sending our cardiovascular system into overdrive. But here's the thing: There's only one switch. The fight or flight response we experience when we're told not to make a mistake is the same one that sent us running for our lives while being hunted by lion.

Needless to say, finding creative insights is difficult when your body is responding as if you're on the verge of becoming lunch.

There are times when brief bursts of avoidance motivation can be useful, but research suggests they are best left to tasks that require persistence. In a 2012 paper titled "Necessity Is the Mother of Invention," a group of psychologists in Amsterdam found that when people are in an avoidance mind-set, they work for longer periods, which, at times, can yield a more creative product. However, they also found that participants in an avoidance state had to exert significantly more mental energy than participants in an approach state just to accomplish the same level of work. And that's not all. The avoidance group also overestimated the difficulty of the task before getting started.

Which leads to an interesting conclusion: When avoiding failure is a primary focus, the work isn't just more stressful; it's a lot harder to do. And over the long run, that mental strain takes a toll, resulting in less innovation and the experience of burnout.

Ironically, allowing for mistakes to happen can elevate the quality of our performance. It's true even within roles that don't require creativity. And, as we'll see in this next section, sometimes it can mean the difference between life and death.

WHY SUCCESSFUL TEAMS MAKE MORE MISTAKES

In the mid-1990s, Amy Edmondson was analyzing the data to what she thought was a fairly straightforward study when she noticed something peculiar.

She was exploring team dynamics within hospitals, as part of her graduate work in organizational behavior at Harvard University. The question at the heart of Edmondson's research was this: Do nurses with better colleague relationships perform fewer errors?

She expected a fairly open-and-shut case. It made sense that working in a collaborative environment would allow nurses to better focus on their job. Of course they'd make fewer mistakes. *Duh!*

Except, they didn't. In fact, what Edmondson found was the exact opposite trend. The better the nurses' relationship with their manager and coworkers, the *more* errors they appeared to make.

How could this be?

Edmonson was dumbfounded at first. But slowly the answer revealed itself. Nurses in tightly knit groups don't actually *perform* more errors—they simply *report* more of them. The reason is simple: When the consequences of reporting failure are too severe, employees avoid acknowledging mistakes altogether. But when a work environment feels psychologically safe and mistakes are viewed as a natural part of the learning process, employees are less prone to covering them up. The fascinating implication is that fearful teams avoid examining the causes of their blunders, making it all the more likely that their mistakes will be repeated again in the future.

Having a team that's afraid of admitting failure is a dangerous problem, particularly because the symptoms are not immediately visible. What appears on the surface to be a well-functioning unit may, in fact, be a group that's too paralyzed to admit its own flaws. In contrast, teams that freely admit their errors are better able to learn from one another's mistakes. They can also take steps to prevent repeating those mistakes by tweaking their process. Over the long term, encouraging employees to acknowledge mistakes is therefore a vital first step to seeing improvement.

As Edmondson points out in her more recent research, not all mistakes are created equal. Some mistakes are caused by inattention and lack of ability, while others are caused by uncertainty or experimentation. The challenge for many organizations is that the pressure to avoid failure is so strong that hardly anyone bothers examining the root cause. It's when intelligent failures are treated exactly the same as preventable ones that learning and creativity grind to a halt.

And when that happens, the results are grim: A culture of innovation is overtaken by a culture of self-preservation.

So what's an organization to do?

Tell employees that it's fine to mess up? Encourage mistakes? Reward failure? A surprising number of prestigious organizations believe the answer to that provocative question is a resounding *yes*.

THE RIGHT WAY TO REWARD FAILURE

In 2011, ad executive Amanda Zolten took a serious risk.

She and her team at Grey Advertising were about to pitch an important client. A major kitty litter manufacturer was looking for a new agency and Zolten wanted badly to win. To stand apart from the competition, Zolten knew her team would have to show some serious originality, and she wanted to do more than simply leave it to the agency's creative department.

Within the world of advertising, a strong performance at a pitch meeting can be the difference between a decades-long relationship and never having another message returned. It's a big deal. Which is why Zolten was determined to create a memorable experience that would set her team apart.

So she did something unusual. She decided to experiment with the client's product ahead of time by conducting a little research. She even enlisted the help of her cat, Lucy Belle, the night before the big pitch.

The meeting started out normally enough. Six of the client's top executives were there, seated around a large conference room table. Then, midway through the meeting, Zolten saw her opening. She casually noted how effective the litter was at neutralizing unpleasant odors. And to make her point, she directed everyone's attention beneath the table. There, in the middle of the conference room, was a litter box, complete with Lucy Belle's contribution.

The reaction was not uniformly positive. Several executives reflexively drew back from the table. Two had to leave the room. Among those remaining, an uncomfortable laughter broke out after a palpable silence.

Zolten's boss took notice of her approach. But instead of chastising her for offending a prospective client, he granted her a Heroic Failure award and celebrated her courage in front of other agency members. Grey's president, Tor Myhren, told the *Wall Street Journal* that he decided to establish the quarterly prize for employees who take risks, noting that the sheer size of his agency was perhaps making his employees "a little more conservative, maybe a little slower."

Grey is not alone in rewarding employee failure. Nor is the approach limited to companies in creative industries. Large pharmaceutical companies have begun rewarding scientists for pulling the plug on major research projects, in an effort to discourage researchers from laboring on ineffective products for fear that admitting failure might cost them their jobs. Merck & Co., one of the world's largest drug manufacturers, gives additional stock options to scientists who admit their research is yielding undesirable results. Eli Lilly organizes "failure parties."

The faster scientists fail, the thinking goes, the sooner they can be reassigned to a project with stronger potential. The alternative is throwing good money after bad. As Peter Kim, Merck's former research and development chief, points out, "You can't change the truth. You can only delay how long it takes to find it out."

SurePayroll, an Illinois-based payroll-processing company, added a Best New Mistake category to its list of annual employee awards. Three winners (gold, silver, and bronze) are selected each year by the company's management team and given a cash prize. "If you don't encourage people to take risks, then you end up with incrementalism forever," says Michael Alter, the company's president. "Mistakes are the tuition you pay for success."

Software development company HCL Technologies takes it one step further by inviting executives to create a Failure CV. To enter the firm's highly coveted internal leadership program, applicants are required to list some of their biggest career blunders and then explain what they've learned from each experience. It's the organizational equivalent of Edward Burger's approach to classroom grading. To advance their careers, potential leaders must first show that they have the ability to turn failure into progress. Those who can't seem to identify any mistakes are presumably told they now have something to put on future applications.

It's an interesting approach. One that begs the question: What would the Failure CV of someone like Babe Ruth or William Shakespeare or Steve Jobs look like? And how would their Failure CV compare to yours?

One thing we can predict with some certainty is that the Failure CV of most high achievers tends to be surprisingly lengthy. Which, when you think about it, is quite refreshing. We don't often think of those at the top as a bunch of chronic failures. But in a way, that's precisely what they are. It's what enabled their success in the first place.

It's a lesson with strong implications for the workplace. When organizations communicate that failure is not an option, they incur an invisible cost: one that triggers a psychological reaction that restricts employee thinking, rewards lying, encourages cover-ups, and fuels the proliferation of more mistakes. It's an approach that ignores a basic reality of how learning and innovation really happen.

We want to believe that progress is simple. That success and failure provide clear indicators of the value of our work. But the path to excellence is rarely a straight line.

If there's one unifying insight we can draw from the experience of extraordinary achievers it is this: Sometimes the best way to minimize failure is to embrace it with open arms.

The Lessons of Failure
Action Items for Managers

Reward the attempts, not just the outcomes. Want to see creativity in the workplace? Then incentivize employees for trying new approaches and occasionally taking risks. When successful outcomes are the only things that are recognized, employees fall back on a conservative approach, sticking with what's worked in the past. The only way to promote risk-taking is to reward the attempts, reinforcing behaviors you want to encourage.

Mine failures for opportunities. When a team's efforts fall flat, it's natural to want to move on by burying your nose in your next assignment. But expert performers know that failure often contains powerful clues for improvement, especially when the focus is on what can be improved in the future. Be careful, however, not to turn postmortems into witch hunts by fixating on *who* made the mistake. Far better to ask future-oriented questions like, "What's one thing we can do better next time?"

Play the long game. No one likes failure. And tolerating setbacks as a manager is certainly a risk. But successful companies know that creating the space for intelligent failure is an investment, one that can yield major rewards in the long run. Think like Google. Or Gretzky. Or Jobs. It's not just about your organization's performance today. It's about its performance in five years.

The Lessons of Failure
Action Items for Emerging Leaders

Ask yourself, "What have I failed at today?" High achievers don't see failure as a personal indictment. They view it as a sign that they're on the brink of growth. If everything you do at work comes easily, consider this: You may not be pushing yourself hard enough. Developing your skills is like waging a negotiation. If the opposition says yes right away, it might mean you've aimed too low.

Anticipate the J Curve. We like to think of progress as a straight line, where one development builds on top of another, leading to steady and unswerving improvement. It's a comforting model. But when it comes to complex creative endeavors, it's also unrealistic. The relationship between creativity and progress is messy and often looks less like a straight line and more like a J, with a heavy dip at the start, representing early challenges and setbacks. Anticipating your early struggles makes it easier to stick around for later gains.

Failure not an option? It may be time to go. In a knowledge economy, unless you're acquiring new skills, you're slowly becoming obsolete. Some organizations want employees to repeat the same behaviors again and again without variation. This is not in your interest. Workplace experimentation is the only path to developing the skills you need to remain both relevant and valuable.

TWO

The Power of Place

How Office Design Shapes Our Thinking

Imagine a hallway with three doors.

Behind door number one is a room that enhances your creativity. Behind door number two is a room that sharpens your attention to detail. Choose door number three and you'll find yourself ready for collaboration.

Sound like science fiction? It's not. In fact, thanks to a flurry of new studies, it may represent the future of the modern workplace.

The last few years have witnessed stunning breakthroughs in knowledge about the way design affects our thinking. Already, organizations like Google, Intel, and Cisco are pouring millions of dollars into redesigning buildings, tearing down walls, and reconfiguring conference rooms. It's not simply for the sake of giving employees an appealing environment—it's driven by a newfound recognition that there is a connection between space and innovation.

The research suggests they're onto something big.

Consider a 2007 study, in which one hundred Rice University students were asked to take a test of abstract thinking, a vital precursor to creative insight. Half of the participants completed the exam in a room with ten-foot ceilings. The other half took the test in an identical room with eight-foot ceilings.

Could a room's height influence people's responses? The idea is not quite as farfetched as it first sounds. Throughout history, many of the world's most impressive architectural structures—from the Taj Mahal to the Eiffel Tower—have relied on height to inspire observers. The same is true for churches and synagogues, which often use tall, spacious interiors to create a sense of awe, as do many distinguished cultural institutions, like museums, opera houses, and arenas.

It seems obvious that people feel differently inside the Sistine Chapel than they do in a claustrophobic elevator. And it's also logical to infer that the contrast in mood can affect their thought process. But would a modest adjustment of just two feet have an effect?

The study's investigators suspected it could, arguing that when people enter high-ceilinged rooms, they feel relatively free and unconstrained, which influences their mode of thinking. They tend to process their environments more openly, making them better at seeing how different ideas relate to one another.

And this is what the experiment was designed to test. To ensure that the test takers noticed their room's height, the researchers attached a few decorative lanterns to the ceiling. They then randomly assigned subjects to rooms, without mentioning a word about the variation in height. The results were striking. Participants in rooms with taller ceilings were significantly better at finding connections between seemingly unrelated objects than those whose ceilings were slightly lower.

The room's dimension had inspired big thoughts.

Height, of course, represents just one element of interior design. It's a single violin within a rich symphony of an office landscape. Over the last decade, studies have revealed that many design elements we take for granted strongly influence our thinking, and that we're often unaware of their impact.

Take color, for example. Research shows that brief exposure to the color red, which our minds automatically associate with stop signs, alarm signals, and blood, stimulates parts of the brain that make us more sensitive to failure. Seeing red causes us to become more alert and vigilant. Depending on the situation, that can either harm or benefit our work. One study found that proofreaders are more successful at picking out errors when using a red pen. Another, published in *Science*, found that while people exposed to red were much better at tasks that require accuracy and attention to detail, they were also much worse at tasks involving free association and big-picture thinking.

Sound is another surprisingly powerful influencer. A 2012 study found that background noise, which many of us try to minimize when we're doing hard work, can actually improve our performance of certain activities. When we're slightly distracted by the noise around us—as we are at a café, for example—we process information more abstractly, which can enhance our creativity.

In contrast, quiet environments are slightly unsettling. The human ear evolved to detect predators, which is why we become a little more aware of our surroundings when we're in a space that's completely still. Our hearing goes into overdrive, amplifying sounds we would normally ignore, because in the past, heightened attention alerted us to potential threats. Extreme quiet intensifies focus, which like the color red can be useful in the right context. When the task we're doing requires precision and minimizing mistakes, the enhanced sensitivity can benefit performance, but when our work involves creative thinking, total silence can be surprisingly detrimental.

Even furniture can sway our thinking. A 2013 experiment found that when people enter a room with chairs arranged in a circle, they become focused on intergroup belonging. But when the seating includes an angle—as it often does in many office conference rooms—the focus shifts to expressing uniqueness and being distinct. In part, it's because a room's layout communicates the type of interaction that is expected, leading us to act accordingly.

Why are we influenced by so many seemingly trivial features of our environment? It's because automatically adapting to our surroundings is actually quite advantageous.

Think of it as cruise control for the brain. We don't have to pause and reflect on how to act every time we encounter a menacing red signal or enter a room we've never been in before. Our mind does it for us, reading our environment and adjusting our thinking so that we can conserve our mental firepower for more important matters.

The upshot is this: The human mind does not operate in a vacuum. It is constantly scanning its surroundings, scouring it for clues and using the data to select an ideal mental approach. Where we are affects the way we think.

Look around. What effect is your location having on you right now?

A BRIEF HISTORY OF OFFICE DESIGN

When we think of inventors, we think of the success stories: Leonardo da Vinci, Alexander Graham Bell, Bill Gates. But not all inventors are equally proud of their work. Some live long enough to see their creations go awry, leaving them to question the true value of their contribution.

Such is the heartbreaking case of Robert Propst, who for decades watched his invention veer hopelessly off the rails before his passing in 2000.

A former professor of fine arts, Propst was hired in the late 1950s as head of research at Herman Miller, a furniture manufacturing company headquartered in Michigan. The position was new, and Propst was given considerable leeway. He'd been handpicked by Herman Miller's founder, D. J. DePree, and told he could research anything that might facilitate the company's growth.

Almost immediately, he gravitated to the idea of reinventing office furniture.

At the time, most workplaces looked almost nothing like they do today. The typical office consisted of a vast open space, with rows and rows of identical desks crammed tightly together. Employees were afforded little in the way of privacy, which was by design. The bullpen office, as it was known, was a natural extension of the factory floor. The goal was to keep everyone visible, as a means of ensuring that they stayed on task.

Propst tackled his new assignment with the intellectual curiosity of an anthropologist. He observed employees as they worked, interviewed them about their experiences, and consulted a range of experts, including psychologists, architects, and mathematicians. He studied the way information flowed among staff members and examined the ways office layout affected their productivity. Following extensive analysis, Propst issued his conclusions. His assessment was bleak. "Today's office is a wasteland," he reported. "It saps vitality, blocks talent, frustrates accomplishment. It is the daily scene of unfulfilled intentions and failed effort."

The modern workplace, Propst argued, was in desperate need of an overhaul. One that minimized distractions, offered privacy, and gave employees some control over the way they worked.

His solution? The Action Office.

Laboring alongside designer George Nelson, Propst developed a new vision for office furniture; one that incorporated his research insights and introduced a workstation that was built around the needs of employees.

Among its features: a selection of work surfaces, including two desks and a small table, allowing employees to spread out their assignments and stretch their legs throughout the day. There were ergonomically correct chairs, standing desks, and movable units to create privacy and offer room for displaying ongoing work. The model also offered customizable furniture combinations, inviting employees to mix and match arrangements, finding a layout that suited them best.

Released in 1964, the Action Office received rave reviews from top-tier business magazines and earned a number of prestigious industry awards. But commercially, it was a total flop. Employers complained that it took up too much room, was difficult to assemble, and cost considerably more than they wanted to pay. There were some features that appealed to buyers (like the notion of separating workers), but overall, the consensus was that in its current form the Action Office was a nonstarter.

Reluctantly, Propst slunk back to the drawing board. He knew that he was onto something, but his current approach wasn't selling. Something would have to change.

Four years later, he returned with a modified version of his invention—one that addressed employers' feedback. It was called the Action Office 2, though if you're like most people, you probably know it by its less formal name: the cubicle.

Gone were Propst's insight-driven prescriptions of increased space, a variety of work surfaces, and employee-driven customization. In their place, this newer unit featured vertical partitions (to minimize distraction) which arrived as part of a single, easy-to-assemble unit that cost a fraction of traditional furniture.

Propst's second attempt was an incontrovertible smash. Within just two years, the Action Office 2 generated an astounding $25 million in sales. Recent estimates suggest that since 1968 it has grossed Herman Miller more than $5 billion.

It's ironic, of course, that Robert Propst's invention facilitated the exact opposite of his intentions. Cubicles were introduced to address the need for personal space and privacy. They achieved neither. Today nearly 70 percent of American organizations utilize some version of the Action Office, and they're using it to cram more employees into less space. In the 1970s, the average worker was allotted 500 square feet of office space. In 2010, that number was down to 200 square feet.

Privacy is hardly fairing much better. While a cubicle's panels may prevent employees from making eye contact, privacy consists of more than just not seeing someone who sits a few feet away. Acoustic privacy is equally vital. Hearing someone you can't see can often be more of a distraction than having them in full view.

Studies show that working in a cubicle can be mentally draining, psychologically stressful, and physiologically harmful. Being subject to constant disruption, high noise levels, and a lack of personal space elevates our anxiety levels and raises our blood pressure, which takes a toll on the body's immune system. When employees are continuously stressed, their motivation, performance, and satisfaction are bound to plummet, because they have less energy to bring to their work.

Propst himself couldn't help but voice disdain for the way his invention has reshaped the corporate landscape. Just three years before his death, he expressed considerable bitterness at how his work had been co-opted to reduce cost at the expense of employee well-being, comparing the modern workplace to "monolithic insanity."

"Not all organizations are intelligent and progressive," he said in 1998. "Lots are run by crass people who can take the same kind of equipment and create hellholes. They make little bitty cubicles and stuff people in them. Barren, rat-hole places."

To be fair, the alternatives to cubicles have plenty of downsides of their own. Private offices eat up a lot of real estate, seal employees off from one another, and introduce barriers to communication. Frequently, the higher up in an organization you go, the more space you're allotted and the more inaccessible you become. Status begets isolation, which can have a crippling effect on teams whose work depends on collaboration. Innovation, it is often argued, comes from spontaneous interaction. It's hard to have those unplanned encounters when seeing other people requires an Outlook meeting invitation.

In recent years, a growing number of organizations have begun rejecting both the cubicle and the corner office, embracing an open-plan layout similar to the one that Robert Propst was so fervently against. Advocates contend that placing everyone in the same location promotes collaboration and fosters better communication. It's an egalitarian approach that affords every staffer the same amount of space. In a world where success is predicated upon effective teamwork, what better way of making sure people work together than by eliminating obstacles to communication and ensuring that everyone is treated equally?

It's a noble idea. But does it work? The research raises some serious concerns.

While open-plan designs may increase communication between colleagues, they often do so at a cost to individual work. The same drawbacks that inspired Propst's redesign back in the early sixties— overheard conversations, visual distraction, a lack of privacy— continue to plague open space workplaces. When our office is riddled with disruptions, we end up consuming the very mental resources we need to think clearly.

Ironically, the frustration we experience when we're not getting our work done inevitably interferes with our ability to collaborate. It's hard to feel cheery toward teammates when you constantly feel like you're behind.

Some also question whether having colleagues so accessible is really such a good thing. As management professor Anne-Laure Fayard told the *New York Times*, "Many studies show that people have shorter and more superficial conversations in open offices because they're self-conscious about being overheard." So sure, open spaces might get you a larger number of conversations, but not all communication is equally valuable. And even if communication were an unqualified good, it's worth remembering that collaboration represents just one facet of what it means to be productive.

All of which should make one thing abundantly clear: For all the advances that have revolutionized the modern workplace over the past fifty years—from personal computing to the Internet to mobile technology—design is not one of them. Most organizations continue to rely on one of three traditional office layouts, each of which carries significant risks of undermining employee performance.

Cubicles are depressing. Private offices are isolating. Open spaces are distracting.

So what's a company to do?

THE CAVEMAN'S GUIDE TO BUILDING
A BETTER OFFICE

Ask the average CEO how to optimize a workspace and they might suggest you consult with an interior designer. Ask the same question of an evolutionary psychologist and he'll direct you to a very different set of experts: our ancient ancestors.

Evolutionary psychologists argue that many of our current design preferences can be traced back to our shared history on the savanna. We're drawn to environments that promoted our survival as hunter-gatherers, and feel uneasy in situations that would have put our forefathers at risk. These preferences, they argue, are largely unconscious. We simply experience safe settings as pleasurable and dangerous ones as repellent, without being able to identify exactly why.

One example: Most of us instinctively enjoy sitting in sheltered locations that overlook expansive areas like parks and oceans. Think waterfront property or apartments overlooking Central Park. In the past, the desire for settings that offered security and a view of our surroundings kept us alive and positioned us to find our next meal. Locations offering prospect and refuge are inherently pleasing, while areas that deny us shelter or a view tend to generate discomfort. We no longer need these features in order to survive, yet we can't help but prefer them.

Brain imaging research demonstrates the deep-seated nature of these preferences: Our desire for prospect and refuge is so strong, it even affects our perception of art. A 2006 study found that the pleasure centers of the brain consistently light up when we're viewing landscapes, especially when their vantage point is one of refuge.

Our desire for safe locations also explains why sitting with our backs exposed can leave us feeling tense. We don't enjoy having others sneak up on us and seek to minimize potential threat. As environmental psychologist Sally Augustin points out, this is one reason that restaurant booths fill up more quickly than freestanding tables. Mafia folklore has it that it's best to sit with your back to the wall. It seems our ancient ancestors felt the same way.

Another evolutionary insight: We're happiest when we're close to the outdoors. As hunter-gatherers, being outside was essential to our survival. It meant proximity to food, water, and other people. An extensive body of work reveals that nature is essential for psychological functioning. A 1984 study, for example, found that surgery patients require fewer painkillers and shorter hospital stays when assigned to a room overlooking trees. Scenes of nature, researchers argue, reduce our anxiety and lower muscle tension, which helps our bodies heal.

Having a view of the outdoors has also been shown to promote performance in the workplace. Employees who sit near a window are better at staying on task, show greater interest in their work, and report more loyalty to their company. A 2003 study found that when call center employees—who often rotate seats—are placed near a window, they generate an additional $3,000 of productivity per year. Research even suggests that the amount of direct sunlight entering an office can reliably predict the level of employee satisfaction in a workplace.

What is it about access to nature that makes us feel better?

Some experts believe exposure to sunlight plays a major role. Daylight regulates our circadian rhythms, affecting our bodies' functioning. Deprived of sunlight, we experience an imbalance in serotonin and melatonin, upsetting our ability to get a good night's sleep and compromising our immune systems. To wit: A 2013 study found that employees whose offices have windows sleep an average of forty-six minutes more per night than those laboring in windowless rooms. Another study published the same year found that after the sun's rays hit our skin, our bodies release nitric oxide, a compound that dilates the blood vessels and lowers our blood pressure.

Others believe that the benefits of nature extend beyond the physiological. A number of researchers argue that natural settings are also cognitively rejuvenating and help us restore our mental resources. In contrast to the overwhelming stimulation we often encounter at work, where we're frequently inundated with calls, e-mails, and text messages for hours on end, natural settings engage our interest but demand very little of our attention. We have the freedom to let our minds wander, noticing as much or as little as we like, entering a state that psychologists term "soft fascination." The result is an elevation in mood as well as replenished mental energy that improves our memory and enhances our creativity.

Studies show that the mere presence of plants can also provide surprisingly large benefits. Office workers report feeling healthier and more energized when their workplace features live plants and fresh flowers. A 2011 study found that randomly assigning participants to rooms with indoor plants led to significantly better performance on tasks requiring sustained attention and concentration.

When views and plants aren't available, even reminders of nature appear to help. Research suggests that access to aquariums and fireplaces put us at ease and open us up to connecting with others. Pictures of landscapes make us less anxious. Brief exposure to blue and green, colors ever-present in fertile environments rich in vegetation, water, and nourishment, make us feel safe and improve our creative output.

It's not hard for the evolutionary psychologist to see why so many offices fail to engage their employees. Depriving people of sunlight, restricting their views, and seating them with their backs exposed is not a recipe for success—it's a recipe for chronic anxiety. So is placing workers in expansive rooms, inundating them with stimulation, and failing to provide them with an area for refuge, where they can recover from attention fatigue.

We tend to assume that employee engagement is about the work, that so long as we give talented people challenging tasks and the tools to excel, they will be happy. But that formula is incomplete. Our mind responds to the signals in our environment. And the less comfortable we are while doing our work, the fewer cognitive resources we have available.

And this is why design ultimately matters. It's because engaging employees is about creating an environment that positions people to do their best work. Paleolithic man may be long gone, but he can still teach us a few things when it comes to designing a better workplace.

USING SPACE TO TELL A STORY

Building a workplace that supports employees' performance is clearly a worthwhile endeavor. But it's not the only way of using workplace design to benefit an organization.

Cornell University management professor Franklin Becker compares a company's use of office space to its "organizational body language." It's a fitting analogy. When a person says one thing and their body communicates another, listeners are left confused. The same can be said for organizations that claim a particular characteristic but fail to follow through in their interior design. They come across as inauthentic to their employees, whose impressions inevitably trickle down to clients.

The more a company's message is reinforced in a workplace environment, the easier it is for employees to integrate that vision and relay it to the people they meet. This is why so many top organizations are now investing in designing interiors that are culturally distinctive and deliver a consistent message—one that the company wants to communicate with the outside world.

Workplace design has also become an important tool for attracting and retaining top talent. Studies show that employees use the quality of an office environment to draw inferences about the competence of an organization's leaders. When a workplace is well designed, employees' confidence in their management team lifts, as does their willingness to stay on in the years to come.

How do you use design to make an organization feel distinct?

One approach is to borrow a practice used by many successful retailers that involves creating a touchpoint map. Touchpoint maps anticipate every element of a customer's experience, from the instant they walk through the door to their final steps back to their car, identifying communication opportunities along the way. The goal is to turn every consumer interaction into a brand experience that reflects the retailer's message.

If you've ever visited an Apple Store, you've probably noticed how different it feels from other electronics shops. The decor is clean and uncluttered. There's no middleman between customers and access to Apple's products. Registers and the long lines they produce have been eliminated; at the Apple Store just about any employee can cash you out.

Every aspect of the Apple Store's design reflects its brand message: simplicity.

In the same way Apple uses its space to communicate a message to its *external* customers, organizations can use the workplace environment to send a message to their *internal* customers. The key is to first identify a message the organization wants to convey—say, innovation, insight, or caring—and then design employee touchpoints that bring that concept to life.

Lobbies and hallways represent key touchpoint opportunities, ones that can be used for sharing an organization's history, traditions, and achievements. Steve Ferretti, an environmental branding expert and creative director at Ferretti Designs, has written about the value of using organizational touchpoints to create an emotional hook. Some years back, Ferretti was hired to design a lobby exhibit for a medical device manufacturer. The obvious approach would have been to put up a few respectful images of the organization's founders alongside a brief history of the equipment they've produced. But Ferretti wanted something more evocative: a touchpoint with emotional punch. So he set up a glass display featuring a solitary pair of ice skates.

To anyone entering the building, the skates felt dramatically out of place; this was, after all, a company that produced dull technical devices. And that was the point. Only after reading the caption would visitors discover the reason for the display. The skates had belonged to Olympian Bonnie Blair, an athlete whose career was extended thanks to the technology made possible by the organization's employees.

While entryways can help set the tone, it's worth remembering that they represent only a tiny sliver of a workplace experience. Often companies limit their design investments to their lobby because it's the element of their environment that's most visible to clients. This is a mistake. Anytime there is a disconnect between the front of the house and the heart of the house, there's the potential for employees to wonder whether their organizational message is simply a façade.

Many successful companies have begun using behind-the-scenes space to highlight a commitment to their employees. For example, Daxko, a software consulting company headquartered in Alabama, has created a "favorites wall" where they display photos of team members holding up some of their favorite books, movies, or sports team jerseys. A related approach, often used by organizations in creative industries, is to put employees' artwork up on display, presenting them much like an exhibit.

Another way of using a space to engage employees is by getting them personally involved in the design of their workplace. When Bliss Integrated Communication, a Manhattan marketing firm, moved into their new office space in 2012, they were committed to having their employees play a role. So they commissioned a summer-long photo contest on two themes central to their company brand: New York City and the media. Every employee was invited to submit their photos, which were then put up for a companywide vote. The winning photos are now displayed throughout the agency.

Naming conference rooms is another tool for making a workplace feel unique. When we label a space we create expectations in the minds of visitors that shape their experience. A spa I recently visited has a locker room that's no different from any other I've seen—except they don't call it a "locker room." They call it "The Sanctuary." It's a clever approach. Research shows that when we anticipate having a positive experience, we're more likely to do so.

Locker rooms are gross. Sanctuaries are refreshing.

Most organizations use generic names for their meeting spaces, like Conference Room A and Conference Room B. Not at Poggled, a Chicago company selling Groupon-like bar and club gift certificates. The company is committed to delivering memorable nightlife experiences, which is why, if you're looking for Poggled's management team, you'll likely find them in one of two locations: the "It's 5 o'Clock Somewhere," or the slightly less formal "Stay Thirsty, My Friends."

Another workplace touchpoint: office furniture. Earlier, we saw the way seating arrangements can subtly influence people's thinking. How rooms are furnished communicates an implicit message about which behaviors are appropriate. Interestingly, it's not just the layout of furniture that affects our experiences—it's also the physical composition. A 2010 experiment conducted by researchers at MIT, Harvard, and Yale found that people seated on hard wooden chairs are less willing to compromise than those seated on chairs with soft cushions.

What this finding suggests is that the furniture an organization selects can have an impact on the way a workplace is experienced. Rather than simply choosing furniture based on its aesthetic appeal, it's worth considering the way it feels and the message it communicates.

Law firms, for example, are often partial to bulky wooden tables and stiff leather chairs. The traditional decor helps communicate stability and trust, which may be useful when conducting a negotiation or persuading a prospective client to use their services. What it's unlikely to do, however, is help visitors relax, silence their inner censors, and come up with out-of-the-box ideas.

Which goes to show: What's right for one location can be entirely wrong for another. The key is to first think about how a room is going to be used and then build an experience that's consistent with that objective.

One organizational touchpoint that often gets mysteriously overlooked: the bathroom. Most office restrooms are bleak and unwelcoming. But for many employees, it's one of the few opportunities they have for stepping away, letting go of trivial details and refocusing on the bigger picture. Instead of treating bathrooms with disdain, some cutting-edge organizations are now using them as an opportunity for stimulating creativity, by displaying interesting artwork, leaving out thought-provoking magazines, or playing unusual music.

At Google, for example, bathrooms are where employees go to learn. Back in 2007, a group of engineers started posting interesting articles on bathroom stalls as a means of educating their colleagues about new methods of code testing. The idea caught on, and soon their coworkers began complaining when the material wasn't being updated quickly enough. To this day, when an engineer at Google says, "Excuse me, I need to go read about testing," it's clear exactly where he's headed.

On the surface, that might seem like just a quirky anecdote. But what it demonstrates is how even a simple bathroom visit can be used to reinforce a company's commitment to intellectual growth.

A final touchpoint worth considering is the design of an organization's gathering spaces. Lunchrooms, locker rooms, and coffee stations serve important logistical functions, but they also double as vital social hubs. When communal spaces are lacking in a workplace, the quality of employee relationships suffers. In fact, research conducted by Gallup shows that organizations that neglect to build gathering spaces have *half* the number of employees with a best friend at work as those that do.

We often give a lot of thought to formal meeting spaces. But often it's the *informal* spaces that can have a bigger impact on the quality of our workplace relationships. Offering appealing indoor or outdoor spaces for employees to gather is a vital organizational touchpoint in just about any industry—one that can bolster employee relationships, create networking opportunities, and spark creative interactions.

THE LESSONS OF TELECOMMUNICATING: WHY EMPLOYEES ARE OFTEN MORE PRODUCTIVE AT HOME

While I was writing this book in early 2013, Yahoo! CEO Marissa Mayer came under considerable criticism for eliminating her company's flexible work from home policy, mandating that employees show up at the office every day. Mayer's reasoning, which no doubt was influenced by her experience working at Google, was simple: Creativity and innovation thrive on serendipitous encounters. And those interactions can only occur when people are collaborating together in the same place.

The decree hit a nerve. Almost immediately, a national uproar erupted over the merits of telecommuting. Pundits wrestled over whether employees are better suited to working from home or at the office.

"A workforce culture based on long hours at the office with little regard for family or community does not inevitably lead to strong productivity *or* innovation," wrote sociologist Jennifer Glass in an impassioned *New York Times* op-ed. *U.S. News & World Report* columnist Susan Milligan was more sympathetic: "Technology is great; it helps us do things more efficiently and cheaper. But it has also led to a breakdown in human interaction that is bad not only for humankind in general, but for business."

Watching all this unfold, I was struck by how much of the debate seemed to be centered on the wrong question. Instead of asking whether employees are more productive at home or at work—to which the obvious answer is, it depends on the specific individual and the particular task—what we should have been asking is what home environments can teach us about building a better workplace.

Numerous studies have found that in many cases, employees who have the option of telecommuting are more productive than their office-bound counterparts. But what is it about working from home that often boosts our output? And more important: How do we apply those insights to the office so that employees can be more effective at work?

In fairness, some comforts of home just can't be replicated, no matter how hard a company tries. Take shaving two hours off an employee's commute. Eliminating travel time reduces employees' stress levels and allows them to spend the best hours of their day doing their job. It's a legitimate benefit that deserves serious consideration.

But there's more to working from home than simply less travel.

Consider access to a quiet, private space, for example. It's impossible to excel at challenging mental work when we're under a constant barrage of e-mails, conference calls, and meetings. Our brains can only handle so much. The cognitive bandwidth we each have is limited, which is why distractions can be so harmful. Allowing disruptions to consume our attention leaves us with fewer resources to attend to the work that matters.

Workplace distractions also slow us down more than we might recognize. A quick visit from a colleague might only take thirty seconds, but the cognitive reverberations of that diversion can last much longer. A University of California–Irvine study found that when we're distracted from an activity in which we are fully immersed, it takes us an average of more than twenty minutes just to regain our previous momentum.

Unlike in the workplace, there's also less pressure in a quiet home environment to multitask. While we like to believe that we're good at multitasking, research suggests it's rarely an effective strategy.

What appears to us as tackling several activities at once often involves simply shuffling between tasks, for which there are serious consequences. When we multitask, our performance suffers, and our stress levels spike. In part, it's because redirecting our attention from one task to another depletes our cognitive resources, leaving us with less mental energy than if we had simply devoted our full attention to one activity at a time. Researchers are also finding that chronic multitaskers— those of us who can't help but read e-mails while talking on the phone, for example—are especially prone to experiencing boredom, anxiety, and depression.

Another benefit of working from home: personalization. At home we get to control many aspects of our environment—everything from the setup of our office to the lighting of our desk to the temperature in our room—which improves our comfort level and allows us to direct our focus to our work.

But personal comfort isn't the only reason personalization is important. Human beings are territorial animals. When we have the freedom to shape our surroundings, we experience a heightened sense of personal control, which reduces stress and improves our confidence. In contrast, believing that we lack control over our environment leads to a decline in motivation.

Psychologists have found that organizations that encourage employees to customize their workspaces tend to have happier workers. Not only does decorating an office make employees feel more comfortable, it also promotes a sense of personal ownership and belonging.

In one experiment, researchers measured a 32 percent increase in performance among people who were allowed to customize their offices, compared to those whose offices were kept bare. Another study reported that employees who *don't* personalize their offices (when personalization is allowed) are typically the ones who are the least happy with their jobs. Findings like these help explain why companies such as DreamWorks and Etsy have started providing new hires with a modest budget for decorating their workstations. A small investment in personalization can go a long way.

When we work from home, we also have access to restorative experiences, like glancing out a window, going out for a run, or taking a nap. At most organizations, opportunities like these are rare. Having the freedom to recharge in ways that many workplaces discourage undoubtedly plays a role in facilitating a telecommuter's productivity.

It's no wonder so many employees believe they are more productive from their home office. It's because in many cases, they are. When we're placed in an environment that's conducive to complex thinking, our minds respond.

But the real lesson of telecommuting, the one that every CEO would do well to consider, is that there's something deeply wrong with the design of a workplace when the only way for an employee to feel productive is to physically leave the building. When coming in early, staying late, and working weekends become implicit requirements for keeping up, this much is clear: The current model is broken.

So what's the alternative?

CAVES AND CAMPFIRES

What the research tells us is that we can enhance employee performance by leveraging their surroundings. That we can foster better outcomes by designing environments that help employees meet the cognitive demands of their work.

Unfortunately, that's far from the way most offices are designed. Instead, the vast majority of organizations embrace a one-size-fits-all approach, asking every employee to toil in the same setting, regardless of their actual work assignments. Marketers, accountants, and salespeople are all lumped together into identical office spaces and expected to excel at their jobs, with little to no environmental accommodation.

But there's an alternative to this approach. And it's one that's rapidly gaining favor in the technology sector—an industry that's been at the forefront of applying psychological insights to workplace design. For many cutting-edge companies, such as Google, Cisco, and eBay, the model for the modern workplace is no longer an evolved version of the factory floor, but a modified version of the college campus.

What can companies learn from a college campus? How to create an environment that fosters self-direction, for one thing. Within a college setting, students receive a set of expectations at the beginning of the semester. How they approach their work is up to them. If they succeed, they are rewarded with good grades and the prospects of a better future. If they fail, they may be asked to leave.

Universities offer students a range of settings, from private and semiprivate dorm rooms to quiet libraries to communal spaces like cafeterias, a quad, and the gym. The campus serves as a tool. It's up to students to utilize the facilities and develop their own formulas for success.

Many organizations are now designing workplaces that embrace a similar approach, offering employees a variety of settings and giving them the option of choosing their own paths. Employees receive a desk of their own, access to a selection of locations designated for quiet focus work, and a range of communal spaces that facilitate collaboration, as well as spontaneous interactions. Depending on the type of work a company does, they can also choose to incorporate some fun, eclectic designs, creating an assortment of vibes (a café, a quiet library, an inspiration room) that employees can draw upon to match their project.

The value of this method is that it allows employees to adapt their setting to the demands of their work, instead of the other way around. When companies offer employees a choice of location, they don't just create an environment that better positions workers to succeed—they empower their team members, demonstrating trust in their decision-making abilities.

There's another benefit to providing employees with a spectrum of options, and that's creating an environment that's rich in both *caves* and *campfires*. Gary Jacobs, an architectural illustrator and design consultant, uses these terms to describe our evolutionary penchant for both quiet, restorative spaces and interactive, group settings. He argues that some of us have personalities that make caves more appealing, while others have personalities that draw us to campfires. But we all need access to both settings in order to thrive, which is what the campus model delivers. It allows people on both extremes to find their preferred environment in a single workplace.

A campus approach may sound complicated or expensive, but it doesn't need to be. Sure, having the Googleplex's twenty-six acres at your disposal would make it easier. But even smaller offices can zone spaces according to activity. Turning the corner office into a public "thinking space" where employees come to focus can do far more for a company's ROI than using the same room for barricading its most talented executive. And when spare rooms aren't available, room dividers and sound machines can be used to create distinctive spaces with a unique feel.

Earlier in this chapter we encountered a difficult question: How do you choose among cubicles, private offices, and open spaces when all three present significant downsides?

There is a simple answer: You don't.

By breaking free of the single space mind-set, organizations can leverage many of the productivity insights we've discovered in this chapter. One thing the research has taught us is that no single environment is conducive to every task. By offering a selection of options, companies can support both focus work and collaboration, using the space they have to enhance their employees' efforts.

Which brings us back full circle . . .

Imagine a hallway with three doors. Door number one leads to a room with plants, tall ceilings, and expansive views. It's where you go to find big ideas.

Behind door number two is a small soundproof room with bare walls and a healthy supply of red pens. It's where you go to tweak, edit, and root out mistakes.

Enter door number three and you're in an open-plan space, where you and your colleagues can park your laptops, grab a snack, and do your thinking in the company of others. It's where you go when you're looking for a collaborative spark.

We can continue fantasizing about this workplace. Or we can build it.

The Lessons of Workplace Design
Action Items for Managers

Design with the end in mind. Some activities require disciplined, distraction-free attention. Others benefit from instant communication and collaborative interactions. The best companies design workplaces with the end in mind, creating spaces that facilitate the work their employees do. No single environment is effective for every task, which is why more and more companies are creating hybrid spaces that offer employees a range of uses.

Think like a caveman. Many of the insights shared by evolutionary thinkers can be easily applied to enhance office settings. Some design elements, like the addition of plants, aquariums, and images of nature, are relatively inexpensive. Others, like offering plenty of natural light and seating with views of the outdoors, are worth considering when selecting or designing a new space.

Brand your workplace experience. Great companies do more than make their employees comfortable. They craft experiences that make their workplace distinct. A unique workplace communicates an organization's priorities, demonstrates managerial competence, and grows employee engagement. You can start by mapping out your organizational touchpoints (like your lobby, bathroom, and break room) and find ways of enhancing each employee experience in a way that is consistent with your brand.

The Lessons of Workplace Design
Action Items for Emerging Leaders

Invest in your psychological comfort. Many employees rarely give much consideration to the decor of their workspaces. Research suggests that they might be more productive if they did. The more comfortable we are, the more cognitive resources we have available for focusing on our work. Which is why taking the time to personalize your workspace (to the extent that you can), from modifying the layout and direction of the furniture to making even modest changes, such as adjusting the height of your monitor or the amount of lighting available at your desk, can have a reliable effect on your productivity.

To replenish your attention, step outside. Much of the work we do requires deep concentration, of which we have only a limited supply. But studies show that we can replenish our mental resources by going outdoors. When we're in natural settings, it's easier to let our attention wander and allow our minds to recharge. No matter how well your office is designed, leaving it for brief periods can help make you more effective.

Create a workplace soundtrack. We often take for granted the noise levels in our environment, yet studies reveal that sound can influence our performance in surprisingly powerful ways. Leaving the office not an option? A pair of headphones can do the trick. Websites like Coffitivity.com re-create the low hum of a café, which research suggests can provide a creative boost, while Simplynoise.com offers the constant swish of white noise to mask distractions when your work requires deep concentration.

THREE

Why You Should Be Paid to Play

On a Thursday evening in April 2011, less than nine months away from a potential New Hampshire primary, Barack Obama sat in the White House Situation Room facing one of the most difficult decisions of his career.

It was just before 7:00 p.m. and all his top military advisers had assembled to receive the president's orders.

Eight months earlier, intelligence operatives had identified a mysterious complex in northeast Pakistan. Initially, it was assumed to be the home of a low-level terrorist courier and his extended family. But when photographs revealed an eighteen-foot concrete wall and barbed wire surrounding the residence, suspicions grew.

Why would a simple courier require that level of protection? And how exactly could he afford to pay for it?

The CIA wasted no time setting up intense surveillance. There had to be something more going on. On the other side of that wall, they reasoned, must be a high-value target.

At first there was nothing. Then, a break. Aerial projections of a slender figure in traditional Pakistani garb. The length of his shadow suggested that the man was tall, far taller than the courier or anyone in his family.

Who was this man? Almost nothing was known, except this: Several times a day he would circle the compound's courtyard. None of the images were close enough for anyone to make out his face, and so investigators gave the man a nickname. *The Pacer.*

The president had been briefed about the compound months ago. His instructions were clear: Map out a detailed action plan of next steps. Now his advisers had returned, narrowing the president's options to two.

The question facing Obama was this: Send in Navy SEALs and attempt a capture, or deploy stealth bombers to obliterate the building?

Both choices had their drawbacks.

Executing a ground invasion was clearly the riskier option. The SEALs could be spotted in the air, leaving the compound's inhabitants enough time to escape. Worse, this would all be taking place on foreign soil without the Pakistani government's consent. U.S. aircraft could justifiably be shot down going in and coming out. The president would be risking an international incident while gambling with the lives of the military's top personnel.

Jimmy Carter had staked *his* political future on a covert operation in 1980. It did not go well.

The alternative—bombing the facility—presented its own disadvantages. This was a residential neighborhood in the middle of Pakistan. The CIA had tallied a total of three families inside the compound, many of them children. A drone attack would be a death sentence to every single one.

Reducing the building to rubble also meant the loss of potential intelligence and, of course, the very likely possibility that the residents' identities would never be revealed.

A decision was needed. Time was running out. At any moment, the Pacer could disappear.

As he often does, Obama asked each of his advisers what they would do in his place.

Defense Secretary Robert Gates, a man who had served seven previous presidential administrations, favored a drone strike. "There is a degree of risk associated with the raid option that I am uncomfortable with," he told the president. The vice chairman of the Joint Chiefs of Staff, General James Cartwright, agreed. Vice President Joe Biden was even more emphatic about not using the SEALs. "Mr. President," he said, "my suggestion is: *Don't go.*"

On the other side of the debate were CIA director Leon Panetta, Admiral Mike Mullen, and Secretary of State Hillary Clinton, all of whom were torn but ultimately favored a ground assault.

The debate lasted for some time. Eventually, Obama spoke.

"This is a close call and *not* one that I'm ready to make now," he said, surprising everyone. "I need to think about this. I'm going to sleep on it."

WHEN THE BEST DECISIONS ARE REACHED UNCONSCIOUSLY

Long before that night in Washington, back when Barack Obama was still a junior senator and the courier's Pakistani compound had yet to be built, researchers in the Netherlands were conducting a set of experiments about complex decisions similar to the one now facing the president. At the core of their research was a simple question: When making a difficult choice, is it better to think long and hard about the problem or to distract yourself by doing something else?

To some, the very notion that distraction might serve as a viable option might seem preposterous. Say you're preparing an important client presentation. You've narrowed your approach down to several possibilities, each of which has its pluses and minuses. You've got a few hours to decide. Surely it's best to direct your full attention to the problem and carefully analyze your choices. What good could possibly come from, say, going to the movies instead?

The Dutch team had its suspicions. Historical accounts are filled with stories of creative insights appearing when least expected, and more than a few intellectual luminaries are renowned for their use of strategic distraction. Albert Einstein turned to his violin whenever he was stuck. Ludwig van Beethoven made it a habit to take hourlong strolls. Woody Allen often changes rooms and takes multiple showers a day for the express purpose of stimulating insight.

Is it possible that conscious deliberation limits our thinking, the researchers wondered? Perhaps it's when we *refrain* from attending to a problem too closely that we reach the best decisions.

To find out, they designed a clever experiment in which participants were asked to imagine that they were out shopping for a car. There were four vehicles from which they could choose. Each came with a list of features that participants were asked to review before making their selections.

In real life, most cars in a given price range are fairly comparable. There's not a whole lot separating, say, a Nissan Altima from a Toyota Camry. One may look a bit sportier and the other might offer slightly better gas mileage. But overall—in the opinion of most experts, anyway—there's no wrong choice, per se.

Here, the experimenters wanted to avoid ambiguity. So they rigged the options. Of the four cars presented, one had significantly more positive features than the other three. The question was: How many participants would select the best car?

Half of the participants received a lot of information about each vehicle (12 features per car, for a total of 48 pieces of information), making their decision complex. The other half of the participants, meanwhile, received considerably less information (4 features per car, for a total of 16 pieces of information), giving them a fairly simple choice.

Now here's where the experiment gets interesting. After reading about the cars, the participants in the study were once again divided into two groups. Half were given four minutes to review their options and carefully deliberate on the problem. This was the *conscious thought condition*. The other half were distracted from thinking about the cars entirely and asked to solve a set of word jumbles for exactly the same amount of time. This was the *unconscious thought condition*.

Which group made the best decision—the conscious or unconscious thought group? When the choice between cars was simple (4 features per car), conscious thinking yielded the best results. No surprise there: Being able to closely examine the limited options helped. But when the decision was complex (12 features per car), unconscious thinkers didn't just do better—they were nearly *three times* more likely to select the best car.

The study, which appeared in one of academia's top journals, *Science*, in the winter of 2006, came with a sobering conclusion: "Conscious thought does not always lead to sound choices."

Why would conscious thinking backfire in the case of complex decisions? One reason is that our conscious minds have limited capacity. We can only process so much data at one time. When we're faced with more information than we can handle, we try to simplify our decisions, often by focusing on only a small subset of facts. As a result, we tend to overinflate the importance of minor features at the expense of the bigger picture, which leads us astray.

Consider your own experience of choosing a home. You might start off with a fairly broad set of criteria—for example, a two-bedroom apartment in downtown Brooklyn. Perhaps after touring a few places, you narrow your decision down to a few options. How do you choose among them? It's virtually impossible to weigh the relative merits of every important feature—cost, location, view, age of building, distance from public transportation, kitchen size, lighting, noise level, floor number, etc.—which is why it's so easy to get sidetracked. Before you know it, you're deciding where to live based on the decor of the lobby; a feature that was of no concern at the beginning of your search and that will likely contribute very little to your apartment satisfaction.

Research suggests that unlike conscious attention, which is limited in capacity, the unconscious is far better at processing large chunks of information simultaneously. And that's not all. More recent studies have added surprising evidence that unconscious thinking is also well suited for creative problem solving.

The reason? When we try to solve a problem consciously, we tend to think in a rigid and linear fashion. But when we absorb a problem and then set it aside, the ideas that pop into our heads are far less obvious. The unconscious mind is less constrained in its approach, stumbling upon associations that are often inaccessible when we're focusing too hard.

One study asked people to list as many uses for a brick as they could think of in sixty seconds. Bricks can be used to build homes, of course, but they can also be used as a paperweight, a weapon, and a musical instrument. As in the car-buying experiment, participants were divided into conscious and unconscious thinking groups. But importantly, a third group was added in this study. Participants in this control condition were instructed to simply list their ideas right away. By including a neutral group, the experimenters could compare their results with the other two groups to determine whether unconscious thinking elevated performance or if conscious thinking simply made it worse.

Surprisingly, conscious thinking did virtually nothing to elevate creativity. Participants who were given three minutes to think before starting (the conscious thinking group) performed no better than those who answered right away (the control group). As for participants who were told to distract themselves with an unrelated task before responding (the unconscious thinking group)? Results showed that their solutions were more creative than either of the other two groups.

The idea that our mind is unconsciously working on problems we're trying to solve, even when we're off doing something else, has inherent appeal. But is it true? Perhaps these studies merely reflect the benefit of taking a break. Or giving an old problem a fresh look. Maybe what we're really seeing is that it's useful to relax before making an important decision.

For a long time the answer was unclear. The only way to know for sure appeared to be getting inside people's heads. Then, in 2013, a Carnegie Mellon University brain-imaging study did just that.

A research team led by J. David Creswell took a group of adults and asked them to choose between the same set of cars presented in the original Dutch study. But before allowing the participants to finalize their decisions, they distracted them by having them memorize a sequence of numbers. Throughout the experiment, neuroimaging tracked the blood flow in their brains.

The scans were revealing. As expected, the brain regions active in memorization shot a bright red, indicating that those areas were being utilized. But surprisingly, even though participants were fully immersed in memorization, their prefrontal cortex—the area of the brain responsible for decision-making—also lit up, suggesting that deliberation continued.

The conscious mind may have been diverted, but the unconscious mind kept chipping away.

HOW PLAY MAKES PROBLEM SOLVING EASIER

What the research demonstrates is that when it comes to solving a difficult problem or looking for a creative solution, working too hard can backfire. Conscious attention narrows our focus, preventing us from processing complex information and seeing the big picture. We get stuck. And the longer we wrestle with a particular problem, the more difficult it becomes to consider novel alternatives.

What that effectively leads us to is an unlikely conclusion: Sometimes, what appears to the outside world like slacking off is actually the path to smarter decisions and more innovative ideas.

Frequently our most brilliant insights come in the gaps *between* hard work, when we let our guard down and allow disparate ideas to emerge. In those moments when we distract ourselves with a walk to the restroom, the commute home, or the in-flight movie on a business trip.

Think back to your last truly great work-related idea. Now ask yourself: Where were you? Chances are that you weren't sitting behind your desk.

In many ways, problem solvers are like artists. Taking a few steps back provides painters with a fresh perspective on their subject, lending them a new angle for approaching their work. Problem solving follows a similar recipe, but it's not always the physical distance that we need as much as the psychological distance—mental space for new insights to bloom. Walking away doesn't just put our unconscious to work: It helps us see our problem with a new perspective. We become less emotionally attached and free ourselves from the influence of those in our immediate surroundings.

One way many organizations—particularly those whose employees are engaged in high-level thinking, like Google and 3M—leverage this insight is by deliberately scheduling play into the workday. Play may seem like the domain of children, and in some ways that's the point. We are naturally creative when we're young, in part because our brains have not quite developed the capacity to prejudge and censor our ideas.

Putting ourselves in a childlike mind-set opens us up to alternative ways of thinking.

In a fascinating study published in 2010, psychologists at North Dakota State University asked a group of college students to imagine that their classes for the day had been canceled. Next, they asked students to answer a few questions: *What would you do? Where would you go? How would you feel?*

Students in a second group were given the same task, with one key difference. Embedded within their instructions was a brief phrase that led them to think differently about their day off: "You are 7 years old."

Participants in both groups were then asked to complete a series of creativity exercises. Would placing themselves in the shoes of a seven-year-old make any difference? The results were remarkable. Those who first thought of themselves as a child scored significantly better on a variety of creativity measures, suggesting that if you're looking for out-of-the-box thinking, tapping into a childlike mind-set can be quite productive.

As we age, we're trained to believe that play is wasteful, that unless we're producing or consuming information, our time is being squandered. But as the complexity of our work increases, play can actually serve as a vehicle for innovation, by providing opportunities for unconscious thinking to occur.

But there's more to play than simply distraction. When we engage in play we're rewarded for exploring new possibilities, for practicing problem solving, and for taking risks. All of which helps us cultivate an attitude of curiosity and interest, often benefiting our work. Feeling playful also makes us more optimistic, which increases our willingness to take on challenges and helps us maintain a flexible mind-set.

What's the right way of incorporating play into the workplace? Twitter has a climbing wall, Zynga lines its hallways with arcades, and Google boasts several volleyball courts. Does that mean workplace amenities are the solution to getting employees playing regularly? As Stuart Brown, a psychiatrist and the founder of the National Institute for Play, points out, not necessarily. Play, he argues, is a mind-set, not an activity. It has less to do with a fun diversion that happens to take place at the office than it does with the attitudes managers express toward taking time out for exploration.

Ultimately, what's important is for employees to feel safe about pursuing the occasional tangential interests without having to worry relentlessly about outcomes. That's what contributes most to a playful atmosphere.

Sure, it's nice for employees to have access to exciting activities at the office. It certainly makes the opportunities for play more common. But placing a $5,000 billiards table in your break room won't guarantee a playful work environment—especially if members of your management team barely touch it and there is an unspoken stigma about taking breaks.

WHY EXERCISE MAKES US SMARTER

All this talk of fun and games might lead you to believe that our best insights come when we let ourselves rest. But as it turns out, sometimes the best approach to jump-starting the mind is to strain the body.

Most of us have come across research showing that exercise improves mood. Recent studies have found that a regular workout regimen is an even more powerful mood elevator than prescription antidepressants. What's less well known, however, is the profound impact exercise has on learning, memory, and creativity.

To understand how exercise can influence your productivity at work, it helps to consider what our bodies were originally designed to do. As physician John J. Ratey points out in his excellent book *Spark: The Revolutionary New Science of Exercise and the Brain*, the human body was built to expend a great deal of energy on a daily basis. Our ancient ancestors had to walk between five and ten miles a day just to find enough food to survive. Today, of course, most of us spend the majority of our day in front of a computer, sitting. And that relative lack of mobility creates an imbalance in the body's functioning.

It's not the only way we differ from our ancestors. Compared to Paleolithic man, our life is considerably *more* nerve-racking. Sure, our environment is no longer plagued by free-roaming predators, but at the same time, the number of stressors we're exposed to on a daily basis has increased exponentially. Many of us have very little control over our schedule. We face deadlines on a constant basis. And thanks to a twenty-four-hour news cycle, we're continuously reminded of every murder, plane crash, and weather disaster that happens to coincide with our existence on the planet.

On the whole, there's a lot more for us to get worried about. And the tension adds up. Encountering threatening events activates a fight-or-flight response, releasing chemicals into the bloodstream that propel our body to move into action. When we deny it that instinct, we risk incurring side effects that include anxiety, attention deficits, and depression.

Exercise restores the balance. The body was designed to burn off excess energy through physical exertion. Emotional buildup requires physiological relief.

Interestingly, when we exercise, we not only heighten our moods with endorphins but also prime our brains to absorb more information. Neurological studies show that when we exert ourselves physically, we produce a protein called brain-derived neurotrophic factor (BDNF) that promotes the growth of neurons, especially in the memory regions of the brain. A 2007 study found that just two three-minute sprints were enough to elevate BDNF secretion in runners, corresponding to a boost in memorization by a stunning 20 percent.

Why would exercise promote better memory? Ratey summarizes it nicely:

> The body was designed to be pushed, and in pushing our bodies we push our brains too. Learning and memory evolved in concert with motor functions that allowed our ancestors to track down food, so as far as our brain is concerned, if we're not moving, there's no real need to learn anything.

The cognitive jolt we experience following exercise can also yield a more creative product. A 2005 study, for example, found that just thirty minutes on a treadmill led to improved creative performance, and that the benefits endured for a full two hours. Running has also been linked with greater cognitive flexibility. The improvement in mood, coupled with increased blood flow to the brain, provides joggers with a significant mental boost.

To their credit, a number of organizations have taken these findings to heart and looked for ways of incorporating exercise into the workplace. At many companies it's no longer surprising to enter an office and discover a receptionist sitting on a large rubber ball. Or to learn that her manager has given up sitting altogether and now stands all day in front of an elevated desk.

Some organizations, such as Salo, a financial staffing firm in Minneapolis, have even fitted their conference rooms with treadmills facing one another, so employees can jog together while talking through their quarterly projections. It's a trend that appears to be catching on. Texas Health Resources, for example, has extended the approach to a meeting room filled with stationary bikes.

There's a lot of appeal in the notion of combining exercise with work. Unfortunately, it doesn't always work.

John Osborn, CEO of one of New York City's leading advertising firms, BBDO, was an early adopter of an increasingly common sight in many workplaces: the treadmill desk. "I got the treadmill because I heard it's super healthy and can make you burn calories and add years to your life," he told *Ad Age*. To keep Osborn motivated, his boss (BBDO's global CEO) hung a chocolate glazed doughnut from the ceiling so that it dangled just above Osborn's computer. A little visual cue of what could soon be his if he maintained his ambitious regimen.

Early results looked promising. Osborn spent almost 80 percent of his day on the treadmill, and even appeared to be losing weight. But then, almost inexplicably, the reverse happened. The continuous exercise began to alter Osborn's metabolism, making him insatiably hungry.

Before he knew it, he had gained six pounds.

But the thing that really made Osborn question the value of office treadmills (and undoubtedly contributed to him reducing daytime walking to a minuscule 10 percent of his routine) was the effect it had on his performance: "You quickly realize how difficult it is to type anything longer than a sentence."

What Osborn discovered, and what other employee-athletes are bound to find out, is that multitasking physical activities is rarely an effective strategy.

A 2009 University of Tennessee study put treadmill walking to the test by measuring its effect on common workplace activities. For his dissertation, health science professor Dinesh John simulated office work by having participants use their mouses to click on objects, drag and drop, type sentences, and solve basic math problems. Half were seated during the experiment, while the other half walked on a treadmill desk set to a modest speed of one mile per hour. The result? Treadmill walkers performed significantly worse on every task.

It's possible, of course, that with extended practice, treadmill walkers can adapt to the constant motion and regain the proficiency they once had while sitting. A study published in 2014, for example, tracked treadmill walkers for a full year and found that in many cases a rebound effect does occur. But on average, the recovery in performance only appears after an initial dip lasting several months.

Given the body's limitations for juggling multiple physical activities at the same time, a wiser approach involves finding opportunities for employees to exercise away from their computers, in ways that allow them to work out their bodies without jeopardizing the quality of their workplace performance.

Most organizations can't afford an in-house gym. But they can afford to give employees wireless headsets that allow them to walk around their office during long conference calls. Another low-cost approach: offering employees free weights they can use over the course of the day. Rewarding daytime gym-goers with an extended lunch can also benefit workplace performance. According to a 2004 Leeds Metropolitan University study, on days when employees exercised during lunch, a majority reported interacting more with colleagues, managing their time better, and meeting deadlines more effectively.

The gym isn't the only place employees can get their exercise fix. San Francisco software developer Atlassian, for example, keeps bikes in the lobby so that employees can go for a ride during lunch. In Chicago, toy manufacturer Radio Flyer encourages employees to bike to work by offering them an incentive of fifty cents per mile.

Another method is enticing employees with a desirable destination to head to by foot. A complimentary art gallery membership to which workers can go for a quick stroll is one example. Organizations can also offer to reimburse teammates who take an internal meeting on the road and pass a nearby café. Walking meetings may not be ideal for every conversation, but they are likely to spark new ideas by taking employees out of the office and exposing them to a different environment.

The shared elevation in heart rate that comes from walking together can also provide an added benefit: better workplace relationships. As we will discover in Chapter 5, increased arousal in the company of others often fosters interpersonal bonding. Exercising with a colleague can therefore do more than improve your health. It can also make you more likable.

THE CREATIVITY DIET

So far we've seen how unconscious thinking, play, and exercise can all contribute to a smarter workplace. But when it comes to fostering innovation, is that really all it takes?

The answer, of course, is no.

A well-timed diversion can help employees process information they already have in a way that leads to better insights. But when you're looking for outside-the-box solutions, sometimes what you really need is a way of encouraging them to be mentally adventurous.

Consider this example of two regional marketing managers at a nationwide flower distributor—Bob and Jeremy—both of whom are tasked with maximizing their team's profitability. Both are go-getters with impressive track records. But they use strikingly different approaches for developing recommendations.

Bob immediately dives in, interviewing everyone on the team, studying his company's offerings, and devouring previous marketing materials. He looks at past trends and holds meetings with the operations team. He uses his time on the train home to pore over sales forecasts. Within a few weeks he is a product expert. He knows exactly where his team has been, how they're preparing for the upcoming holiday season, and the precise quantity they're likely to sell over the next twelve months.

Jeremy goes about it differently. He uses his first few days to examine his company's offerings, but only until he feels like he understands them well enough to form a general assessment. He then extends his search into other industries and unrelated products: candy, greeting cards, lingerie. He uses his commute home to peruse magazines, looking for connections between other companies' marketing strategies and ones he might use.

A month into their tenures both Bob and Jeremy are summoned to corporate headquarters and asked to deliver their recommendations. Who is likely to offer a more creative approach?

In reality, this is a false choice. Product knowledge and cross-industry expertise are not mutually exclusive. A good marketing manager does both. But it does illustrate an important point: *What we create is a function of the information we consume.*

Our minds naturally search for connections between ideas. And where we direct our attention determines the combinations we find. When we stare at a problem using a single lens, being creative is difficult. We get stuck in old ways of thinking. To uncover new solutions we need to break our mental frames.

A diet of diverse mental stimulation is a vital component of creative thinking. Remember psychologist Dean Simonton, the researcher who discovered that creative geniuses have a surprisingly high failure rate? Well, that's not all he found. His studies also show that on average, creative geniuses tend to have more unusual interests and hobbies than their less successful peers, which likely contributes to their seeing problems differently.

Steve Jobs, arguably a modern-day genius, had this to say about creativity in a 1996 interview with *Wired* magazine:

> Creativity is just connecting things. When you ask creative people how they did something, they feel a little guilty, because they didn't really do it, they just saw something. It seemed obvious to them after a while. That's because they were able to connect experiences they've had and synthesize new things. And the reason they were able to do that was that they've had more experiences or they have thought more about their experiences than other people.

The more ideas we're exposed to, the more likely we are to find novel solutions. Provide enough inputs and new outputs will emerge. As Todd Henry, author of the highly regarded book and podcast *The Accidental Creative* points out, "If you want to regularly generate brilliant ideas, you must be purposeful about what you are putting into your head."

The challenge in most workplaces is that employees are exposed to the same information day after day, making it difficult to come up with new and innovative solutions. But a growing number of companies, inspired by well-known success stories at Google, Yahoo!, and Facebook, are trying to break that mental rut. They've begun inviting employees to set aside a portion of their time each week for free-form exploration and for pursuing projects of their choosing. The only requirement is that their efforts have the potential for benefiting the company in some way.

The practice isn't quite as unstructured as it first sounds. At Google, for example, where developers devote up to 20 percent of their time to self-authored projects, employees are encouraged to work together in groups. The interpersonal dynamic and shared responsibility make productive team projects a point of pride. Employees naturally want their team's contribution to stand out, because, among other things, it means elevated organizational status. At 3M, employees present their work to the rest of the organization using cardboard posters, similar to an annual science fair. And top innovators at Qualcomm are rewarded with cash and stock prizes.

Handing employees the keys to 20 percent of their time may not be workable or even advisable in every industry. But it does have a few undeniable benefits that are worth considering, no matter what business you're in.

By asking employees to identify a work-related interest and empowering them to actively deepen their knowledge base, organizations like Google are turning employees from order takers into job cocreators. It's an approach that helps employees feel autonomous, motivates them to keep an eye out for new business opportunities, and turns every employee into a developer.

With 20 percent time, there's *always* another product in development.

For Google the gambit has clearly been paying off: Gmail, Google News, Google Earth, and AdSense—an advertising vehicle that nets Google $10 billion in revenue a year—are just some of the products that were developed during 20 percent time.

Which raises the question: Would Google be nearly as profitable if its employees sat around waiting for Larry Page and Sergey Brin to tell them what to do?

A PRODUCTIVITY BOOST STRONGER THAN COFFEE

It's 2:14 p.m.

Your eyelids are feeling heavy, and now you're stifling a yawn. A few minutes ago you arrived back in the office, fresh off a satisfying lunch. But now you're in the throes of what is undeniably a midafternoon crash.

You reach for your coffee mug and head for a refill when a coworker stops you in the hall. He's discovered an alternative treatment, he tells you. Like caffeine, it improves concentration and alleviates drowsiness. But it won't give you heartburn or heighten your blood pressure. It's also been clinically proven to elevate your mood, enhance your creativity, and improve your memory.

Sound too good to be true?

It turns out that you used to use this technique all the time. So did your ancient ancestors. It's called napping.

Now, before you dismiss the idea of workplace napping out of hand (as I did before conducting the research for this book), consider the facts. As sleep researcher Sara Mednick notes in her book, *Take a Nap! Change Your Life*, twenty-to-thirty-minute naps have been shown to:

- boost productivity
- increase alertness
- quicken motor reflexes
- raise accuracy
- heighten perceptions
- strengthen stamina
- improve decision-making
- elevate mood
- enhance creativity
- bolster memory
- lower stress
- reduce dependence on drugs and alcohol
- lessen the frequency of migraines and ulcers
- promote weight loss
- minimize the likelihood of heart disease, diabetes, and cancer risk

Not bad for about the same amount of time it takes to visit a Starbucks.

Some studies have shown that learning after a nap is as effective as learning after an entire night's sleep. So why do most of us scoff at the idea of a mental reboot when our bodies signal the need for rest?

In part, it's because we misunderstand napping.

Because our energy levels dip after lunch, we tend to think feeling drowsy is a consequence of having eaten too much. However, research shows that people are equally drowsy eight hours after waking, whether or not they've had lunch beforehand. If you find this hard to believe (as I did), consider the way you feel after breakfast. The first meal of the day energizes us. Why not the second?

Another napping misconception stems from the fact that people occasionally wake up from a midday rest feeling groggy, or find that it disrupts their evening sleep cycle. This problem arises if you allow yourself to sleep too deeply. Unlike nighttime rest, which involves all five stages of the sleep cycle, napping is most effective when we wake *before* our bodies descend into deep sleep.

We have a biological need for rest that is no less pressing than our biological need for food or water. When we're tired, less blood flow reaches the areas of our brain that are critical to thinking. We're also less capable of forming long-term memories. Sure, we can power through the midday slog when we need to—but only at a reduced level of functioning.

Perhaps the biggest reason that we continue to look down on naps, as Tony Schwartz, author of *The Way We're Working Isn't Working*, has noted, is that we have been misled into equating hours on the job with productivity. If you believe that performance is entirely a function of effort, you see anyone who takes a break as a slacker.

In the past, this view had merit. Line workers' value *was* tied to the amount of hours they put in on the factory floor. But the vast majority of us don't work in a factory anymore. In today's knowledge economy, it's the quality of your thinking that matters most, and quality thinking is directly tied to energy level.

A related argument can be made for the growing importance of maintaining a positive mood. In a world in which most jobs involve building interpersonal connections and fostering collaborations, feeling irritable can have serious implications for performance. Research shows that when we're tired, we get into more disagreements, and not just because we're less patient. It's because our ability to read other people diminishes.

A brief midday rest recharges our minds and allows our memories to consolidate. It relaxes our mental filters and allows unconventional ideas to surface. It reenergizes our ability to concentrate and restores our emotional composure.

Slowly the tide is changing on workplace napping. In fact, some organizations are so convinced that sleep improves performance, they're investing thousands of dollars every year in encouraging employees to literally sleep on the job. Among the more generous spenders are *Huffington Post*–AOL, P&G, and Cisco, all of which have installed Energy Pods in their offices. Retailing at about $8,000, the Energy Pod represents the Rolls-Royce of napping accommodations. Climb into the futuristic-looking capsule and you'll find yourself reclining on a leather couch that tilts your feet above your heart, improving circulation. A visor prevents light from entering, while ambient sounds slowly lull you to sleep. After twenty minutes of peaceful restoration, a timer goes off, waking you with a gentle vibration.

Yahoo! and Time Warner outsource their napping to local spas that allow employees to recharge in private rooms, complete with aromatherapy and a selection of nature soundtracks. Zappos, Ben & Jerry's, and even Nike (Nike!) designate in-office "quiet rooms" for employees to sleep or meditate.

Not every workplace is fortunate enough to have sufficient space for a quiet room. But that didn't stop Workman Publishing. The New York City publishing house distributes yoga mats and eye masks, and encourages employees to nap behind room dividers or underneath their desks (George Costanza–style).

Midday napping may sound like an extravagant indulgence that coddles workers. And it's true that employees reap considerable advantage. But the ultimate beneficiaries of allowing for rest are the companies that create the conditions for optimal functioning.

No reasonable person expects to visit a gym and lift weights continuously without a break. We openly acknowledge the limitations of our muscles. But we don't do so for our minds. Declining performance is not as readily visible to us in the office as it is in the weight room, and so we continue plodding along, oblivious to the fact that we are contributing at a fraction of the rate we were earlier.

Ignoring the body's need for recuperation or drugging it into submission may keep workers awake. What it won't do is position them to deliver their best performance.

WHY DISCONNECTING IS SO MUCH HARDER THAN IT LOOKS

How often do you check your cell phone after leaving work? The answer might reveal your future productivity.

According to a 2010 study published in the *Journal of Applied Psychology*, the less employees detach psychologically during off-hours, the higher their emotional exhaustion in twelve months' time.

Staying connected is addictive. It helps us feel needed, in the know, productive. But constant communication comes with a cost. An onslaught of e-mails, text messages, and phone calls breeds a sense of perpetual emergency, fostering an ongoing stress response in the brain. And as we've seen, continuous pressure has a damaging effect on the way we think and feel.

When we can't fully log off, we can't fully recover.

Jim Loehr is a sports psychologist who has coached some of the world's top athletes. Early in his career, Loehr spent countless hours studying elite tennis performers, trying to pinpoint what makes them better than everyone else. What he found was surprising. According to Loehr, the key difference can't be found in players' serves, their volleys, or their play at net. It's not even their experience or innate ability that sets them apart. It's what they do *between* points. Some athletes are better at calming their nerves and restoring their focus, and they're the ones who tend to win most.

Loehr's observation is as applicable to the workplace as it is to the tennis court. A careful balance of work and recovery is as vital for mental athletes as it is for those whose job it is to excel at physical skill. In both cases, when we deny ourselves the opportunity to recuperate, our performance invariably suffers.

In many organizations, being available around the clock has become an unspoken expectation. When a manager sends late-night e-mails, he implicitly endorses a round-the-clock work culture, paving the way for after-hours stress that spills over into the home, where a curt e-mail can spoil a dinner or ruin a weekend.

While there are undoubtedly instances when staying connected is a legitimate necessity, it's rare for a business to require that every team member stay logged on continuously. Moreover, it's in a company's interest to allow employees to recover. If an associate is frequently working late into the night and through the weekend, she is likely doing so at a cost to her long-term engagement.

It used to be the case that managers had to push employees to work harder. Today the opposite seems to be happening. In many industries, a key to retaining top talent involves protecting employees from working nonstop, which is why some pioneering organizations are starting to take matters into their own hands, leaving employees little choice but to recharge.

Volkswagen, for example, has begun turning off its e-mail server thirty minutes after the end of a shift and turning it back on just before the start of the next one. They're not alone in limiting access. Other organizations, like Empower Public Relations in Chicago, are also adopting an e-mail blackout policy, because they find that it helps employees arrive at work fresher the next day.

Daimler, another German automaker, has programmed its server to automatically delete e-mails received during employee vacations, telling senders who they can contact in an employee's absence. Even the highly regarded Boston Consulting Group has begun monitoring employee paid time off (PTO)—not to identify employees who take too much personal time, but to flag individuals who accrue too many hours without taking a break.

A surprising number of companies have stopped limiting vacation time altogether, including IBM, Evernote, and Netflix. It's a way of communicating trust in their employees and encouraging them to take the time they need when they need it.

But the workplace with the most outrageously pro–time off policy? Without a doubt, that title belongs to FullContact, a Denver software company that in 2012 implemented a program that actually pays employees $7,500 to take their family on vacation. There are, however, a few strings attached. To receive the bonus, employees must first agree to three strict provisions, as outlined on the blog of Full-Contact CEO Bart Lorang:

1. You have to go on vacation, or you don't get the money.
2. You must disconnect.
3. You can't work while on vacation.

And just why are they being so generous? Lorang put it this way: "We'll be a better company if employees disconnect."

HOW TO CATCH A TERRORIST

On the morning of April 29, 2011, Barack Obama gathered a number of his top aides in the White House Diplomatic Reception Room. The mood was tense. No one had a clue what he would say following the previous night's discussion.

Before any of them could speak, the president delivered his answer.

"It's a go," he announced. They all knew what it meant. He was sending in the SEALs.

Two days later, Special Forces descended upon the Pakistani compound. When the operation was over, the Pacer, whose identity was confirmed as Osama bin Laden, was among the casualties. His body was later buried at sea so that a shrine could not be built by his admirers.

What convinced Obama to authorize the raid? In part, it was by stepping back and seeing the bigger picture.

There was no denying that a ground offensive would endanger American lives. And it was true: In comparison, an unmanned drone strike would be considerably safer. When viewed from this perspective, the decision appears to hinge on a single factor: Is the risk justified? Should the president gamble with American lives in order to attain confirmation of bin Laden's identity and secure access to any intelligence that might be stored within the compound?

However, there is something this analysis is missing: context.

What the high-risk/low-risk dichotomy leaves out is the frequency with which Navy SEALs face hazardous circumstances. To them, entering life-threatening situations is not uncommon. It's the norm. Just how often are Navy SEALs involved in dangerous missions? As former chairman of the Joint Chiefs of Staff Mike Mullen later pointed out, invading bin Laden's compound wasn't even the only SEAL operation taking place *that night*. There were several units engaged in comparable missions, some considerably more dangerous.

What may not be known is in addition to this operation that night, this specific one, there were multiple operations just like this going on in Afghanistan. Some of them actually more difficult than the one that got bin Laden. And when I say more difficult, I don't think higher strategic risk, certainly not more important, but physically more difficult, more dangerous than the one that our great Special Forces executed.

On the surface, the Obama decision appeared to center on whether or not the president should put the Navy SEALs at risk. But the reality is, Navy SEALs are constantly at risk, and this mission was not outside the norm of what they regularly do. It was the realization that invading bin Laden's compound, albeit dangerous, was within the realm of the SEALs' expertise that swayed Obama's thinking.

"The reason I was willing to make that decision of sending in our SEALs to try to capture or kill bin Laden rather than to take some other options," he told NBC's Brian Williams, "was ultimately because I had 100 percent faith in the Navy SEALs themselves."

It would be naive to suggest that the president's choice to get some sleep is the reason the world's most wanted terrorist is no longer alive. Obama had spent months grappling with the issue, debating the pros and cons with advisers, weighing the political ramifications, evaluating the military and diplomatic risks. The decision to invade "on the ground" was a long time coming. And despite the considerable benefits of sleep, no serious scientist would suggest that rest (or the unconscious thinking it can facilitate) is a legitimate substitute for the hard work of fact-finding, careful analysis, and intellectual scrutiny.

What it does reflect, however, is the decision-making style of a man who is accustomed to processing an inconceivable amount of data and delivering choices that often prove successful.

Obama doesn't do his job by working endlessly. He does it by collecting information, evaluating his options, and, critically, taking frequent breaks.

Six days a week, his first order of business is exercise: forty-five minutes, alternating between weight training and cardio. He makes time for play, fitting basketball and golf into his weekly schedule. He reads history and nonfiction, but also literary fiction, noir mystery, and modern poetry. During his first four years in office, Barack Obama took 131 vacation days, averaging more than a month off per year.

"Nothing comes to my desk that is perfectly solvable," Obama told *Vanity Fair*'s Michael Lewis in 2012. "Otherwise, someone else would have solved it. So you wind up dealing with probabilities. Any given decision you make you'll wind up with a 30 to 40 percent chance that it isn't going to work. You have to own that and feel comfortable with the way you made the decision."

You don't need to be president of the United States to face a similar level of uncertainty at your job. Often our days are filled with complex decisions in which the right solution is anything but obvious. And while the choices we make may not determine the fate of the free world, that doesn't mean we take them any less seriously.

Which is why it's helpful to know that smart thinking and time off are not incompatible. And that, in fact, there are instances when the most effective approach to achieving great work is simply to stop.

When complexity abounds, hard work can sow the seeds for insights. But it's the occasional distraction that makes them bloom.

The Lessons of Play
Action Items for Managers

Take up gardening. Relying exclusively on leaders to come up with groundbreaking solutions is a remnant of the past. How do today's innovative companies stay successful? By fostering creativity from the bottom up. Following an interview with Amazon CEO Jeff Bezos, *New York Times* columnist Thomas Friedman took away this insight on leadership in the information age: "'You have to think of yourself not as a *designer* but as a *gardener'*—seeding, nurturing, inspiring, cultivating the ideas coming from below, and then making sure people execute them." If great ideas are important to your company, start by creating the conditions that promote innovative thinking. Integrating play, exercise, and the occasional break have all been shown to spark creativity.

Distract strategically. Exposing people to new and unexpected ideas makes them more creative. How do you put that insight to use? By setting aside time each week for a group viewing of an employee-nominated TED talk, or by scheduling a monthly show-and-tell on industry trends. You can also start a "You Don't Have to Read the Book" club (as they did at Mercedes-Benz) to stimulate discussion on new ideas. Creativity doesn't happen when we sink into a routine. It's when we make exploration a habit that we find unexpected solutions.

Redirect your inner workaholic. As a manager, if you sit at your desk for twelve hours a day and spend your weekends churning out e-mails, the message is clear: Disconnecting is bad. To get the most from your team and keep them engaged, give your employees the space to recharge. Go ahead and send those evening and weekend e-mails if you want to, but program them to arrive during work hours, so that your employees can spend their off-hours being present at home.

The Lessons of Play
Action Items for Emerging Leaders

Put your unconscious to work. Conscious deliberation is useful for solving simple problems, but when the challenge facing you is complex, you're more likely to find clearer insights after a period of incubation. To get the most out of unconscious thinking, do the work of getting clarity about your goal and absorbing the data at your disposal. Then, distract yourself by taking a walk, reading an article, or working on something unrelated. Research suggests a thirty-minute diversion is often ideal. When you return to your original assignment, you're likely to see things differently than before you left.

Use mornings for learning and look for insight at night. The same internal clock that causes your body to feel sluggish in the afternoon also influences other aspects of your performance. Studies show that cognitive skills are sharpest in the morning, when working memory peaks, but that as the day wears on we tend to retain less. Feeling tired also has its upsides. The more fatigued we are, the weaker our internal mental filter, which means more unusual associations come to mind. When you're looking for a creative solution at work, try reexamining it later in the evening. You're likely to discover a novel and unexpected way of seeing things.

Reframe exercise as part of your job. Exercise doesn't just improve your health; it gives you a mental edge. Many of us neglect going to the gym, especially during weeknights, when we're concerned about falling behind at work. But what recent research shows is that regular exercise can boost your memory, elevate your creativity, and improve your efficiency. In short, it can make you a better employee. The more complexity you deal with at work, the more value you can derive from keeping your body physically fit.

FOUR

What Happy Workplaces Can Learn from a Casino

When I was nineteen years old, I had a life-altering experience inside a casino.

I was somewhere in the mid-Atlantic, onboard a Caribbean cruise that my parents had booked for a family vacation. The ship itself was stunning, with no shortage of entertainment options: hot tubs, ping-pong tables, a basketball court. The food was as plentiful as it was delicious. Outside, the weather was sun-kissed perfection.

But once we reached international waters, none of that seemed to matter. Because now, the casino was open for business.

I'd heard that there was a casino onboard and I had come prepared. A week earlier, after discovering that the ship permitted gambling for anyone over the age of eighteen, I wasted no time picking out a book that promised to reveal the secrets of blackjack. I studied it religiously, devouring it several times over while making notes along the edges.

By the time we were boarding, I was more than ready. I had developed a system.

My approach was simple. I would bet the table minimum of $5 on the first hand. If I won, I would stick to this amount, continuing to play $5 hands. However, the moment I lost, I would double the size of each ensuing bet, chasing the previous loss. First I would bet $10, then $20, and finally $40. The idea was to give myself four chances of coming out a winner. After the fourth loss, I would accept defeat, reverting back to the original $5 level.

If you assume that the chance of winning a hand of blackjack is roughly equivalent to a coin flip (50 percent), then the chance of losing four hands in a row is 6.25 percent (50 percent × 50 percent × 50 percent × 50 percent). That means that as a bettor, you have a 93.75 percent chance of winning each time. Even before passing my first stats class, I could tell these were pretty good odds.

On the first night of the cruise, while my family was enjoying calypso music by the pool, I placed my first table bet and won. My goal was to collect $50 and then leave. In retrospect, that doesn't seem like a particularly lofty financial goal, but at the time I considered it a princely sum, large enough to cover even the most lavish of meals at a local McDonald's. In less than twenty minutes I had made my nut (a gambling expression I had picked up from my book) and bolted back to the cabin elated.

The next few evenings brought similar results: $55 one night, $65 the next. By the sixth day I was up over $300. I was not raking in a fortune, but I was winning consistently. Which seemed like definitive proof: My system was working.

Then came the final night of the cruise.

For reasons I couldn't understand, my technique wasn't working its usual magic. Before that evening I had lost four consecutive hands just once. But now, a mere forty minutes into my visit, I had already done it three times. I watched in horror as half of my week's winnings disappeared.

My system called for me to buckle down. Play conservatively. Slowly work my way back into the black using a steady regimen of $5 bets. But I no longer had the patience. My discipline was completely gone. And before I knew it, all of the chips that I had accumulated over the previous six days were on the line.

I had bet it all on a single hand.

WHAT CASINO OPERATORS KNOW

A funny thing happens to your brain inside a casino.

Rational thinking becomes elusive. Logic and self-control fade. You suddenly find yourself gripped with a hunger for immediate gratification.

The emotional roller coaster of winning and losing is one reason it's hard to maintain your poise, but there's more to it than that. Casinos also play a role in promoting a risk-taking mind-set. They do so by using subtle techniques that sway our moods, shape our thinking, and gently nudge us in the direction of gambling.

Some methods are more obvious than others. Take chips, for example. Casinos minimize the use of real currency, because it makes gambling more palatable. It's painful to remove a crisp twenty-dollar bill out of your wallet when you're ready to place a bet, and even harder to watch a dealer take it away. Betting with colorful plastic chips makes losses abstract and allows gambling to feel like more of a game.

In recent years, casinos have shrewdly been working to widen the psychological distance between gamblers and their money. Slot players no longer walk around with coin-filled plastic cups. Instead, their money is converted into electronic "units" and recorded on paper vouchers. Coinless slot machines make gambling faster—meaning there's less time wasted waiting for players to pick up a coin and place it in the slot—and eliminate pesky cues that make losing more obvious. Casino visitors no longer have the benefit of seeing their coin stack shrink or feeling their cup getting lighter.

Slot machines can be tricky in other ways as well. It used to be that you'd walk up to a slot machine, pull the lever, and hope for three cherries. Today single-row slots are exceedingly rare. Most machines allow for a large number of winning combinations across multiple rows. On the surface, it sounds great. But the payout on cross-row combinations is much lower and often results in players "winning" a fraction of their original bet.

Why would casinos bother telling players they've won when they clearly haven't? Because the frequent, irregular payouts promote the *feeling* of winning, which leads gamers to continue betting.

If all of that weren't enough, casino floors bombard the senses. Blinking lights and colorful sounds excite, overwhelm, and disorient. Visual icons of fruit, cartoons, and popular TV shows are used to lull visitors into feeling safe. And all the while, scantily clad women dressed as bunnies parade up and down the aisle, distributing free alcoholic drinks.

What casinos are doing is leveraging a series of psychological techniques that increase people's tolerance for risk, enhancing their willingness to gamble.

So what's all this got to do with the workplace? More than you think.

In most organizations, risk-taking is obviously of limited value. But there exist certain mind-sets that *are* worth promoting among employees. Like happiness.

Research shows that happy people tend to be more effective at their jobs. When we're feeling good about our lives, we connect with others more easily, think more optimistically, and free up valuable mental resources to focus on novel ideas. Happiness also breeds confidence. Positive moods make our situation feel more controllable, which can give us the grit to power through challenging tasks.

How exactly do you foster happiness in the workplace? By taking a cue from casinos and embedding psychological triggers into the employee experience that promote a positive mind-set.

In recent years, scientists have made tremendous strides in understanding the conditions that foster happiness. As it turns out, when it comes to sustaining happiness, a few minor changes can have a surprisingly large impact. In this chapter we'll take a look at some of the more intriguing discoveries and examine ways organizations can apply these findings to the workplace.

WHY WORKPLACE HAPPINESS IS HARD TO FIND

One of the more distressing facts about human nature is that we are not particularly good at staying happy. Positive emotions wear off. Whether we've earned a promotion, landed a new client, or moved to the corner office, with time we tend to return to our happiness baseline.

Often the process doesn't take very long. Consider what happens when you order a wonderful dish at a new restaurant. The first bite is exquisite. The second is very good. By the third, you're ready to share. The more you eat, the less enjoyment you derive from your meal, until after a certain threshold you couldn't bear another bite.

Chances are, the next time you return to the restaurant and order the same dish, it will taste like it's missing something. It is: novelty.

The good news about our inclination to adapt is that the same psychological process responsible for acclimating us to positive events is also at work when we experience a tragedy. Studies show that lottery winners, for example, return to their happiness baseline roughly one year after receiving their windfall. Accident victims show a similar pattern. Just twelve months after losing the use of their legs, paraplegics estimate that they will feel just as happy in the future as they did before their injury.

Our brains are programmed to adapt to our circumstances, and for good reason. Too happy and we'd lack any ambition; too sad and we'd never leave our beds.

To some, learning about the existence of a happiness baseline can feel incredibly liberating. It means that no matter how badly you screw up your next project, inevitably your disappointment *will* wear off, and you'll return to your happiness set point. So why not take some risks? After all, you're working with an emotional safety net.

To others, it can seem downright depressing. If happiness is fleeting, what's the point of even trying? It's the reason some researchers have equated the human condition to a "happiness treadmill." We struggle as hard as we can, only to remain stuck in the same emotional place.

Recently psychologists have begun examining ways of slowing the adaptation process as a means of prolonging happy experiences. If we can prevent ourselves from habituating too quickly to positive experiences, the reasoning goes, we can sustain the initial high for longer periods of time.

How do you delay adaptation? Here's a look at what we've learned so far.

INSIGHT #1: *FREQUENCY* IS MORE IMPORTANT THAN *SIZE*

Every positive experience takes some getting used to. And the more positive events we have, the longer it takes us to return to baseline. Which leads us to our first happiness insight: *Small, frequent pleasures can keep us happy longer than large, infrequent ones.*

What this means from a practical perspective is that bringing home a ten-dollar arrangement of flowers every Friday for a month is a wiser happiness-promoting strategy than purchasing a single forty-dollar bouquet. So is spacing out weekend getaways over the course of a year instead of taking a single two-week vacation.

The more frequent our happiness boosts, the longer our mood remains above baseline.

The implications from an organizational standpoint can be profound. For one thing, we may be better off splitting up positive annual events into quarterly ones. Companies often hand out bonuses at the end of the year, but delivering smaller, quarterly bonuses may be a more effective strategy. The same logic applies to parties. Instead of spending lavishly on a single holiday party, it may be wiser to divide spending into smaller increments, providing seasonal get-togethers.

The importance of frequent positive events also provides a new lens for appreciating the psychological value of office perks. Offering employees relatively inexpensive workplace benefits—for example, by purchasing a high-end espresso machine or stocking the refrigerator with interesting snacks—is more likely to sustain day-to-day happiness levels than the sporadic pay increase.

From the employee perspective, access to office perks can often do more than temporarily elevate mood: It also sends an implicit signal that an organization cares about them. While financial bonuses tend to be viewed as payment for performance, perks communicate on an emotional level and provide a motivational boost. Studies show that when employees feel cared for, they are inclined to reciprocate by working harder. A 2012 experiment conducted by behavioral economists at the University of Zurich, for example, found that on-the-job rewards are significantly more motivating than cash bonuses of identical value.

In 2013, executives at Pictometry, an aerial imaging company based in Rochester, New York, made the decision to set aside $2,500 a week toward feeding their 250 employees. Everything from popcorn to cold cuts to microwavable meals were made available for everyone on staff to munch on throughout the day. Employees were even asked to provide input on how they thought the money should be spent.

Then a funny thing happened. One technician asked if he could use a portion of the stipend to bake pies over the weekend, offering to bring them in for his colleagues. Another requested that the office purchase a slow cooker and volunteered to bring in ingredients for a stew. Today it's not uncommon to find staffers at Pictometry sitting together for communal lunches that they themselves have cooked.

To be fair, $2,500 a week is by no means a small expenditure. Multiply that amount over fifty-two weeks a year and you're looking at a bill of $130,000. Is it worth it?

Here it's instructive to look at the alternative: If Pictometry were to abolish its generous meal stipend and divide the money it's now spending among its 250 employees, each one of them would receive a raise totaling just one quarter per hour. Which would you prefer: a salary bump of two dollars a day or access to an unlimited snack bar and the occasional home-cooked meal?

INSIGHT #2: VARIETY PREVENTS ADAPTATION

Increasing the frequency of positive events isn't the only way of delaying adaptation. So is introducing variation.

Because our brains are programmed to habituate quickly to our circumstances, we tend to tune out events that happen repeatedly, no matter how positive. Our minds slip into autopilot when our environment is predictable, conserving mental energy for when changes occur. We need new experiences to keep us emotionally engaged.

From an evolutionary perspective, it's a process that's served us well. The inevitable boredom that arises once we adapt to our circumstances is what keeps us striving for bigger and better, no matter how much we've achieved. What it hasn't done, however, is make us very good at savoring positive experiences when they happen. The more we do the same enjoyable things, the less attention we pay them. Which teaches us an important lesson about happiness: Sometimes, in order to continue enjoying something we love, we need for it to temporarily disappear.

This is one reason traveling can feel so rewarding. When we go away, we break the routine of everyday life. Not having access to your bed, your car, or your favorite reading corner might hardly be noticeable when you're traveling. But when you return, you suddenly have a newfound appreciation for the little things that contribute to your comfort. In some ways, the real benefit of a vacation is in helping us recognize the pleasures of being home.

Variety helps prevent adaptation, which is why creating a happy workplace involves more than just repeating the same enjoyable activities again and again.

One way of introducing variety into the workplace is by linking certain happiness boosts to specific seasons. At Plante Moran, an accounting and business advisory firm, employees take breaks in the warm months to enjoy ice cream together, and share apple cider and doughnuts when the temperature drops. Summertime barbecues, fall clambakes, Halloween pumpkin–carving contests, and winter chili cook-offs are just a sampling of seasonal events that can quickly become office traditions.

Some workplaces take it one step further and design unique seasonal events that reflect their company culture. Santa Clara's Hitachi Data Systems, for example, marks every summer with an annual Dog Day, on which employees not only bring their dogs to work but get to treat them to an assortment of activities that include grooming, professional training, and a talent show. It's a way of elevating morale and highlighting the company's commitment to family. Qualcomm is another organization that has adopted seasonal activities. During summer months they invite local farmers to set up shop on their lawn for a weekly farmers' market, giving employees access to fresh fruit, honey, and flowers before heading home for the evening.

By connecting positive events with certain months of the year, organizations can enhance an activity's emotional impact while creating an additional layer to the experience: giving employees something to look forward to.

Another way of ensuring variation involves adopting a technique similar to one used by Admiral Group, an insurance provider with offices in Canada and the United Kingdom. The company has created a "Ministry of Fun" that rotates employees on a monthly basis, giving fresh voices an opportunity to chime in with new activities to make the workplace more enjoyable. While the "Ministry of Fun" moniker might not suit every organization, the idea of enlisting the help of employees on an ongoing basis has considerable value. Novel suggestions are a lot easier to come by when every member of a company is invested in finding new ways of elevating the workplace experience.

INSIGHT #3: UNEXPECTED PLEASURES DELIVER
   ## A BIGGER THRILL

Picture this: You arrive at the office on a Monday morning and discover that your lobby is covered in a sea of balloons. A local band is playing by the elevator. Tuxedoed waiters are handing out breakfast hors d'oeuvres.

What would you think?

When something surprising happens, our brains automatically pay closer attention, lending unexpected events greater emotional weight. We're motivated to make sense of events we haven't predicted and devote more mental energy to thinking about them after they occur.

In this way, surprises provide an emotional exclamation point, enhancing the impact of any event—good or bad.

In *The Myths of Happiness*, psychologist Sonja Lyubomirsky writes that one reason the start of a romantic relationship is so alluring is that every encounter reveals something new about your partner. With each shared activity comes a new revelation about his or her interests, history, and goals. The constant flow of surprises keeps us engaged.

But with time, we get to know your partner. The discoveries stop, and it's at this point that many relationships are at risk of losing their glow.

The same can be said for most jobs. When we first join an organization, each day involves meeting new people, exploring new locations, and learning new practices. Then one morning the surprises stop. We know almost everything about our workplaces, and suddenly our jobs are predictable.

Given that surprises enhance the impact of an event, it's ironic that most workplaces only use surprises to communicate negative information. A colleague is fired; a department is reorganized; a product is discontinued. Some bad news is clearly unavoidable, and there's no changing the fact that certain information is better kept under wraps. But when events like these are unexpected, it causes us to stand up and take even more notice than we normally would.

By leveraging positive surprises in the workplace, organizations can get a bigger emotional bang for their buck. How do you surprise your employees? One idea might be renting out a movie theater and taking everyone out for the premiere of a major release. Or hiring a massage therapist to walk around the office for a day. Or paying a professional impersonator to call an employee on her birthday.

The goal is not just to improve mood temporarily but to create an environment of positive expectations. The more employees anticipate good things happening, the more likely they are to find them.

INSIGHT #4: EXPERIENCES ARE MORE REWARDING THAN OBJECTS

Suppose you've just wrapped up a successful year. Your client base has expanded and your revenues have soared. It's just been announced that you can expect a larger budget in the next fiscal year. Things are going well in your division, and you want to be sure you retain your current team.

What's the best way of investing the money to make your employees happy?

When it comes to choosing between different purchase options, one line of research worth consulting is the emerging science of smarter spending. In recent years a number of psychologists have begun looking at the happiness ROI of various products and services. What they've discovered is that purchasing life experiences (for example, a hot-air balloon ride, a wine-tasting class, or a vacation to Italy) tends to provide a greater happiness boost than spending a comparable amount on material objects (for example, a flat-screen television, a fancy suit, or a purse).

Why is this the case? For one thing, it's because experiences tend to involve other people, and being in the company of others elevates our happiness. Experiences also expose us to new ideas and surroundings, growing our intellectual curiosity and expanding our horizons. Material objects, on the other hand, are often used in private, when we're away from friends and family, and rarely entail novel adventures.

Unlike material objects, experiences tend to improve with age. Think back to a vacation you've taken in the past. Did you have a good time? Research shows we remember events more positively the further they are in our rearview mirror. But that overpriced watch buried in your dresser? It's suffered a few scratches and no longer seems quite as chic as the day you bought it.

When facing a choice on departmental spending, it's worth keeping this insight in mind. Investing in employee experiences—by sending staff members to conferences, sponsoring exciting group outings, or giving away a weekend getaway in place of a small bonus—can yield a bigger happiness boost than investing in new furniture or upgrading your phone system.

One cautionary note: If your office equipment is a constant source of frustration and prevents your employees from doing their jobs, investing in your business infrastructure makes good sense. But if your team is relatively satisfied with their office setup, it's then that you should favor experiences. Not only are experiences likely to lift the moods at your office, they can also foster stronger connections among colleagues and help them see their workplace as a vehicle for continued growth.

INSIGHT #5: WE DON'T ALWAYS KNOW WHY WE'RE HAPPY

As we discovered in Chapter 2, our environment often has a powerful impact on our behavior. Our minds absorb an enormous amount of information about our surroundings and use it to guide our thoughts, feelings, and behaviors. And much of this process happens outside of our conscious awareness.

One feature of our environment that we rarely pay attention to is scent. Research shows than when we're exposed to positive scents—as we are standing outside a café, a candle shop, or a bakery, for example—we tend to become happier and we don't know why. Interestingly, the change in mood often affects our behavior. We become more helpful, less competitive, and show greater generosity.

A Washington State University study found that stores that spray pleasing scents through their ventilation systems (a practice known in the industry as aroma marketing) are rated as more colorful, cheerful, and modern. Shoppers also perceive the products sold at these locations as "higher quality" and more "up-to-date," which explains why they're more willing to return to scented stores than their unscented competitors.

The fact that scents can unconsciously put people in positive moods hasn't escaped the attention of casinos. It's no accident that many of the world's most successful gambling destinations continue to pump fragrances onto their gaming floors, despite the fact that smoking at their facilities (which used to be the main reason for modifying a casino's scent) has been banned for years. Research shows that slot machines near pleasing scents rake in a stunning 50 percent more than those in unscented locations.

Music can also lift our mood unconsciously. Our heart rates tend to synchronize to the sounds we hear, which is why techno can send our pulses racing while the slow croon of Frank Sinatra can help us relax. Retailers often use music as a tool for influencing shoppers, and the research shows it's effective. When the music in our environment is slow, we tend to move accordingly. Studies show that customers linger in stores and restaurants that play relaxing music, which often leads them to purchase more. For bar owners, however, a different strategy applies. The faster the music, the more quickly people drink, and the larger their tab.

Obviously no office wants to smell like a casino or sound like a bar. Yet the findings do hint at subtle ways ordinary workplaces can tweak their environments to promote better moods. Lavender sachets in the break room or fresh flowers near the entrance can provide a modest psychological boost. So too can jazz music in the hallway or a collection of employees' favorite tunes playing in the restrooms.

No one change is enough to single-handedly transform a work environment. But together, they add up.

INSIGHT #6: A GRATEFUL MIND IS A HAPPY ONE

There's another thing we can do to foster happiness in the workplace: train ourselves to be grateful.

It's a lot harder than it sounds. In many ways, we're implicitly encouraged to tune out the positive when we're working. Much of our day is consumed with thinking about future deadlines and tasks we have yet to accomplish. The process can take a toll. Over time a continuous focus on *what's missing* trains our minds to center on the negative.

It's rare that we pause to savor what we've achieved. The moment one grueling project ends, the next begins. But by taking a moment to direct our attention to things that are going right, we enhance our enjoyment and stave off the process of adaptation. Gratitude helps us appreciate positive events when they happen, making them last longer. We restore a balance to our thinking that elevates our moods and prevents negative emotions like resentment, envy, and regret from creeping in.

Psychologists have found that simply asking people to identify specific aspects of their lives for which they are thankful alters their perspectives in powerful ways. When we build appreciation for our current circumstances, we feel happier about the present and more optimistic about the future, which improves the quality of our work. Grateful people also recover from stress more quickly and behave more generously toward those around them.

An activity that researchers recommend for cultivating gratitude in our lives is jotting down positive events, either electronically or in a notebook. The simple practice of keeping a gratitude journal has been shown to promote a healthier mental outlook and lower one's chances of growing depressed.

While journaling may work well for individuals, implementing the practice on an organizational level presents considerable challenges. The moment you start requiring employees to document positive events, the practice gains all the appeal of filling out time sheets.

So what can you do to help employees—and yourself—feel grateful?

One solution involves setting aside time every few weeks for employees to share their recent accomplishments as a group. Think of a traditional staff meeting—with an important twist.

In most organizations, staff meetings involve a small subset of colleagues discussing tasks that have not been completed. It's designed to bring everyone in a department up to speed on current projects and create plans for the week ahead. While traditional staff meetings certainly have their place, their focus on *what's missing* does little to promote a sense of gratitude. An alternative to this approach is to include a broader group, inviting employees from a range of departments for a planned get-together. Instead of asking everyone to talk about what they haven't done, use the meeting as an opportunity for staff members to share what they are most proud of having accomplished since the group last met.

It's fascinating to watch the process unfold. When people are asked to talk about their accomplishments in front of others, they often try to shift the focus away from themselves. Inevitably, during meetings like this an employee will thank a colleague for a contribution he or she has made. And when that happens, others are likely to mimic this behavior by recognizing their coworkers and the help they've provided. Soon the practice of expressing gratitude—not just about the employees' own circumstances but toward their colleagues—catches on.

By subtly shifting the focus from *what's missing* to *what's been achieved*, progress-focused meetings allow employees to reflect on aspects of their work that are going right, instead of falling for the *what's missing?* trap. In their 2011 book, *The Progress Principle*, Harvard Business School professor Teresa Amabile and researcher Steven Kramer present compelling evidence that the experience of progress is the single most important component of a satisfying workday. And yet, in most organizations, it is rare for employees to consider the goals they've accomplished or the growth they've achieved.

Progress-focused meetings make these experiences easier to notice and more fully appreciate. What's more, they also expose employees to the work of their colleagues, building a sense of connection between teammates, while helping everyone recognize the way their efforts are linked.

THE DARK SIDE OF HAPPINESS

I remember feeling queasy the moment I let go of my chips.

An entire week's winnings was about to vanish and all because of some stupid impulse. It took forever for the dealer to start the hand. I couldn't help but wince at the ship's rocking, which had suddenly grown more noticeable.

My eyes widened when I saw my cards: a king and a queen, for a total of twenty. Not bad. For a second I sensed a wave of undeserved relief, the way it feels after you accidentally blow past a stop sign without attracting the police. I looked up at the dealer's hand. He was showing a five of hearts—one of the weakest starting positions for a player. Slowly it dawned on me that I was facing a choice. I could play it safe and stick with my twenty, or I could "split" my king and queen into two separate hands, requiring me to double my initial bet, but also giving me two chances to win. The book I had read made it absolutely clear: A starting hand of five results in a dealer's bust more than 40 percent of the time. It would be foolish not to split my cards, tantamount to blackjack malpractice.

Reluctantly, I reached for my wallet and emptied it out, barely meeting the required bet.

The rest of the hand is something of a blur. But I do remember this much: It got very quiet when the dealer turned over his second card and found a six. And then, it got very loud when he drew a ten, yielding an unbeatable total of twenty-one.

The walk back to the cabin was agonizing. Not only had I failed to profit after investing six nights in a casino, I was now leaving it practically broke. The mix of humiliation, disgust, and self-pity lasted for some time. But it was in that unhappiness that I learned something important about myself: Gambling is not an activity for which I am well suited.

Several years later, after the sting of that casino experience had long abated, I sat down with Professor Ed Deci, whose research on motivation inspired Daniel Pink's bestseller *Drive*. I had applied for a position in his lab and was visiting the University of Rochester for an interview.

"So, tell me about happiness," he said, referring to the essay I'd included with my graduate school application. I replied by summarizing what I had written in my paper: that I was committed to studying happiness because I couldn't think of anything more important in people's lives. To this day I remember Ed's response, verbatim: "Well, I think happiness is a bunch of *crap*."

I was confused. Here was a psychologist who had made a career of studying optimal human functioning. What could he possibly find objectionable about happiness?

Then he explained.

When we're completely consumed with trying to be happy all the time, Ed told me, we overlook the value of unhappy emotions, such as anger, embarrassment, and shame. Those experiences may not feel very pleasant when they're happening, but they exist for a reason. Negative emotions help direct our attention to elements of our environment that require a response. From Ed's perspective, artificially blunting negative emotions comes with a cost. It prevents us from acknowledging errors and adapting our behaviors.

In a fascinating 2011 article echoing Ed's concerns, psychologists June Gruber, Iris Mauss, and Maya Tamir identify other surprising ways that feeling bad can serve our interests. When we feel sad, for example, we send a social signal to those around us that we need help. Think about the last time you saw someone cry. If you're like most people, you felt an immediate impulse to provide comfort and support. It's the sadness that drew you in.

Feeling guilty can also be useful. It motivates us to repair something damaging we've done to hurt a relationship. Even embarrassment has its upside. It tells us we've committed a social infraction and pushes us to make amends (for example, by telling yourself never to gamble again).

Interestingly, research suggests another downside to excessive happiness: an increased tendency for making mistakes. When we're happy, we grow confident, which at times can lead us to overestimate our abilities and ignore potential dangers. We can become more trusting, less critical, and occasionally unrealistic.

In 2007, psychologists Shigehiro Oishi, Ed Diener, and Richard Lucas released an ambitious paper titled "The Optimal Level of Well-Being." In it they describe a study involving more than a hundred thousand people from around the globe, each of whom reported their happiness levels several times over a twenty-year period. The researchers then examined how people's happiness scores related to their life circumstances, including how much they earned, their education levels, and their social relationships.

Their findings were illuminating.

As expected, extremely happy people reported better relationships and more community involvement, but surprisingly, they also lagged in income and education. Who collected the biggest paychecks and earned the highest academic degrees? That distinction belonged to those who were slightly *dis*satisfied.

Because these results are correlational, we can't say for sure whether dissatisfaction causes higher levels of achievement per se. But what we can conclude from the data is this: Higher income and education are more common among people who are not continuously ecstatic about their lives.

So what are we to make of these findings? Several observations are worth noting.

First, happiness in the workplace is beneficial, but only up to a point. As a general rule, employees who are happy at their job are more productive than those who feel dissatisfied. But extreme levels of happiness can also interfere with work quality. Despite what we often hear, happiness in the workplace is simply not an unqualified good.

Second, being in a positive mood can benefit some activities more than others. That means feeling happy can make us better at certain aspects of our jobs while also making us worse at others. Instead of simply assuming that intense happiness will improve everyone's performance, it's wise for managers to first consider the types of activities employees are expected to do. An emotional climate that's advantageous for a team of salespeople is often different from one that's beneficial for a group of accountants.

And finally, when organizations convey an expectation that every employee should feel happy at work all the time, they do their workers a disservice. It's one thing to promote happiness in the workplace but another to make it a job requirement. Studies show that the more pressure we place on ourselves to feel happy, the less likely we are to succeed. And as we've seen, negative emotions can occasionally be useful and actually improve performance on certain tasks, particularly ones requiring persistence and attention to detail.

Psychologist Jeremy Dean notes that we have a name for people who don't experience negative emotions: psychopaths. Which underscores an important point: Incessant cheerfulness is abnormal, unhealthy, and counterproductive.

Is there value to promoting happiness in the workplace? Absolutely.

But it's only by doing so in ways that complement the requirements of employees' tasks and allow them to be authentic about their experiences that we can expect it to drive success.

The Lessons of Happiness
Action Items for Managers

Plan happiness boosts around specific work activities. Research shows that when we're happy, we're better at connecting with others, seeing the big picture, and generating creative ideas. That means that if you're trying to get a group to bond or think flexibly—as in a client meeting or a team brainstorm—elevating people's mood at the start by using refreshments, good news, or an interactive activity can be a wise approach. However, beware of applying the same strategy when your team is tasked with rooting out mistakes or conducting careful analyses. Feeling good can lead them to overlook potential threats, undermining their performance. Remember, positive emotions can help or hurt depending on the task. The trick is to promote a mind-set that benefits the activities you're about to undertake.

Think small. You can get a bigger psychological bang for the buck with small, frequent positive experiences (e.g., workplace benefits that employees experience on a daily basis) than from larger positive experiences that only occur infrequently (e.g., the annual bonus). Modest workplace perks, such as a high-end cappuccino maker or artisan pastries, might appear frivolous, but in many instances they pay for themselves by elevating employees' moods, making a workplace feel distinct, and improving productivity.

Some perks are wiser than others. Organizational perks can do more than sustain positive moods; they can also nudge employees into making better decisions. Having fruit and almonds available in conference rooms, for example, promotes healthy eating. Complimentary passes to a nearby gym encourage employees to exercise. Another smart perk worth considering: incentivizing employees to live near the office. Imo, a Silicon Valley tech company, for example, pays employees who live within five miles of work an extra $500 a month. It's by no means a small amount, yet the company views it as an investment. Shorter commute times mean their employees get better sleep, spend more time with their families, and presumably, have closer relationships with colleagues who also happen to be neighbors. When living near the office is unrealistic, rewarding employees who carpool together can also deliver considerable benefits to an organization.

The Lessons of Happiness
Action Items for Emerging Leaders

Ask for variety. It's easy to grow bored with a job that involves doing a small number of tasks over and over. When the work we do becomes predictable, our attention falters and our engagement slips. Research shows that employees whose work involves a wide range of activities tend to enjoy greater job satisfaction, in part because variety delays adaptation. For a happier work experience, look for new ways of applying your skills instead of hoping that the same old routine will somehow recapture your interest.

Feeling unhappy can be good for you. While the mind is designed to maximize pleasure and minimize pain, research suggests that interludes of unhappiness allow us to better enjoy the positives in our lives when they occur. When we experience anger or sadness, there's typically a good reason for it. Noticing the way you feel and then examining the reasons behind the emotion—whether at work or elsewhere—can help you identify the changes you need to make to foster genuine happiness.

Find a way of making gratitude work for you. Appreciating the things that are going right in your life is a basic requirement for sustained happiness. Yet gratitude is not something that often comes naturally. Journaling about the positive aspects of your day is one approach, and several smartphone apps (like Happy Tapper and Gratitude Journal 365) send automatic reminders that make the process easy. Some even allow users to take photos of positive events, doing away with the writing requirement that turns so many people off. Another simple way of practicing gratitude: working it into your dinnertime routine. It's something we've begun doing at my house. We go around the table and have everyone make a toast about one thing for which they are grateful. We tried it once on a whim and the practice stuck. I recommend it highly. You'll be surprised at how natural it feels, how much you learn about the people you're with, and how quickly the mood improves.

FIVE

How to Turn a Group of Strangers into a Community

In the late 1960s, after nearly twenty years of teaching educational psychology at the University of Nebraska, Donald Clifton made the stunning decision to hand in his resignation.

He had found a better opportunity—in his basement.

Clifton had never quite fit in with other researchers in his field. While most psychologists were consumed with curing mental illness, Clifton had other interests. He was less concerned about ways the mind could go wrong than with identifying what it did when things were going right.

What was different about high performers? Clifton wondered. He was convinced that somewhere in the data lay insights that could help ordinary people achieve more fulfilling lives.

At first, Clifton searched for answers in academic studies. He spent years analyzing outstanding teachers and counselors. Eventually he came to realize that his objectives were better suited for the corporate world, where there was a strong appetite for understanding the factors that contribute to people's success. And so, at the age of forty-five, Clifton gave up his cushy job as a professor and started a company that specialized in finding exceptional employees.

Clifton died in 2003, but you might recognize the name of his company. It has forty offices in twenty-seven countries and more than 2,000 employees. It's called Gallup.

Less than two decades after Clifton began offering his services, his firm had grown so prosperous that it was able to acquire the well-known polling company, and wisely assumed the Gallup name.

Before his passing, Clifton developed a survey that in many ways represented the culmination of his life's work. It's known as the Q12, and to this day it is one of Gallup's signature offerings. Clifton's measure is made up of twelve survey items that he believed were the best indicators of employee engagement. Among them is one question that has attracted a little more attention than all the others—and not all of it has been positive. In fact, Gallup's researchers freely admit that more than a few senior executives have balked at using the Q12 altogether, because they couldn't quite understand why the item was there in the first place.

The question at the heart of the controversy: *Do you have a best friend at work?*

Clifton insisted on measuring workplace friendships for good reason: It's one of the strongest predictors of productivity. Studies show that employees with a best friend at work tend to be more focused, more passionate, and more loyal to their organizations. They get sick less often, suffer fewer accidents, and change jobs less frequently. They even have more satisfied customers.

Why would friends be better at working together than acquaintances?

A joint study by management professors at the University of Pennsylvania and the University of Minnesota offers a clue. Researchers began by asking students in a large course to identify classmates with whom they have a "close interpersonal relationship." They then used that information to assign students to small groups made up of either close friends or mutual acquaintances.

What the researchers wanted to know was this: Could preexisting friendships benefit *some* activities but interfere with others? To find out, they had all the groups complete two different assignments. The first was a decision-making project involving collaborative thinking, and the second was a model-building task involving repetitive manual labor.

The results were definitive: Friends outperformed acquaintances on *both* tasks. The reason? Friends were more committed at the start of a project, showed better communication while doing the activity, and offered teammates positive encouragement every step of the way. They also evaluated ideas more critically and gave one another feedback when they were off course.

Acquaintances, on the other hand, took a different approach. They appeared to prefer working alone, engaging one another only when it was absolutely necessary. They were also less comfortable seeking help and resisted pointing out when one of their coworkers was making a mistake. Instead of fusing into a group and leveraging one another's strengths, their lack of connection was holding them back. They were operating in silos.

Research suggests that workplace friendships yield more productive employees, and it's not just because friends are easier to work with. It's also because there is more on the line. Feeling a connection with colleagues can motivate employees to work harder for a simple reason. When colleagues are close, a poor effort means more than a dissatisfied customer or an unhappy manager. It means letting down your friends. The social pressure to do a good job can often serve as a stronger motivator than anything a boss can say.

Workplace friendships also benefit organizations for another reason: Employees with better friendships tend to stay on with their company for longer periods of time. In today's world, loyalty to an

organization has become an antiquated concept, one that rarely determines people's career decisions. But when our coworkers are our
friends, it suddenly becomes harder to leave. Often it's our loyalty to
our colleagues that keeps us from accepting higher salaries and better
titles with another company.

What happens when there's a lack of friendships in the workplace?
Psychologists call it *process loss*, and if you've ever worked with a difficult colleague, you've probably experienced it firsthand. The technical
definition is "wasted energy and loss of productivity caused by interpersonal difficulties." We all recognize the symptoms. The mild version involves the occasional miscommunication. More acute cases are
rife with unresolved tension, breakdowns in collaboration, and eventually full-on turf wars. Instead of focusing all your attention on your
work, you find yourself sidetracked by interpersonal drama, which
invariably makes you worse at your job.

Clifton was onto something when he insisted that businesses in-
quire about the state of their employees' relationships. And not just
because workplace friendships predict higher employee engagement
but because organizations lacking them are *leaking profits*.

Perhaps instead of asking *if* businesses should measure workplace
friendships all these years, the real question Clifton's detractors
should have been asking was this: How much is it costing businesses
to leave employee friendships to chance?

HOW LONELINESS MAKES YOU STUPID

Part of the reason so many executives have a hard time taking the
importance of employee friendships seriously is that it's easy to
confuse the concept of friends at the office with the notion of fool-
ing around. Informal colleague relationships are often perceived as
sources of gossip, interpersonal favoritism, and general workplace
distractions.

But research suggests that this is a misguided way of thinking about what happens when we're working with friends. Meaningful connections are vital to our psychological and physical well-being. So much so, in fact, that many scientists now believe it's impossible to be healthy *unless* we're feeling connected to others.

Studies show that loneliness can have a crippling effect on our bodies. Lonely people have weaker immune systems, stiffer arteries, and higher blood pressure. They experience more stress, have a harder time relaxing, and derive less pleasure from the possibility of reward. Often they lose sleep, which precipitates further mental deterioration. Over time, extended bouts of loneliness can lead to cognitive decline in the form of memory and learning deficits.

Left untreated, chronic loneliness can threaten your life.

A 2011 study demonstrates that loneliness in the workplace isn't merely an uncomfortable personal experience—it can interfere with the performance of an entire team. Management professors from California State University and Wharton Business School interviewed hundreds of employees twice over a period of six weeks. The lonelier an employee felt at the start of the study, the weaker their performance at the study's conclusion on three separate levels: their individual execution at work; their effectiveness at communicating with others; and their contribution to their group. When employees experience loneliness, they grow more disconnected from their colleagues. Their ability to focus deteriorates and their desire to succeed plummets. Often they waste valuable cognitive resources attempting to hide their loneliness from others, leaving even less mental firepower for doing their work.

In short, they become less capable of doing their jobs.

Which leads us to the big elephant in the room: Even if friendships *are* vital to workplace performance, what can organizations possibly do about it? Friendships, after all, are voluntary. You can't persuade people to become friends.

Or can you?

THE SCIENCE OF MAKING FRIENDS

As it turns out, organizations have a lot more influence over employee friendships than they recognize. To understand how companies can promote bonding between coworkers, let's first examine some of the common ingredients at the core of successful friendships.

What makes people like one another? Research suggests that there are three basic building blocks and they're all surprisingly straightforward. The first is evidenced in a classic social psychology study conducted in an unusual location: the training academy of the Maryland State Police. When police cadets first report for duty, most are strangers to one another. But after an intense training program lasting several weeks, it's not uncommon for close friendships to take hold.

What leads cadets to bond with some colleagues but not others? To find out, researchers surveyed them at the end of their program and asked everyone to list their close work friends. At first glance, the results seemed puzzling. The O'Briens tended to list the O'Malleys and the Fosters tended to mention the Franklins. But the chances of an O'Brien connecting with a Foster or an O'Malley clicking with a Franklin were much lower.

The question was why.

The reason, researchers discovered, was simple. Both dorm room and seating arrangements at the academy had been assigned based on alphabetical order. The cadets' last names determined who they spent time with, and the longer recruits were together, the more likely they were to become friends.

This highlights the first ingredient for friendship: *physical proximity*. Initially, physical proximity might sound like an obvious requirement for friendship, one hardly worth mentioning, except its implications are profound. Consider the number of close friendships you've formed while living, studying, or working near people you now hold dear. How many of those relationships would have developed if the seating arrangements had been slightly different?

The same observation applies to the realm of romance. Think you and your spouse were made for each other? Maybe. But if of the seven billion of the world's inhabitants you and your soul mate just happened to share a zip code when you first met, cosmic destiny may have had less to do with your relationship than the principle of proximity.

When a coworker is often nearby, your chances of hitting it off are far greater than if the two of you work in different departments. There might be someone at your company sitting at their desk right now who could be the best friend you will ever have. But if your opportunities for interacting with that person are limited, you may live your entire life without knowing it.

A second friendship requirement: *familiarity*. On average, we tend to like people the more we see of them, and often the effect is unconscious.

Take the results of a clever study, in which experimenters asked four equally attractive females to sit in on a large lecture class over the course of a semester. To test the effect of familiarity, the researchers varied the number of times each woman attended the class. The first woman visited the class 5 times, the second 10 times, the third 15 times, and the fourth not at all. None of the women said a word all semester. They simply arrived a few minutes before class, sat near the front, and took notes.

At the end of the semester, students in the course were asked if they remembered seeing any of the women. Nearly everyone said no. Yet the more often a woman visited, the more students said they liked her picture.

How do we account for these findings? Psychologists call it the *mere exposure effect* and argue that our minds are designed to distrust the unfamiliar. There's an uncertainty we feel upon meeting someone for the first time. But with repeated exposure we develop a sense of safety and comfort around them. Which is why familiarity tends to breed liking.

Studies show that the mere exposure effect doesn't just affect our impressions of people. It also applies to paintings, songs, and consumer products. Ever wonder why Coca-Cola still bothers advertising when nearly everyone on the planet has already sampled their beverage? The mere exposure effect offers one perspective: The more often we see a logo, the more we tend to like (and therefore buy) the product.

The third and strongest contributor to friendship is *similarity*. The more we have in common with others—whether it's a college major, a favorite TV show, or even the same birthday—the more we tend to like them. As writer C. S. Lewis once observed, "Friendship is born at the moment when one person says to another, 'What! You too? I thought I was the only one.'"

Why is this the case? Because similarity is reaffirming. If I like Malcolm Gladwell and you like Malcolm Gladwell, your opinion validates my own and makes me feel good about myself.

In a study of best friends who managed to stay close for nearly twenty years, researchers found that the strongest predictor of long-term bonding is the level of similarity when friends first meet. The same principle applies to intimate relationships. Romantic comedies and sitcoms may try to convince us that opposites attract, but the research is conclusive: When it comes to long-term relationships, similarity beats differences every time.

While all friendships are founded on the pillars of proximity, familiarity, and similarity, psychologists have discovered that you can have all three elements and still not see a blossoming friendship. There's still something missing, a vital ingredient that sparks the relationship process.

That ingredient? Secrets.

HOW TO TURN ACQUAINTANCES INTO FRIENDS

The year was 1997 and relationship expert Art Aron was facing a problem.

He and his colleagues had spent decades studying the science of human bonding, authoring groundbreaking papers on romance and friendship. But Aron wasn't content. Something, he felt, was missing.

At the time, the majority of the studies on close relationships relied on comparisons between couples: romantic versus platonic relationships, happy versus unhappy couples, successful versus unsuccessful marriages. The findings were intriguing but relied too heavily, in Aron's view, on relationships that had been established *before* couples arrived at the lab, rendering many critical relationship processes invisible.

All good scientists aim to minimize ambiguities, and Aron was no different. So he asked a provocative question: Can we re-create the friendship process in the lab?

To find out, he and a group of colleagues invited one hundred volunteers who had never met before and assigned them into pairs. They then asked them do one thing over the next forty-five minutes: talk.

Aron had a theory about the development of friendships. He believed you could induce people to connect with others, even if they'd only just met. The key was making sure they talked about the right things. To test his hypothesis, he and his team divided the pairs into two groups and provided each with a list of questions to help launch their conversations.

See if you can spot the ones that led to greater closeness at the end the study.

Sample Questions from List A
- How did you celebrate last Halloween?
- Describe the last pet that you owned.
- When was the last time you walked for more than an hour? Describe where you went and what you saw.

Sample Questions from List B
- Given the choice of anyone in the world, whom would you want as a dinner guest?

- Would you like to be famous? In what way?
- Before you make a telephone call, do you ever rehearse what you are going to say? Why?

From Aron's perspective, not all conversations are created equal. Some are more meaningful and engrossing than others, and his procedure helps elucidate why.

The questions in List A, which Aron referred to as the "Small Talk" condition, were designed to promote an exchange of factual information, keeping personal revelations at a minimum. The other half of participants was given the questions in List B, which were written with the goal of encouraging couples to open up and share emotionally sensitive information.

If you want two people to connect, Aron argued, factual exchanges aren't enough. What you need is for people to reveal intimate information about themselves in a reciprocal fashion. Having one person talk and the other listen won't get the job done; it will simply leave one person feeling exposed.

For intimacy to develop, both partners need to self-disclose.

Another important feature that Aron incorporated into his study is the observation that in close friendships the level of self-disclosure tends to escalate over time. When we first meet a friend or colleague, the revelations we make tend to be fairly superficial. But as we grow closer, we become more comfortable sharing intimate details and expect our partners to do the same.

The progression is important. Without deeper revelations a relationship can stall.

To replicate this process in the lab, Aron slowly ratcheted up the intensity of the disclosures by providing three rounds of questions. The questions above were taken from the first round, during the first fifteen minutes of the interaction. By the third round, Aron had participants answering questions that included:

- When did you last cry in front of another person? By yourself?
- If you were to die this evening with no opportunity to communicate with another person, what would you most regret not having told someone? Why haven't you told them yet?
- Of all the people in your family, whose death would you find most disturbing?

Needless to say, if Aron had started his study with these questions, more than a few participants might have bolted for the door. But thanks to the shared bonding that had occurred during previous disclosures, there was a willingness to discuss difficult topics that would otherwise have been unimaginable.

By the end of the study, participants who took turns self-disclosing reported feeling significantly closer to one another than those who had spent an equal amount of time engaging in small talk. They also reported greater interest in collaborating with their partner on future projects. Some even became long-term friends.

In a way, what Aron had done was re-create the formation of intimacy. By requiring participants to take turns sharing information and gradually escalating the level of disclosure, he was able to condense a process that typically takes years into under an hour, successfully turning complete strangers into close friends. And all it took was a few questions about the right topics.

SELF-DISCLOSING IN THE WORKPLACE

How relevant are Aron's observations to workplace friendships? After all, self-disclosure might be a good way of bonding with a buddy at the gym or a new neighbor. But in a competitive work environment, where everything we say and do reflects on our level of professionalism, shouldn't we be a little more discreet? Is opening up and sharing emotionally sensitive information with coworkers really a wise approach?

Research conducted by Washington State University professor Patricia Sias suggests it is, at least if your goal is to make friends. Sias and her colleague Daniel Cahill investigated the development of workplace friendships by asking employees to identify one coworker with whom they have a close relationship. They then interviewed both colleagues to determine how the two initially became friends.

What they discovered is that close workplace friendships tend to follow a distinct pattern that is marked by three key transitions.

The first is the transition from *acquaintance* to *friend*. Sias and Cahill report that, for the most part, all it takes for this transition to occur is working near a colleague for a period of about a year and occasionally collaborating on team projects. How can you tell if coworkers are friends? Ironically, by the amount of time they spend discussing nonworkplace topics. The more frequently colleagues talked about nonwork matters, the closer they tended to be.

There's an important lesson here for anyone interested in growing their influence in the workplace: When all you do at the office is talk shop, you might develop a reputation for being competent, but you're not likely to end up with a whole lot of friends.

The real surprise in Sias and Cahill's study came when they looked at the second and third transitions, the ones that turned *friends* into *close friends*, and *close friends* into *best friends*. Here the proximity and common ground that prompted the first transition were nowhere near enough to catalyze a strong connection.

What was? Sharing problems from one's personal, home, and work life.

The self-disclosure that Aron's research indicated was so critical for generating interpersonal closeness was also, as Sias and Cahill discovered, at the core of long-term relationships at work.

The challenge for many of us, of course, is that proactively sharing potentially embarrassing information is a little like visiting an emotional casino. If your listener reciprocates with a few revelations of their own, the payoffs can be big: You stand to win a deeper and more satisfying relationship. But if your disclosure isn't reciprocated—or worse, if it's criticized—you end up feeling exposed. And that experience is painful.

The irony is that close relationships are often built upon a foundation of shared risk. It's when we reveal our vulnerabilities that we acquire new friends.

WHAT EVERY MANAGER CAN LEARN FROM A PARTY PLANNER

We know a lot about the formation of friendships, yet we seem to apply very little of that knowledge to cultivating relationships in the workplace.

Consider what happens when an employee joins your company. In many organizations, surprisingly little thought is given to the way onboarding can contribute (or undermine) a sense of connection between team members.

When I joined a New York City consulting group after graduate school, my onboarding process consisted of me showing up on the first day and my manager removing a few boxes from a desk and saying, "You can sit here for now." He was a brilliant guy working at a highly successful company. But he was far too busy to give onboarding much attention.

On the other end of the spectrum is a process that overcompensates, exposing newcomers to the corporate equivalent of speed dating. Meetings are stacked back-to-back at breakneck speed so that new employees can introduce themselves to important leaders in their company.

While well intentioned, it's an approach that forces employees to pinball from office to office, answering the same superficial background questions and leaving them little room to absorb information. By the end of the day, faces have blended together and any meaningful connections that might have developed are squandered.

Both extremes miss the mark for the same reason: They design onboarding from the perspective of the organization and not the employee. And in so doing, they miss a key opportunity for fostering close friendships.

Remember how you felt on your first day on the job? Proud, excited, perhaps a little anxious . . . You didn't want to be ignored, but you certainly didn't want to feel overwhelmed. What you really wanted was to find a way to show your coworkers—and especially your manager—what a shrewd decision they had made by hiring you.

Intelligent onboarding reflects the needs of employees as well as those of their companies, by addressing two concerns that often weigh heavily on the mind of new hires: demonstrating their competence and connecting with their colleagues.

Entering an organization is like joining a party that has been going on without you for years. Some people are naturally drawn to mingling, but many struggle over what to do. The first few minutes are especially critical for guests, because the longer they feel isolated, the more they need to rationalize their experience with negative thoughts like, "Everyone here is so boring" (defensive) or, worse still, "These people must not like me" (self-critical).

A considerate host plans ahead, finding ways to maximize people's chances of interacting, strategically placing food in different locations, carefully positioning the bar, and occasionally enlisting the help of a few guests to introduce newcomers, highlighting what they have in common. Smart workplaces use a similar approach. They recognize that it is the responsibility of the "host" to establish subtle techniques for integrating coworkers from the moment of their arrival.

One key to getting onboarding right is stretching out the process, allowing new employees the space they need to find their bearings, organize their thoughts, and get more out of their time with coworkers. Onboarding doesn't have to begin with an employee's first day of work. It can start the moment they accept a job, when their enthusiasm for a position is at an all-time high. Instead of asking HR to set the process into motion, assign a teammate or two to introduce themselves via e-mail and offer to go out for coffee. Encourage them to share information about past projects and help their new colleague learn about the significance of their role. The more context new employees have before starting, the easier it is for them to feel competent and appreciative of their teammates on their first day.

Another technique for helping colleagues connect: Introduce new hires by revealing more than just their professional background. Talk about their hobbies, their favorite TV shows, or an unusual talent of which they're particularly proud. Remember, similarity sparks friendships. What might appear to you as a trivial detail can serve as the basis for a close colleague relationship.

Snagajob, a Virginia-based recruitment company and winner of the Great Place to Work Institute's Best Companies to Work For award in 2011, has made personal interests a key feature of their onboarding practices. Every Snagajob employee fills out a survey called Snagger Confessions, which includes a series of questions about their personal interests. Managers at the company then use the responses to provide a colorful introduction, making it easy for teammates to have non-workplace topics to talk about the first time they meet.

When employees first arrive on the job, it's tempting to get introductory meetings out of the way as quickly as possible. Resist this urge. Far better to scatter them over a few days or weeks. That may feel inefficient at first, but not if you want new hires to be mentally present and primed to make connections.

It also pays to think carefully about a new hire's first assignment. You can use it to do more than simply get a new employee up to speed; you can use it as a tool for deepening relationships. Start new hires with a series of modest, collaborative projects that discourage isolation and allow them to collect early wins. The shared accomplishment will bolster connections while fostering a sense of team pride.

If stretching out and customizing the onboarding process sounds complex, that's because it is. And it should be. Building lasting relationships takes time. At parties, a well-handled introduction can mean the difference between guests remaining late into the night or using any excuse to leave. The same is true of the workplace. How employees feel when they first arrive shapes every impression they develop thereafter.

THE KEY TO LASTING WORKPLACE RELATIONSHIPS

What do you do when the onboarding honeymoon is over? When the meet-and-greets have ended and colleagues who were once new and exciting recede into the background of the daily grind? As a leader, what can you do to continue to promote new employee connections and help sustain old ones?

As we've already seen, decades of research reveal that the recipe for friendship is simple. Proximity, familiarity, similarity, and self-disclosure all play a role. The trick is to create the conditions that naturally foster these elements and integrate them into the work environment.

After-work activities represent one approach. Many of the companies that appear on *Fortune* magazine's annual list of top workplaces now offer seed money for relatively inexpensive activities that range from after-work yoga to wine-tasting classes to improv training. From a financial perspective this can seem wasteful. Yet the value these activities yield to interpersonal connections—and therefore to employee productivity—makes them a wise investment.

Shared activities catalyze workplace friendships in ways few interactions can. They foster *proximity* between employees who rarely meet, boost their level of *familiarity* with one another, highlight *similarity* of interests, and leverage informal, nonwork environments to prompt *self-disclosure*.

By allowing colleagues to direct their attention to a common task, shared activities create opportunities for dialogue without the pressure of forced conversation. In this way, they're the antidote to a more traditional and often less successful approach to after-work socializing: the cocktail party.

What's wrong with cocktail parties? Nothing at all. Unless, of course, you're interested in fostering meaningful connections.

Cocktail parties tend to isolate people into groups of those they already know, trapping them in conversations that often feel strained and rarely result in close bonds. Partly it's because there's nothing to do *but* talk. For many people, taking the focus off the conversation and placing it squarely on an activity itself reduces self-consciousness and makes connections easier to grow. This can be especially true for the introverts in a group, who are often more comfortable bonding shoulder to shoulder with a colleague than face to face.

When shared activities include a physical component, such as running or dancing, they have the added feature of increasing physiological arousal. Research indicates that when we experience a rush of adrenaline in the company of others, we like them more, and even find them more attractive. The more opportunities employees have for sharing in physical activities, like softball, volleyball, or even fishing, the easier it is for them to get along.

There's a reason why so many close business connections are forged out on the golf course. Ironically, it's what we do together outside the office that frequently offers the biggest boon to our relationships at work.

ABOLISH THE "THEY"

Another insight for sustaining workplace friendships comes to us from an unlikely source: research on conflicts that go horribly—and sometimes violently—wrong. Take this classic social psychology experiment conducted by Muzafer Sherif, who in 1954 decided to single-handedly orchestrate a war.

The scene was a remote campground, deep in the sunny woodlands of Oklahoma, where a group of eleven-year-old boys were enjoying what they thought was a typical summer camp. What they didn't know was that their "counselors" were actually researchers and that they were secretly running an experiment. One that would make their summer camp a staple of psychology textbooks for generations to come.

When the boys arrived, everything seemed normal enough. Their first few days were filled with quintessential camp activities. They put up tents and paddled canoes. They played softball together, went swimming, and took long hikes. After several days of bonding, they were invited to give their group a name, which they got to stencil on their shirts and flags.

They called themselves the Eagles.

Everything was going well for the Eagles that summer until they learned something their counselors hadn't told them. Something unnerving: They weren't alone. Just a short walk from the Eagles' cabin lived another group of eleven-year-old boys, and they too had shirts and flags and a name. They called themselves the Rattlers.

Now this is where the experiment gets a little diabolical.

One day Sherif brought the two groups together for some friendly competition. Then he did it again. And then again.

Soon friction emerged. Lots of it.

First there was name calling. Then there were cabin raids, the burning of one another's flags, and the use of improvised weapons (rock-filled socks). Within days the boys were refusing to eat in the same room. Not long after that, an all-out brawl threatened to erupt, and the counselors were forced to step in and physically separate the groups.

This was, of course, no accident. Sherif knew competition would escalate tension and harm group relations. And that's exactly what he wanted. What interested him is not what led to the groups' conflict but whether he could repair it once it occurred.

Here was his chance. Sherif's first attempt involved having the boys relax together by watching a movie. It didn't work. Then he tried giving them something fun to do by inviting them to light fire-crackers together on the Fourth of July. (Remember, this was 1954.) Still, no luck.

His third approach proved to be the winner: He introduced what he called *superordinate goals*.

As it turned out, Sherif had been going about it all wrong. Instead of using shared enjoyment to promote friendship, what he really needed was a shared struggle. Sherif discovered that the key was in presenting a challenge so big that it could only be resolved through collaboration.

To get the groups working together, Sherif had to manufacture a crisis, which he did, masterfully.

One stifling summer afternoon, while the boys were out playing, Sherif had the camp's water supply sabotaged. He'd arranged for the water tank to be turned off and for two large boulders to block access to the valve. When the boys realized that none of the faucets worked, they quickly grew alarmed. It had been a long day, and nearly all of their canteens were empty. There was no water anywhere.

The counselors claimed it was the work of vandals who, they said, were known to heave rocks at the camp from time to time. Normally the valve to the water tank could be turned on easily. But this time the rocks made the valve impossible to reach. The only way for the water to be restored was if the boys could somehow figure out a way to clear a path.

Immediately the boys got to work. Without realizing it, they began plotting together. They talked with one another, shared suggestions, and helped one another execute ideas. The boys weren't entirely successful in their efforts (the counselors eventually had to step in), but that didn't matter. The collaboration had changed them. And when the water finally came through, both sides cheered.

Sherif noticed a thaw in their relations after the water tank episode. And so he proceeded to devise other challenges that made superordinate goals essential. By the time camp ended a few weeks later, there was no sign of the earlier hostilities. Quite the contrary. Before heading home the Rattlers even offered to buy the Eagles a round of chocolate malts.

As Sherif's work demonstrates, superordinate goals can serve as a powerful tool for defusing tension in times of conflict. Just as important, they can also be used to inoculate coworkers *before* disagreements erupt. When colleagues feel like they're working toward a common objective, a sense of shared purpose naturally softens the conditions for friendships.

The challenge in many workplaces is that superordinate goals are often surprisingly difficult to identify. In a world in which every employee is a specialist, colleagues can sit next to one another for years and not know what their coworkers are doing. At many offices an employee's contributions are only visible within their team.

How do you leverage superordinate goals under these conditions?

The first step involves helping employees understand the way their colleagues' work contributes to their own success. It's when that connection isn't evident that teams tend to splinter into factions, making friendships harder to foster. As innovation expert Tom Kelley points out, anytime employees view colleagues in another department as a "they" rather than an "us," you have a problem. In psychological terms, what they're really saying is, they're lacking a superordinate goal.

Some organizations work to abolish the "they" right at the start of an employee's tenure, building cross-departmental understanding right into the onboarding processes. Genesis Fertility Centre in Canada, for example, includes a Day of Osmosis in which new employees get to shadow members of other departments during their first few days on the job. Other companies, like Toronto's Construction Control Inc., offer a department rotation program that gives employees exposure to the work of their colleagues.

Making existing superordinate goals more visible is one approach. Another is creating new ones. That's what executives at the Hilcorp

Energy Company did in 2010 when they announced that every employee would receive a check for $100,000 if the company's production and reserve levels doubled by 2015. Sound impossible? Not to the employees at Hilcorp. Thanks to a previous challenge, hundreds of them drive to work every day in a $50,000 car.

Another opportunity for superordinate goals in the workplace is starting cross-departmental competitions and assigning employees who don't normally work together to the same team. One example is the office version of the Biggest Loser, a game that rewards the group that collectively loses the most weight with a cash award. Participants can only win when their coworkers are successful, leading them to support one another's weight-loss efforts, share strategies, and plan meals around a common goal. Even better are wellness programs that reward colleagues for the amount of exercise they undertake collaboratively, encouraging teammates to work out together in groups.

Superordinate goals also naturally emerge through joint volunteer efforts, sports teams, and the establishment of a company band. Ultimately, the activity itself is not important. What matters is bringing together employees who rarely interact and putting them in situations where collaboration is the only path to success.

SOWING THE SEEDS FOR A WORKPLACE COMMUNITY

In 1997, psychologist Sheldon Cohen invited 276 healthy volunteers into his lab and infected every one of them with a virus. But first, he had them fill out a brief questionnaire. What he and his team wanted to know was this: Do people's social networks affect their ability to fight the common cold?

The findings, which appeared in the prestigious *Journal of the American Medical Association*, revealed a fascinating conclusion. Because germs are contagious, many of us assume that the more people we're around, the more likely we are to contract an illness. But Cohen's results turn that assumption on its head. As it turns out, the more types of relationships a person has, the *less* susceptible they are to developing a full-blown cold, even after direct exposure to a cold-causing virus.

Cohen's research highlights a surprising benefit of robust social networks. When people have a wide range of connections, it provides them with a sense of psychological security that buffers them from day-to-day stress. And because they experience stress less often, their bodies are better conditioned to fend off physiological challenges when they occur.

Workplace connections offer similar benefits. When we feel supported by our colleagues, we are less likely to experience challenging events as stressful, knowing that our teammates are there to back us up. Minor hiccups appear less intimidating, which helps us keep our emotions in check and enables us to make better decisions in the face of crisis.

Studies show that the way we perceive our social network is vital to our mental health. When we believe that those around us are available to provide social support—by offering assistance, advice, and emotional reassurance—we tend to be healthier both physically and psychologically.

One obvious path to improving perceptions of social support in the workplace involves helping colleagues establish close friendships. But as many organizations are now discovering, the reverse is also true. When a company introduces formal practices that make social support and mutual caring the norm, friendships tend to bloom naturally.

One simple way organizations can help employees support one another is by encouraging them to celebrate important milestones. Research shows that how people react to the positive events in one another's lives is often more important to the quality of a relationship than how they react to negative events. Shared celebrations over a recent marriage engagement, a major birthday, or a recent promotion can magnify positive emotions and strengthen the fabric of a group's bond. The occasional order of cupcakes won't break the bank. Yet in many companies every expenditure requires the approval of a manager. Why not give every employee a modest celebration budget that they can use at their discretion?

There is also value to sharing negative events within a group. Recognizing setbacks, like the passing of a spouse or the development of an illness, can draw employees closer together and allow colleagues to provide one another with social support when they need it most.

Disclosing setbacks publicly obviously requires an employee's permission and considerable tact, but as we saw earlier in this chapter, connecting over struggles can mean the difference between superficial chit-chat and a lifelong friendship. It's when we open up about adversity that we build our closest relationships. And, as a 2011 University of Notre Dame study shows, people who choose to disclose a painful event publicly tend to feel significantly better than those who keep it to themselves.

Organizations can also bolster employees' perception of their support network by encouraging colleagues to pool together resources in a way that helps those confronted with financial emergencies. Starbucks is one company that's taken this step, creating the Caring Unites Partners (or CUP) fund that provides grants to employees in need.

It's when organizations take steps to weave employee connections beyond the office that they set the stage for a workplace community to emerge. And interestingly, it's not just the recipients who profit from the additional support. Research shows that altruism often benefits *givers* more than *receivers*. Helping others—even when we're not particularly close—improves our moods and enhances our perceptions of the support we have available, should we need it in the future.

WHEN CLOSE FRIENDSHIPS GO AWRY: WHAT TO DO ABOUT GOSSIP

No discussion of workplace friendship would be complete without addressing a legitimate concern that many managers hold about encouraging close employee relationships: the spread of office gossip.

When you enhance people's comfort level working together, you also increase their willingness to share thoughts and feelings they might otherwise keep to themselves. Occasionally, those include unflattering impressions of other employees or managers around the office.

Gossip can have a debilitating effect on a workplace. It breeds distrust between colleagues, siphons time away from important projects, and injures company morale. Left unchecked, it can contribute to a culture of fear and anxiety.

So what do you do to prevent office gossip?

The surprising conclusion from a number of psychological experts is that you can't, and that you might be better off not even trying.

Now, before you dismiss this notion, consider the reason researchers believe gossip exists in the first place. Gossip, evolutionary psychologists argue, serves an important function. It provides people with valuable information on how to behave and helps them navigate the world more effectively.

Say I hear a rumor that one of my associates, Cheryl, got dressed down by a client this morning for being unprepared. How does that affect my behavior? Well, first, it informs my approach to dealing with Cheryl on our afternoon conference call. Perhaps I'm a little nicer to her before we launch into our weekly update and offer her some encouraging feedback after she presents her portion. When discussing upcoming projects, I also might think twice before agreeing to let Cheryl take the lead.

The gossip circulating about Cheryl doesn't do *her* any good, but it does make *me* a little better prepared for doing my job.

Score one for gossip.

Another benefit of gossip: keeping people in line. As news of Cheryl's misstep spreads throughout our division, it conveys a subtle warning: Beware, the gossip tells all of us. Arrive at meetings without doing your homework and your reputation will suffer a similar fate.

A 2012 study published in the *Journal of Personality and Social Psychology* uncovered yet another way gossip is beneficial: People are less likely to cheat when there's a possibility others will gossip about their actions. Gossip appears to foster prosocial behavior. When we're concerned that others will find out what we've done, we're less likely to act selfishly and more likely to behave in a cooperative fashion.

When you consider all the value gossip brings, it's no wonder it plays such a pivotal role in our lives. According to discourse analysts, nearly two thirds of conversations contain some elements of gossip. It often goes undetected because we don't all gossip about the same things. On average, men tend to gossip more about high-powered authority figures who include political figures, athletes, and celebrities. Women, on the other hand, spend more time gossiping about family members and close friends.

We gossip, according to anthropologist Robin Dunbar, because in the past our lives depended on it.

Back when our ancestors lived in small groups, they were able to monitor one another's behaviors firsthand. But as group sizes expanded, direct observation was not always feasible. For a while, living in a large group was risky, because you didn't know who to trust. Eventually language entered the picture, and suddenly people had a tool for tracking reputations. Now, if someone behaved unethically, everyone in the group would find out, and soon enough the perpetrator would be shunned.

From Dunbar's perspective, if we didn't need to gossip we may never have learned how to talk.

Gossip is useful, which is why it often feels so rewarding. When your coworker Mike tells you that his boss has been spending a lot of time with a particular intern, he implicitly shows that he trusts you and views you as someone worth inviting into an exclusive social circle. It's a flattering experience. At the same time, Mike gets to demonstrate his moral superiority on the issue of romancing interns while simultaneously proving that he is "in the know." That brief exchange brings you and Mike a little closer and gives both of you a temporary bump in self-esteem.

As much as we'd like to believe we're above gossiping, the reality is that we're all susceptible. It's an inherent part of who we are. But just because we're prone to doing certain behaviors doesn't mean they're necessarily good for business. The more employees gossip behind one another's backs, the harder it is to build team camaraderie and sustain collaborations.

Some organizations try to root out gossip by outlining formal policies or having executives issue explicit warnings. It's an approach that displays a basic misunderstanding of human nature. Asking employees to stop talking about one another is a little like warning your kids never to yell. They can try their best, but eventually they'll slip up, and when they do, it will only increase the distance between you. Ironically, your disapproval makes the transgression a little more exciting when it happens.

The real question—the one that many organizations fail to address—is what's causing workplace gossip to crop up in the first place. We all enjoy a bit of gossip, but some of us participate in it more than others. How come?

Research shows that teammates are particularly susceptible to gossip when they're feeling powerless or insecure. The more people feel like they are out of the loop, the more they traffic in scraps of information.

Gossip in the workplace tends to be the weapon of the isolated and socially disenfranchised. When employees feel disconnected from the broader organization, they resort to forming cliques, drawing some colleagues close by putting other colleagues down. Ironically, it is their need for connections that results in organization-defeating behaviors that ultimately erode a team's trust.

Instead of outlawing gossip, leaders would be better off listening carefully to it instead. People tend to gossip about issues that reflect real workplace concerns. A lack of transparency about important decisions, for example, can breed uncertainty and sow the seeds for organizational chatter. Promoting openness between colleagues and building an environment where people feel safe addressing their concerns reduces the desire for talking behind one another's backs.

Another thing leaders should listen for is the source of the gossip. The more someone gossips, the more powerless he likely perceives himself to be, which is an issue that deserves genuine attention.

There are also those who wield gossip as a weapon, strategically undermining others while attempting to elevate their own status in an organization. There's a term for them in the literature: *workplace terrorists*. It's important to identify strategic gossipers early, before they can inflict too much harm. The challenge, of course, is that when we're handed a juicy piece of gossip, it's easy to be seduced by the feeling that we've gained useful information from someone who is on our side. Which is why it's important to consider the motivation behind the disclosure. Is the speaker trying to help you, hurt a potential rival, or both?

Attitudes toward gossip, like other social norms, are communicated from the top. As we'll see in Chapter 9, leaders have a disproportionate influence over many organizational behaviors, and gossiping is no exception. If, as a manager, you light up when given a piece of gossip, you're likely to have team members who do the same and strive to feed you information. And any manager who resorts to speculating with employees about their colleagues is not only undermining organizational trust, he is also damaging his own stature as a leader. Studies show that those who gossip the most are often viewed as the least powerful.

How do strong leaders respond to workplace gossip? By listening. And then, by encouraging and modeling open communication. It's one thing to hear about Cheryl's unfortunate turn at that client meeting. It's another to find Cheryl and see if you can help.

True friendships can only emerge when there is an openness between colleagues. When teammates have enough confidence in one another to raise difficult topics, even when that means having a challenging conversation.

It's what makes workplace friendships so vital in the first place.

When we see that we're surrounded by people who care about us, it's a lot easier to stay on task.

The Lessons of Friendship
Action Items for Managers

Onboard with an eye toward friendship. Rather than viewing onboarding simply as a tool for getting new hires up to speed, think of it as an opportunity for sparking employee friendships. Consider starting before your new hires arrive, assigning one or two of their colleagues to reach out and give them a head start. Introduce new employees by describing their interests—not just their CV—so that they have something to bond over when meeting with coworkers. And look for collaborative assignments right at the start, so that they can continue to forge connections as part of a team. Remember, *you're* the host. If you want people staying late at your party, you need to give them a reason to stick around.

Empower your team to find mutual passions. Instead of organizing social gatherings that may or may not be engaging, encourage your employees to take the lead by offering to fund activities that appeal to at least five team members. Friendships don't take when managers force employees into awkward social activities—not to mention the fact that you're too busy to play camp counselor. Far better to show your interest in helping employees pursue their passions by asking them to identify fun events they'd like to engage in. Even better: Allow them to bring their significant others along. Encouraging employees to involve spouses in workplace-sponsored events is another way of fostering connections, simultaneously promoting healthier marriages and growing the bond between coworkers' families.

Simplify caring. Employees grow closer when their colleagues are there to celebrate milestones and provide support in times of difficulty. Great workplaces make it easy for teammates to magnify positive events and empower them to get creative and customize their approach to each fellow employee. Here's one example: sending automated team reminders before each colleague's birthday and offering a modest twenty-dollar celebration budget. You might see some birthdays celebrated with a traditional cake, Hawaii-themed office decorations, or the hiring of an amateur opera singer off of Craigslist. Sound ridiculous? That's the point. Helping employees show that they get one another makes them significantly more likely to bond.

The Lessons of Friendship
Action Items for Emerging Leaders

All business all the time makes you a weaker employee. We're more effective at working with our teammates when we're connecting on a personal level. Workplace friendships don't happen when you're buried in a spreadsheet. They emerge in the spaces *between* work, before and after a team meeting—when you and I accidentally discover that we both love jogging and happen to own the same car. Make time for chance connections. Chatting with the new guy in sales may not feel productive in the moment, but it may turn out to be the most valuable thing you do all day.

If you are struggling with a colleague, find a superordinate goal. Often in the workplace, we get locked into our own objectives and see others as a barrier. It's what contributes to the development of turf wars. If you're dealing with a collaborator who seems to view you as competition, look for areas of common struggle, where you need one another. It's easier to connect with someone when it's clear you're both on the same side and neither one of you can succeed alone.

Recognize that gossip is the fast food of social connection. Gossip creates intimacy in the short term. But beware: It also weakens your standing in a group. Research shows that despite the immediate enjoyment people get from listening to gossip, frequent gossipers are viewed as less trustworthy, less powerful, and less likable. There's a Turkish proverb that says, "He who gossips *to* you, will gossip *of* you," and it appears that on some level, people implicitly believe that to be the case. If gossip is your primary means of connecting, it may be time you reconsidered your approach. It might feel like you're bonding with others, but the damage you're doing to your reputation makes it harder for your coworkers to view you as a friend.

PART TWO

Motivating Excellence

The Leadership Paradox

Why Forceful Leaders
Develop Less Productive Teams

The call came at 10:00 p.m.

It was done. Charles Henry's company, Johns Manville, had just sold for $2.3 billion, and he couldn't have felt more relieved. He was beginning to wonder whether he'd *ever* be able to retire. For months his CEO suite had been cluttered with cardboard boxes stacked along the walls, waiting to be shipped to his vacation home on the Savannah coast.

After more than thirty-seven years in the industry, Henry had long since been ready to call it a day. There was just one problem: His company had been on the block for over a year, and still, no takers. A stalled economy had made investors skittish toward manufacturing firms like his. And who could blame them? Two of Manville's biggest competitors had recently gone bankrupt, and in the previous five months alone, company shares had plummeted a full 30 percent.

The year was 2000. The dot-com bubble had just burst. And Johns Manville's prospects were looking decidedly grim.

But now, after a deal with Bear Stearns had fallen through in the final stages, a new buyer had stepped forward with an aggressive bid.

The board had voted to accept, and the timing couldn't have been better. It was five days before Christmas.

"There *is* a Santa Claus," Henry gushed to his employees the following afternoon. "But he's not located in the North Pole, my friends. He's in Omaha."

Henry's company had been purchased by Berkshire Hathaway, a multinational conglomerate that currently owns a wide range of corporations, including GEICO, Fruit of the Loom, and Dairy Queen, as well as parts of Heinz, Coca-Cola, Wells Fargo, and IBM. It has over a quarter million employees and annual revenue of over $180 billion. Its CEO is eighty-four-year-old Warren Buffett.

On the flight to meet his new boss, Henry thought about his wife, Kay, and his four daughters. He fantasized about retirement and what it would mean to finally have the time he needed to be with them. He considered what he'd say at even the slightest hint of a power struggle between him and his new manager.

Sure, Manville hadn't performed at its best in recent years, but so much of that was due to the warped economy. At the age of fifty-nine, Henry wasn't about to be bullied by some rich investor.

He settled on two words, at the ready should it appear that things between him and Buffett wouldn't work out: "I'm gone."

The meeting lasted six hours. Afterward Henry was singing a remarkably different tune.

"I came out totally committed to making this thing work," he told *Fortune* magazine's Carol Loomis. "It's easy to see what happens with Buffett's companies. You end up saying you don't want to let this guy down."

Retirement would have to wait. After meeting Buffett, Henry kept his role at Johns Manville, and not merely until his company had made it through the transition. He gave Berkshire Hathaway another four-and-a-half years.

What was it about Buffett that caused him to change his mind?

Much of it has to do with Buffett's unorthodox approach to management, which involves giving his direct reports complete autonomy over their own decision-making. Rather than supervising employees with weekly calls or monthly meetings, Buffett prefers to leave them in charge of their own affairs and simply makes himself available whenever they would like his input. According to biographer Alice Schroeder, Buffett reserves his morning for reading and spends his afternoons sitting by the phone so that his managers can reach him as needed.

When he does speak with his direct reports, Buffett rarely instructs. Instead, he uses his distance from the day-to-day minutiae to ask clarifying questions that help his managers find their own insights.

Schroeder offered the following assessment of Berkshire Hathaway's managers in her 2008 biography: "[They] were lucky because Buffett largely left them alone, his tricks of management being to find obsessed perfectionists like himself who worked incessantly; then ignore them except for a 'Carnegizing'—attention, admiration, and Dale Carnegie's other techniques—every now and then."

"Most managers use the independence we grant them magnificently, by maintaining an owner-oriented attitude," Buffett wrote in an annual report to investors. As for not micromanaging the affairs of his businesses, Buffett had this to say: "If I thought they needed me, I wouldn't have bought their stock."

Buffett's approach stands in sharp contrast to managerial practices in most workplaces. Within the vast majority of organizations, it is the manager who sets the course and the employees who implement his vision. But not at Berkshire Hathaway. In the words of a 2011 *New York Times* article, Warren Buffett perceives his role less as chief executive officer and more as "delegator in chief."

The idea of allowing employees such a high degree of independence when it comes to doing their work can seem a little unsettling. To some it might even smack of managerial neglect. Surely Warren Buffett knows more about running a successful business than most of his employees. Shouldn't he be telling them what to do?

Perhaps. But from Buffett's perspective, that's not the point. Because the feeling of ownership that's created by allowing employees decision-making freedom is itself an investment, one that pays dividends in the form of better motivation, stronger organizational loyalty, and sustained engagement.

It's a provocative idea. Is he right?

THE MAN WHO TURNED MANAGEMENT INTO A SCIENCE

Long before Berkshire Hathaway grew into one of the world's wealthiest organizations, a peculiar young man who would later become known as the father of scientific management was on the verge of delivering some shocking news.

The year was 1874, and Frederick Winslow Taylor had reached a decision. Ever since he was a boy, there had never been much doubt surrounding the direction of his life. The plan had always been for him to follow in his father's footsteps and become an attorney. And now that he had turned eighteen, a single question remained: Where would he go to school?

Taylor had no shortage of options. As a meticulous student from a wealthy family, he could go just about anywhere he pleased. His parents presumed he would choose Harvard, or perhaps the Massachusetts Institute of Technology. Their hopes were dashed when Taylor revealed that he was quitting school altogether. Instead, he would become a factory worker.

To this day, the rationale behind Taylor's decision is somewhat unclear. Taylor's deteriorating eyesight provided him with a convenient explanation for abandoning higher education. But historians suspect that was simply an excuse. The real motive, many believe, had more to do with his unusual fascination with efficiency.

Growing up, Taylor harbored some unusual quirks. He had always been obsessed with performance, some would say to the point of extreme. According to one childhood friend, as a teenager Taylor was "constantly experimenting with his legs, in an endeavor to discover the step which would cover the greatest distance with the least expenditure of energy; or the easiest method of vaulting a fence, [or] the right length and proportions of a walking staff."

In all likelihood, it was the precision of industry that drew him to the factory floor.

But the transition did not come easily. Commuting from his parents' mansion each morning, Taylor did his best to hide his wealthy upbringing from his coworkers, but no matter how poorly he dressed or how often he cursed, he never quite fit in.

The rejection grew mutual. With time, Taylor became increasingly critical of his colleagues, considering their work habits to be inefficient and lazy. They didn't work fast enough, Taylor thought, and it was costing the factory money.

One day Taylor approached his supervisor with an idea. In addition to his responsibilities on the factory floor, he would conduct an experiment to identify the most efficient way for cutting metal. His method was simple. He would test blades individually, altering their size, angle, and speed, until he identified "the one best way." His results could then be used to standardize the way work was done in the factory, improving its output and productivity.

Taylor got his wish.

Six months later he shared the findings of his research and received approval to carry out more experiments, which he did, enthusiastically.

Slowly, Taylor's studies evolved. He became less interested in the operations of the machines and turned his attention to the factory's men.

How long did it really take workers to do their jobs? Which tasks were eating up the majority of their time on the factory floor? What happened when management paid them a little extra?

Taylor carried around a stopwatch and measured compulsively, breaking down individual jobs into their component tasks. He then presented his findings, offering painstaking analyses and recommendations for eliminating waste and enhancing performance.

With each study, Taylor's influence grew. He had started as an apprentice. By the age of thirty-one he was promoted to chief engineer.

Once in a position of management, Taylor had the authority he needed to implement his vision. In his view, the key to getting the most from workers was to standardize work by detailing how every aspect of a job should be performed, down to the precise physical motions.

Thinking, from Taylor's perspective, was the concern of management. Doing was the domain of workers. Once best practices had been established, management's responsibility was simple: enforcing regulations that require employees to do their job in a formally prescribed way, without deviation.

To ensure compliance, Taylor believed in motivating employees using both the carrot and the stick. Pay in Taylor's factories was not determined by job title or experience, as the labor unions might have wished. Instead it was directly tied to an employee's performance. The faster workers produced, the more income they earned. And the moment their output dipped there would be repercussions. Taylor had little patience for waste, and developed a reputation for being quick to send workers packing.

Naturally, Taylor's approach fostered a great deal of resentment among employees. But few could argue with his results. At the Midvale Steel Company he *doubled* the machinists' output. At Bethlehem Steel Works he shrank the number of employees from 500 to 140 without *any* drop in production.

With time, word of Taylor's success began to spread. By his midthirties he was leading a management consulting firm that proved far more lucrative than his prior work as an employee. The diversity of his experiences offered him a unique platform, which he leveraged skillfully, including the release of a number of bestselling books, such as *The Principles of Scientific Management*. It became one of the most widely read texts in all of business and came to epitomize the way the role of management was understood for generations.

At the core of Taylor's thinking was a mechanistic view of human behavior. Taylor saw employees the way we see a car: as machines in need of a driver. Among his central assumptions was the notion that employees are inherently unmotivated to work hard. Nor are they intelligent enough to find efficient ways of working. The bottom line for Taylor was this: By allowing employees the freedom to choose how to do their jobs, too many businesses were leaving productivity to chance. And it was costing them a fortune.

By the time of Taylor's passing in 1915, his ideas had taken on a life of their own. Spurred by the start of World War I, when faster production was a matter of life and death, scientific management became synonymous with efficiency. What had begun as a single man's obsession with numbers transformed not only factory life but the operation of institutions everywhere. An assembly-line mentality was applied to the way restaurants served customers, to the way patients were treated at hospitals, to the way children were educated in schools.

But there was a problem with Taylorism—one that young Frederick Taylor could never have foreseen back in his days as a gang boss on the floor of the Midvale Steel Company.

Somewhere along the way, it stopped working.

WHAT TAYLOR MISSED

In many ways, Taylor was ahead of his time. He was working as a lone experimenter in a world that did not consider human behavior a science. His methods were inventive, and his recommendations clearly achieved results. Back in Taylor's day, paying for performance, simplifying tasks, and observing workers closely really did contribute to productivity.

But then something changed. The knowledge economy arrived,

and the jobs grew infinitely more complex. And suddenly, predicting employee performance proved a lot trickier.

Some years back, Duke behavioral economist Dan Ariely and a few of his colleagues ran a study testing one of Taylor's least controversial assumptions: the idea that offering higher pay leads to better performance. On the surface, it seems obvious that the promise of an alluring bonus will motivate employees to work harder. It's why we offer professional athletes millions of dollars when their teams reach the playoffs and reward executives with additional stocks when their companies record higher profits. The more you pay them, the harder they work, and the harder they work, the better they'll do, right?

Except that's not what Ariely's team found.

The group conducted their experiment in India, where favorable exchange rates made it affordable for American experimenters to offer highly lucrative rewards. Participants in the study were asked to complete a series of memory and concentration tasks and were offered a bonus if they did especially well. The amount of the bonus varied depending on the group to which participants were assigned. There were three conditions in the study: a *low bonus* condition, in which the incentive for good performance was the equivalent of one day's pay; a *medium bonus* condition, in which the incentive was two weeks' pay; and a *high bonus* condition, in which the incentive was a knee-buckling five months' salary.

In which condition did participants perform best?

It turned out there wasn't much difference between the low and medium bonus groups, both of which did fairly well. The high reward group, on the other hand, did differ significantly and *not* in the direction Frederick Taylor's theories would have predicted. Surprisingly, participants offered five months' salary performed dramatically worse, despite having been offered 150 times the amount of money as those in the low bonus group to do the exact same work.

Why? The prospect of an enticing reward, Ariely argues, can have a debilitating effect. When the stakes are unusually high, our bodies activate a fight-or-flight response, which, as we saw in previous chapters, interferes with our ability to think clearly. This is why it can suddenly become difficult to communicate on a job interview or a date, when basic questions like, "Tell me about yourself" can render you speechless.

In sports it's called choking, and the term isn't strictly a metaphor. The more psychological pressure you experience, the more your muscles unconsciously tighten, making even the most basic motions (like breathing) more difficult to execute.

In a follow-up study, Ariely ran a similar experiment with a slight twist. This time, he and his team had participants complete two sets of exercises. The first—much like the memory and concentration task used in his first experiment—was cognitively taxing (doing a math exercise). But the second was straightforward and simple (typing on a computer). What effect would large incentives have on performance this time around? Once again, the high bonus group performed worse on the cognitively challenging task. However, when the task was easy, the adrenaline boost of a high reward was quite useful, leading to better results.

Higher rewards do result in better performance, but only when the task is simple. When the work is complex, large rewards often backfire, undermining the very outcome they are intended to elevate.

TAYLOR VERSUS BUFFETT: THE TRUTH ABOUT MOTIVATING TOP PERFORMANCE

Overwhelming arousal isn't the only downside to making rewards a central focus. So is the way the rewards alter the quality of an employee's motivation.

From Taylor's perspective, motivation was about one thing: *quantity*. Employees were either highly motivated or they weren't. And it was up to managers to energize them, by enticing them with seductive bonuses and threatening them with losing their jobs. It's a perspective that continues to be popular in many organizations today. But a growing number of motivational experts argue that this view is not only simplistic—it's actually wrong.

Here's why. Motivation, we now know, varies not just in *quantity* but also in *type*. Some employees are motivated by the intrinsic enjoyment they derive from doing their work, while others are motivated by the lure of extrinsic factors, like the appeal of money or an important title.

To the outside observer, the motivation energizing an employee's behaviors is invisible. But the internal psychological experience it produces has a significant impact on a worker's thinking, which then influences his on-the-job performance. Studies show that the more intrinsically motivated people feel, the more creative, engaged, and energized they are while working. And what's more, they stay motivated for longer periods of time.

Interestingly, when the work is itself rewarding, an emphasis on rewards can have an unexpected effect. It *reduces* intrinsic motivation. That's because the moment rewards take center stage we begin to view our work as a means to an end and start enjoying it less. Economists call it the "crowding out" effect. We stop focusing on the enjoyment the work brings us and become fixated on receiving our reward. Consequently, the more emphasis an organization places on salary and bonuses, the less likely its employees are to enjoy the work for its own sake.

To be fair, there are times when using extrinsic rewards to increase motivation makes sense. For example, when the work itself is repetitive and uninteresting, like the factory jobs Taylor was hired to oversee. But when the goal is to grow engagement and improve performance on intellectually challenging tasks, managers are far better off fostering intrinsic motivation than supplementing motivation with extrinsic rewards.

How do you get employees intrinsically motivated about their work? One vital component, according to psychologists Edward Deci and Richard Ryan, involves taking a page out of Warren Buffett's managerial playbook and helping people feel autonomous while doing their job. When people are empowered to make their own decisions at work, they naturally feel motivated to excel for one simple reason: Autonomy is a basic psychological need.

Deci and Ryan's research shows that the experience of choice is inherently energizing and fundamental to psychological well-being, across geographic and cultural boundaries. It's also pivotal to succeeding at goals well beyond the workplace. Dieters who pursue weight loss for autonomous reasons lose more weight than those who feel pressured by others. Smokers who choose to stop smoking are more successful than those who feel forced to stop. Patients are more likely to stick with their medication regimen when they understand and endorse the need for treatment.

Ultimately, the value of autonomy is that it allows people to fully embrace their goals and see the investments they make as their own choice. It's that feeling of personal ownership that inspires employees to be driven by their own interests, curiosity, and desires to succeed. And when that happens, when the interests of the manager and an employee overlap, the need for the policing Taylor recommended disappears.

WHAT DISAPPROVING PARENTS AND MICROMANAGERS HAVE IN COMMON

We know that experiencing choice in the workplace boosts intrinsic motivation and enhances performance on complex tasks. But what happens when a manager puts limits on the autonomy of his employees? When suddenly even the most rudimentary decisions need to be approved by a committee or a higher-up. In other words, how do we react when our autonomy at work is thwarted?

In a classic experiment examining how people respond to limits on their freedom, researchers at the University of Colorado conducted a study on a decision most people expect to reach on their own: their choice of romantic partner. Psychologists interviewed couples in relationships of varying lengths (both dating and married) and asked each partner to rate how much they loved their significant other, the degree of trust they felt in the relationship, and how often they disagreed. Then they asked the couples a few questions they weren't expecting. What was their parents' reaction to their relationship? Were they critical of their partner in any way? Had they ever said anything that might imply they hoped the relationship would end?

The findings suggest that dissatisfied parents would do well to keep their mouths shut.

The more parents disapproved of a romantic partner, the more in love the partners said they were. The effect was strongest among dating partners, who presumably had more of a choice about whether to continue or end the relationship. There was something unnerving about a parent's meddling that appears to have motivated their children to rebel.

The finding, known within social psychological circles as the "Romeo and Juliet effect," is part of a broader tendency. It's not just lovers who show a stubborn streak of defiance. The same goes for the rest of us. Anytime we're told we can't do something, the idea of doing it suddenly grows more appealing.

Psychologists have a term for this: *reactance*. It's what happens when you feel your freedom or control is threatened. You're motivated to try and restore it, often by defying the very instructions you have been given.

Studies show reactance occurs in a wide variety of domains. Therapists who try to persuade their clients by talking more and offering more advice tend to have lower success rates. Smokers who are shown graphic warnings about the consequences of inhaling tobacco are more resolute about continuing to smoke.

Think back to the last time you were on the receiving end of a hard sell. Chances are, you suddenly found yourself digging in your heels, unwilling to budge.

The harder we're pushed, the more we resist.

Within the workplace, micromanagement can trigger reactance in ways that are not immediately visible to a supervisor. Customers might be made to wait a little longer. An employee's cell phone suddenly "dies" just when his manager needs to reach him. And, of course, the ultimate act of defiance: employee turnover. Studies show that the less autonomous workers feel, the more likely they are to consider taking another job.

Limiting people's autonomy does more than simply spark the occasional act of rebellion. It creates a cycle of dependence that prevents employees from taking a proactive approach to their work. When managers attempt to control too much, their employees learn to sit around and wait for further instructions. On the assembly line, that may have been fine. But in a knowledge economy, it prevents employees from taking the initiative, which, ironically, costs managers even more time in the long run.

Leadership can be a zero-sum game. The more a manager demands from his employees, the less his employees are able to demand of themselves. Which leads to a relationship pattern that's similar to a helicopter parent and his overdependent child. With every controlling directive comes a demoralizing message: "Only *I* know what's best."

THE ART OF FOSTERING AUTONOMY

In some ways, providing autonomy presents a formidable challenge to managers. How do you consistently promote a sense of autonomy when the reality at most companies is that choice isn't always an option?

Take, for example, an event many managers face all too often: the client emergency.

Your cell phone is ringing. It's an important client and he's got a crisis on his hands. The upshot? Your team will need to turn around a last-minute assignment right away. Their workload is already at capacity. You'll need your staff to work well into the night, and it's your job to break the news.

What do you say?

Psychologists offer a number of recommendations for promoting the experience of autonomy, even when real choice appears to be lacking.

Provide a meaningful rationale. The first requirement to endorsing any behavior, whether it's crafting a report at work, running three miles every morning, or taking a prescribed medication, is having a good understanding of why you're doing it. Managers often assume that they and their employees have the same knowledge and background about a project and therefore share an understanding about why a task is valuable. That's simply not the case.

Research shows that when people are given a meaningful rationale, they're more likely to invest more effort and to view their contribution as important. But not just any rationale will do. The key to crafting an effective rationale is communicating how a successful outcome will provide value to the person doing it or someone they care about.

To fully endorse a behavior, we must first see its worth.

Define the outcome, not the process. We experience a task more autonomously when we're given the opportunity to define our approach. When we chart our own path we're more likely to feel a sense of control, experience ownership, and take pride in our work. That's why it's vital to provide employees with some leeway on designing a plan rather than dictating one yourself.

As any manager knows, letting go is often harder than it sounds. In many cases, years of experience have taught you exactly how to tackle a project. Why *wouldn't* you tell your team what to do?

Here's why: Spoon-feeding instructions comes with a cost. Sure, overseeing every detail might speed up productivity on this particular assignment, but that short-term lift is likely to undermine your team's overall experience of autonomy, leading to long-term declines in their motivation.

Micromanagement is the motivational equivalent of buying on credit. Enjoy a better product now, but pay a hefty price for it later.

Use open-ended questions. Inviting employees to explore solutions together and demonstrating that you value their input is another technique for growing an employee's sense of choice. It's one thing to ask your team to develop their own plan and quite another to show that their ideas have merit.

Here are two questions a manager can ask, both aimed at meeting that looming client deadline. See if you can spot the one that's more likely to contribute to an employee's sense of autonomy.

"What solutions do you see for designing a presentation by Tuesday?"

or

"Have you looked at the deck Martha used the last time she presented?"

What's different about these questions? The first is open-ended, meaning it deliberately invites a longer response and asks the employee to think and reflect. The second question is close-ended, meaning it is easy to answer, and limited to the words "yes" and "no."

Open-ended questions—ones beginning with the words "how," "what," or "why"—unconsciously communicate a respectful interest in the way another person thinks. They also allow the respondent to direct where the conversation goes from there.

In contrast, close-ended questions place the responder on the defensive: *Did you check Martha's deck!?* It's a question that can easily be interpreted as an accusation. Unlike open-ended questions, close-ended questions allow the questioner to maintain control of the conversation, leading the responder to feel pressured rather than supported.

Acknowledge negative feelings. What do you do when an employee tells you he is not happy about working late? It can make for an uncomfortable conversation. No one likes dealing with negative emotions in the workplace, especially when they feel helpless to alleviate their coworkers' concerns.

One approach is to ignore the negative comment, or to gloss over it by focusing on the positive ("at least we don't have to do it every night!"). But interestingly, recognizing negative experiences and legitimizing them actually helps sustain people's autonomy.

To understand why this works, it's important to recognize that when people voice a complaint, the first thing they want is to feel heard. The alternatives, which include being told our perspective is wrong or having it ignored, only makes us feel more frustrated. Paradoxically, having our feelings accepted defuses some of the negativity by legitimizing our experience.

Even in cases in which directly addressing a concern is not possible, mirroring an employee's emotion by reflecting back what's been said ("You're feeling frustrated" or "This project is complicated") goes a long way toward helping your colleague feel understood.

Minimize the focus on rewards. Your team might get paid overtime or receive a free dinner for working late, but resist making that the focus. As a manager, you may find yourself desperate for ways of cheering up your team. But remember, long-term interest is better sustained by keeping a focus squarely on the task itself. Earning overtime is great for your bank account but terrible for your motivation.

Unexpected rewards that come at the end of an activity—for example, a bottle of wine the following Friday to show your appreciation for a job well done—*can* keep intrinsic motivation intact. So feel free to offer your team a modest gift, but wait until *after* the project is done. The key is to let success on the task serve as its own reward while the work is getting done.

Psychologists who study autonomy—called "self-determination theorists"—argue that supporting others' experience of choice is a persuasive motivational tool, especially when there is a power differential between two people. That means it's not just managers who benefit. It's also teachers, doctors, and parents.

The bottom line: Anytime you speak from a position of authority, the more supportive you are of others' autonomy, the more likely you are to inspire their best effort.

WHY THE BEST WORKPLACES ENCOURAGE INEQUALITY

When you consider all the steps that contribute to an employee's experience of autonomy at work, a broader theme emerges.

Leadership from the top down rarely sustains people's intrinsic motivation.

It's only when managers create an environment that allows employees to lead themselves that their natural desire to excel takes hold. The key lies in empowering employees to find their best way of working and offering them the flexibility to implement that approach.

Which is why it's strange that so many organizations continue to insist on using an outdated workplace model that requires employees to follow the same workday schedule.

In Taylor's day, a factory's output depended on employees working in shifts. Without a fixed schedule, the assembly line would stall and production would cease. Back then, the workday was designed to maximize the output of a factory's *machines*, not its *people*.

Today, of course, access to workplace machinery is no longer a requirement for being productive. Having a phone and a computer is often enough. Yet for most companies the fixed schedule remains. Despite all that we know about the factors that contribute to productivity, workplaces offering employees the freedom to set their own calendar are still very much in the minority.

From a psychological perspective, requiring all employees to follow an identical schedule and expecting them to do their best work ignores a basic reality of human nature: We are born with biologically based personality differences that lead us to thrive under different conditions.

And it's not just the variations *between* employees that are worth considering. It's also the way our ability to make a meaningful contribution fluctuates with the time of day. As we discovered in Chapter 3, research done in recent years has revealed a trove of data about the physiology of peak performance and the way our bodies' circadian rhythms affect our productivity.

We know, for example, that our memory and concentration tend to be sharpest in the morning and that we are better at seeing abstract connections between ideas later in the day, when we are fatigued. We know that hand-eye coordination and physical strength peak in the late afternoon. We know that the human mind is not very good at focusing for an extended period of time and that ninety minutes pushes the limit of what we can comfortably absorb.

Yet most organizations acknowledge none of this.

In the end, the real consequences of demanding that employees follow a regimented schedule are stress, burnout, and a weaker product. Access to computers at home, coupled with the pressure to be at the office all day (no matter how fatigued or unproductive an employee feels), leads to a focus on *appearing* busy during work hours while doing the real heavy lifting at night and on weekends. Not only does this encourage employees to act disingenuously at work, it also leaves them with less time to unwind and recharge. Ultimately, it is the work itself that suffers.

It's not uncommon for managers to feel wary about allowing employees to determine their own schedules. Without the structure of an eight-hour workday, they fear, employees will lose their focus or put off coming into the office when their work would benefit from their being there.

But if the research on autonomy is any indication, granting employees the flexibility to determine their own schedule is likely to do far more to improve workplace performance by enhancing intrinsic motivation, communicating trust, and boosting employee loyalty. Removing the forty-hour scaffold from organizational life can also be quite revealing, exposing those who are simply pretending to work while bringing the real contributors to the fore.

If the specter of an empty office frightens you, perhaps the following study might lead you to reconsider. Research conducted by Stanford's economics department suggests that rather than employees getting sidetracked at home, their productivity actually rises when telecommuting is required. In an experimental study that randomly assigned call center employees to either work from home four days a week or remain in the office full time, findings showed a 12.5 percent increase in productivity among at-home workers.

The reason? Fewer breaks and sick days and a quieter work environment.

That alone would be impressive. But there's more. Employees assigned to work from home were also significantly more satisfied with their jobs, displayed greater psychological adjustment at the end of the study, and were 50 percent less likely to quit their jobs.

Which goes to show: Sometimes, the less management tries to control, the better the results.

The Lessons of Autonomy
Action Items for Managers

Empower people to find their best way of working. One way of helping people feel autonomous is giving them the flexibility to design their own approach to the work, however they see fit. Encouraging employees to build a schedule for meeting goals instead of requiring that they sit by a computer to meet a predefined schedule sends a powerful message of trust and sets the stage for sustained performance.

Consider motivating by subtraction. Look around at your organization's top performers. Are they responding to a supervisor's demands or driven by an intrinsic desire to succeed? There's a reason people arrive energized and optimistic on day one—long before they've been exposed to a manager's influence—and it's because the prospect of succeeding at a job is inherently gratifying. Instead of focusing on rewards and punishments that extrinsically motivate, work on identifying and then eliminating barriers that sap your team of the intrinsic motivation they possessed when they first started.

Practice macromanagement. When you're up against a tight deadline and feeling pressured to deliver, it's tempting to micromanage every aspect of a project. Don't. Micromanagement is an autonomy killer that diminishes your team's long-term development and deprives them of the space to lead themselves. Instead of obsessing over process, ask your team to chart their own path. Your job is to ask questions and provide feedback, not steer the ship.

The Lessons of Autonomy
Action Items for Emerging Leaders

Feeling micromanaged? Turn the tables. When supervisors micromanage, it is often because they're feeling overwhelmed. We all want a sense that life is controllable. When we don't, we experience unease, which some supervisors express in the form of overmanagement. How do you calm micromanagers down? By flooding them with information, proactively reaching out and sharing progress, and asking questions that help them feel like they're in control. Micromanagers are scared. Your job is to reassure them.

Put Taylorism to work for you. Each of us has a unique physiological rhythm, which is why it pays to identify your "one best way" of working. Noticing when you're at your most productive is the first step to building a better schedule. Perhaps you need to block out your mornings for focus work, set a calendar alert to take a midafternoon walk, or activate Freedom, a free software program that temporarily disables your Internet access during hours when multitasking is a temptation. Experimenting with your daily routine can help you identify an approach that reliably brings out your best.

Rank autonomy over wealth. When choosing between jobs, you're better off prioritizing the amount of freedom a role provides over the size of its paycheck. In a 2011 study spanning over sixty countries, researchers found that autonomy is a consistently better predictor of psychological health than income. Ironically, one of the reasons we find money so alluring is that having disposable income brings with it the promise of independence. But beware of pursuing money for its own sake. It's when we sell our autonomy for a higher income that we get ourselves in trouble.

SEVEN

Better Than Money

What Games Can Teach Us About Motivation

On a blustery winter day in 2003, I was making my way to a lecture hall at the University of Rochester with a fellow graduate student, when we both noticed something strange.

We had just entered Wilson Commons, a student activity center that more often than not was the last place you'd find students. There wasn't much attracting them to the building. A few billiards tables, the office to the campus newspaper, an optimistically named "café."

But on this particular afternoon, there was something different about the place.

At first we weren't sure what it was. A large mob of students was cheering, circling around what appeared to be a pair of synchronized dancers. The two of them were standing on an elevated platform, their feet moving at breakneck speed. You could feel the loud thump of techno music as spotlights flashed rhythmically overhead.

"What do you think is going on here?" asked my friend, Arlen. "Some type of performance?"

It certainly looked that way. Except for one thing. Both the dancers and the audience were staring ahead in the same direction, eyes fixed on a television screen.

"What are they looking at?" I remember asking.

The answer, as we later found out, was Dance Dance Revolution (DDR), a Japanese arcade game that would soon become a worldwide sensation.

Most video games reward players for hand-eye coordination. But DDR introduced a new approach to gaming, extending the genre to their feet. To succeed, players have to follow a sequence of steps that appear on a screen by stomping on a motion-sensitive platform. When they do well, they accumulate points, and with enough points, they get to play faster, even more challenging levels.

To say that DDR took the gaming world by storm would be putting it mildly. Arcades around the globe reported record-breaking sales. Some outfitted entire rooms with DDR machines, just to keep up with demand. Fan clubs were formed. Tournaments were held. In Norway, DDR was declared a professional sport.

Later, video games like Guitar Hero and Rock Band would popularize the musical video game genre. And in retrospect, it seems reasonable to wonder whether either title would have attracted the development funding it needed had DDR not first made such a splash.

The fascinating thing about DDR isn't just the way it transformed the video game industry. It's the effect it had on its players. Before DDR was wheeled into the University of Rochester, the idea of two undergraduates voluntarily standing up in front of a group of strangers and performing a choreographed dance would have been unthinkable. Now, not only was it happening on a daily basis—students were actually paying good money just to get their turn.

It's a phenomenon that's bigger than DDR. When we're immersed in games, we get sucked into a whole host of behaviors we would normally avoid. We voluntarily sort cards. We enthusiastically rearrange tiles. We compulsively rotate falling blocks. We anguish over defeating cartoon villains and delight at collecting imaginary coins. And often, we engage in these behaviors at considerable personal costs. Bedtimes are ignored. Meals are skipped. Weekends disappear.

Today, thanks to seductive smartphone apps like Words With Friends, Bejeweled, and Angry Birds, many of us instinctively reach for our pocket at the slightest hint of spare time. In many cases, we're not even aware that we're doing it.

Which raises some intriguing questions. If games can convince people to do repetitive tasks for inconsequential rewards, what can they teach us about motivating employees? Can our passion for mastering games somehow be harnessed in the workplace?

But perhaps the most provocative question of all is this: Could the secret to engagement be buried inside a video game?

THE ONE WORKPLACE REWARD THAT
FEELS BETTER THAN A RAISE

Before we uncover some of the factors that make video games so appealing, let's first play a little game of our own.

Suppose that on your way home tomorrow night you pass an elderly street musician. You've always had a soft spot for vaguely Parisian music and the man is playing the accordion. Impulsively, you decide to pull out your wallet and politely place a five-dollar bill in the bowl sitting next to him. Lo and behold, it turns out this is no ordinary performer. It's a genie, and he's feeling quite generous himself. He offers to grant you one wish: You can change anything about your job. What will it be?

If we're being completely honest, the request many of us might make is simple: a higher salary. Who, after all, doesn't want to make more money?

But is earning money really all that important to our experience at work?

In 2010, Timothy Judge, a business professor at the University of Florida, set out to determine the real impact of salary on job satisfaction. To find out, Judge and his colleagues searched journal archives for every published study they could find measuring both salary and job satisfaction. They then combined the results into a single statistical analysis. All told, they looked at eighty-six different studies and evaluated the experiences of more than 15,000 employees.

Their conclusion: "Level of pay had little relation to either job or pay satisfaction."

Now, if you're like most people, these results seem deeply at odds with your personal experience. We all know how exhilarating it feels to get a raise or land a job with a big paycheck. And yet the numbers tell us something completely different. How then do we account for these findings?

One explanation, according to Judge and his colleagues, is that people tend to adapt to their level of income surprisingly quickly.

If you earn $80,000 a year and receive word that your manager has just authorized a $10,000 increase, you can expect to feel pretty elated. The question is, how long will that feeling last? A few days certainly. Maybe even a week. But three months from now, will you still be happier?

It's a bit like driving a new car. You get a genuine thrill out of that first ride home from the dealership. Breathing in the new car scent, you can't help but notice all the ways your new vehicle is superior to your old one. But after a few weeks, it's all background. You go back to being the same person, albeit one holding a different set of keys.

The data suggest that above a certain level of income—around $75,000 a year, according to latest estimates—increases in salary have a very minor effect on our happiness level. We adapt to income—no matter how much we make—yet we continuously yearn for more. The reason? It's because a rise in income really *does* make us happier. It's just that the initial thrill doesn't last.

If higher income doesn't lead to sustained happiness, what does?

One answer, according to Cameron Anderson, a psychologist at the University of California–Berkeley, is status. In a 2012 paper published in *Psychological Science*, Anderson and his colleagues make the case that if we want to predict people's happiness level, instead of looking at their socioeconomic status (or level of income), what we should really look at is the amount of respect and admiration they receive from their peers.

In one of the paper's studies, Anderson and his team measured the happiness levels of MBA students twice: once before they received their graduate degree and then nine months later, after the majority were working full-time jobs. On average, the typical student's income doubled during this period. But the range was broad. Some students found $40,000 jobs, while others were earning three times as much.

If ever there was an opportunity for seeing the impact of salary on happiness, this was it.

So what effect did salary have? Anderson's team found that once you take people's social status into account, the answer is exactly none. As it turns out, the best predictor of happiness is not participants' answer to, *How much do you earn?* It's their answer to, *How much do others look up to you?*

The findings present an interesting lens for viewing why so many people appear to be consumed with earning a higher salary. Perhaps it's not the material possessions they want, but the respect that comes along with it. When you're flush with cash, you command the attention of a lot of people, which may be what many of us are really after.

RECOGNITION, FEEDBACK, AND THE KEY TO A LONGER LIFE

The notion that our happiness is largely driven by the respect we receive from others makes a good deal of sense from an evolutionary perspective. In the past, being a valued member of a tribe meant security, access to attractive mates, and influence over important decisions.

Being recognized feels so good because it's the ultimate sign of belonging.

And while the data suggest that we adapt to money rather quickly, there is also some compelling evidence that we never quite get used to feeling respected. Consider the case of actors who have received the ultimate display of recognition in their field: an Academy Award. Studies show that on average, Oscar recipients live four years longer than other standout performers who have also received nominations but left their ceremony empty-handed. Similar trends have been found among Nobel Prize–winning scientists and Baseball Hall of Famers. Those who achieve the highest levels of recognition in their field tend to live longer than their unrecognized counterparts.

Recognition doesn't just make us feel better—it bolsters our health in significant ways. When we feel accepted by those around us, we experience less stress, get better quality sleep, and recuperate more quickly from illness.

What happens when we fail to receive recognition for our work? Our motivation suffers, we lose interest and eventually experience burnout. It's why, year after year, jobs with the highest turnover rates tend to belong to telemarketers, fast-food employees, and retail associates. Work that involves continuous sacrifice and garners little appreciation is psychologically exhausting.

One reason that recognition is vital to doing good work is that it feeds our need for competence. When we receive positive feedback, we experience an emotional rush. Competence is inherently motivating, which is why feeling like you're good at your job leads you to invest even more of yourself in your work.

Grow people's experience of competence and you'll inevitably grow their engagement.

Take, for example, your choice of career. Many of us pursue an occupation not because of some spiritual connection with a particular line of work, but because we happened to achieve success in a related area early on.

Perhaps in high school you found that you could make other students laugh, and this feedback propelled you to try your hand at stand-up comedy. After a few years of playing open mics, you land a job as a writer, and later go on a few auditions. Today you are the host of *The Daily Show*.

(For the record, this is, in fact, the biographical story of Jonathan Liebowitz, the comedian who changed his last name to Stewart because Liebowitz "sounded too Hollywood.")

Our interests flow from our successes.

Recognition not only shapes our career ambitions, it also increases the perceived value of our work. We often interpret the meaning of our job from the way others treat us. The exact same task can induce feelings of shame or pride, depending on how it is viewed by our colleagues.

Here's one example: plowing snow in the employee parking lot. If a custodian does it, we see it as menial labor. But if our CEO picks up a shovel and does the same thing, we revise our perspective and view it as an act of valor.

When we have evidence that others value our work, we tend to value it more ourselves, leading us to work harder.

Recognition at work is also important because the positive feedback is instructive. If we're deprived of feedback on our performance—positive or otherwise—we lack the information we need to improve. And when we're missing clear direction on what we need to do to succeed, it's just a matter of time before our enthusiasm wanes. It's a fundamental truth of the human condition: Being ignored is often more psychologically painful than being treated poorly.

Which brings us back to the world of video games.

Why are video games like Angry Birds and Bejeweled so engaging? It's because they fulfill so many of the desires we have in our everyday lives. When we pick up our smartphones and settle in with a good game, we immerse ourselves in a world that offers instant feedback on our performance and a sense of accomplishment when we succeed. A world where every task offers an opportunity to grow our competence, enhance our skills, and earn recognition.

No wonder we find so many of them addictive.

The obvious question, of course, is this: How do we make people feel the same way about their work?

HOW *NOT* TO RECOGNIZE EMPLOYEES

Helping the people who work for you feel appreciated seems easy enough. So it's surprising that plenty of workplaces get it wrong.

In many organizations, recognition is rare. Some managers are so focused on preventing mistakes that they neglect to pay much attention to things that are going right. Others are uncomfortable with praise, or feel that it's not their job to be a cheerleader. There is also the fear among some—particularly small business owners—that offering employees too many compliments might confuse them into thinking that they deserve a raise.

What these managers fail to consider is that recognition is not about stroking an employee's ego. It's about providing them with the psychological fuel to feel engaged. We are all dependent on the need for competence. And if we don't fulfill that need during the forty or so hours we spend at work, we will search for competence experiences elsewhere, shifting our mental energy to nonwork activities.

One reason it's easy for managers to underestimate the value of recognition is that they hold high-status positions that are regularly on the receiving end of admiration and respect. It's natural for them to take these benefits for granted, forgetting that less senior employees rarely experience the same level of glory.

At many companies, the standard tool for offering feedback and recognition is the annual performance review. And in a lot of ways it does more harm than good.

On the plus side, performance reviews prompt high-level conversations about an employee's progress and provides an opportunity for dialogue about short- and long-term goals. The information holds tremendous value for employees, but not when the feedback arrives in twelve-month intervals.

And that's the trouble with performance reviews: They mislead managers into thinking they're giving enough feedback. Ironically, they also make it easier to avoid difficult conversations. If an employee is performing poorly, it is easier for a manager to let it slide when he knows that he can just bring it up later in a performance review.

When it comes to growing engagement, an annual or even semi-annual review is exactly the wrong approach. Even negative feedback, which provides clues on ways of improving performance, can be a lot more motivating than silence.

Another way organizations get recognition wrong is by overdoing it and making it routine. Receiving excessive positive feedback is just as bad as having no feedback at all. When everything we do is celebrated, we lack the data we need to adjust our behaviors and build our skills, which interferes with our experience of competence.

Worse, undeserved positive feedback is demoralizing to our team members. When every employee is given the same degree of recognition regardless of effort, we can't help but grow disengaged. An overly grateful manager is a poor manager. As British essayist Samuel Johnson once put it, "He who praises everybody praises nobody."

Some organizations use Employee of the Month awards to show their appreciation, rewarding one high-performing individual with a gift card or a coveted parking spot. While well intentioned, there are a number of reasons to doubt the effectiveness of this technique.

First, Employee of the Month awards turn appreciation into a competition, pitting coworkers against one another in a fight for recognition. When appreciation is a limited resource, and getting ahead means outdoing colleagues, it's natural to become stingy with praise.

Second, the award itself may actually foster more disappointment than glee. If you work in an office of ninety people, for example, you have one winner who walks away feeling good about himself and eighty-nine losers who feel like this month's efforts went unappreciated. The math simply does not favor an engaged workforce.

And finally, when awards are tied to specific timelines rather than behaviors, it's easy to wonder whether you were selected because of something you did or because management needed to fill a slot. In smaller offices, in particular, the award becomes something of a running joke. Employees take turns winning, well, because someone has to.

THE SCIENCE OF PRAISE

With so many pitfalls to providing recognition, it's easy to wonder: How do you get it right?

Psychologists offer a number of guidelines for gaining the biggest motivational bang for the buck out of your positive feedback.

First, feedback is most effective when it is **provided immediately**.

Unlike golf or basketball, performance in the workplace tends to be ambiguous. How well your memo was written or how convincing you were at a client presentation can be open to interpretation. But the longer we go without clear feedback on our performance, the less engaged we become. Delayed praise is still pleasurable, of course. But it is both less motivating and less likely to result in learning than feedback that is delivered right away.

Second, positive feedback is more meaningful when it is **specific**.

"Good job, Mike," is a lot less powerful than, "I was really impressed with the detailed research you did in advance of our meeting." The less generic the compliment, the more we take it to heart. It also shows that you're paying close attention, which is inherently flattering.

Third, as a general rule, you should do your best to **compliment the behavior and not the person.**

When you focus your praise on how smart or talented someone is, you make the recognition about the individual, taking attention away from the task. Praising effort, on the other hand, directs attention to what they did right, encouraging them to do more of it.

Research shows that praising intelligence, for example, leads people to view their abilities as fixed traits, leaving less room for growth. And when people view their success as reflective of their ability, they become less willing to take risks and more willing to cheat in order to protect their reputation.

Fourth, **public praise is more powerful than private praise.**

Complimenting an employee in front of his or her peers will carry greater weight than doing so in a private e-mail. One clever way of taking advantage of this insight involves thanking employees by rewarding not them, but their colleagues in recognition of a recent success. At Akraya Inc., a staffing and recruiting company in Sunnydale, California, for example, the CEO buys everyone ice cream when a new recruit exceeds expectations. It's an effective approach because it offers both competence feedback and gratitude from one's peers.

And finally, when it comes to rewards, **adding a positive is more motivating than removing a negative.**

Many managers reward high-performing employees with time off, but this approach communicates the wrong message. What it says is that hard work is a bad thing, a punishment you escape when you do something right.

Research shows that when it comes to motivating others, introducing a positive reward following a desired behavior is a lot more effective than removing a negative punishment. To grow workplace engagement, instead of taking work away in recognition, try rewarding high performers with *more* responsibility by growing their departmental involvement and including them in major organizational decisions.

THE BUSY MANAGER'S GUIDE TO APPRECIATION

You can know a lot about positive feedback and still be very bad at it. It's not that you don't think appreciation is important. Or that you don't value your employees. It's that, as a manager, you're busy. You're on conference calls or in meetings or traveling. There's not enough time in your day to go around complimenting everyone. And part of you, frankly, doubts whether that would be the best use of your skills.

So what do you do?

For a lot of smart leaders the answer comes down to a simple and powerful solution: outsource praise.

Top-down recognition from a manager isn't the only source of positive feedback available to employees. So is recognition from their peers. As it turns out, there's something a lot more powerful about recognition when it comes from our colleagues. For one thing, while a manager's positive feedback can fulfill our need for competence, the feedback of our teammates can help us feel both competent *and* connected, making it satisfying on a broader level.

As a manager, the more peer-to-peer recognition you can inspire, the easier it is to maintain engagement.

Getting employees to recognize one another isn't a matter of issuing a companywide directive. After all, for gratitude to be effective, it needs to be sincere.

One way to change behavior, which we'll examine more closely in Chapter 9, is by modeling certain actions and adjusting social norms. As a manager, you can lead the way by making it a habit to publicly recognize at least one employee during every group meeting, shifting expectations about how team members interact.

Another approach is to listen for the next time an employee mentions how much a teammate contributed to a project. Encourage her to write a quick e-mail or, better yet, offer to pay for your employee to take her colleague to lunch.

A growing number of organizations are now using social media to facilitate appreciation in the workplace. Web-based platforms such as Yammer and Chatter allow employees to communicate online using sophisticated tools, including organizational polling, picture sharing, and live blogging. They also make expressing gratitude a lot easier with a feature that is similar to Facebook's Like button. In many programs, Thankers get to rate their level of gratitude, and the information they share is then broadcast to the employee's manager and teammates.

By simplifying the expression of gratitude and publicizing it when it occurs, workplace social media tools are helping organizations promote a mind-set of recognition, making it easier for employees to bond while simultaneously fueling their motivation.

But let's face it. You can have all the recognition in the world and still not be all that engaged at your job. It's because no matter how effective you are at the office, it's not always clear that the work you're doing has value.

In a world where most of our day is spent typing away at a keyboard, it's easy to find yourself driving home at night, wondering what exactly you have to show for the last nine hours of your life. It's only natural. The further removed we are from the outcome of our work, the harder it is to identify the point of our contribution.

So what can you do to keep people motivated when being successful isn't motivation enough? As we'll see in this next section, sometimes what it takes is a really good story.

THE SECRET TO MAKING ANY JOB FEEL MEANINGFUL

The average college football team has 125 players, many of whom won't see a single minute of playing time all season. They make the same time commitment as the team's starters, travel to all of the same games, and risk the same serious injuries every time they step onto the field. Yet they receive none of the accolades.

Why do they come back year after year?

One reason is that they tend to believe their sacrifices have value. Within college sports, coaches have become adept at helping bench players see the significance of their role. By allowing starters to practice against opponents who expend every ounce of effort, they facilitate the success of the entire team.

Every organization has a bench of second stringers who hold little hope of receiving the salary or glory of those on the front lines. Which is why companies can learn a few things from the way college coaches use meaning to motivate their players.

In today's economy, it's especially easy to lose track of the value of our work. Unlike the craftsmen and laborers of the past, we no longer benefit from tangible reminders of our contribution. That's why it's important for all employees to have an explicit understanding about the value of their contribution, so that they can stay motivated even when progress is hard to see.

Finding meaning in our work gives us a framework for understanding our sacrifices. When we view our work as meaningful, we are better able to deal with setbacks and persevere in the face of difficulties. How do you make a job feel meaningful? In many ways, the answer has to do with broadening employees' perspective.

We tend to view our work as more meaningful when we can see beyond our day-to-day activities and identify a long-term benefit, ideally one that helps others. Research on workplace experiences bears this out. On the whole, we are happier pursuing long-term rather than short-term goals. We also feel better when our goals center on benefiting others instead of ourselves.

In 2005, Wharton business professor Adam Grant was curious to see whether helping employees find meaning in their job would improve their performance. It's one thing to say that meaning makes a difficult job easier to tolerate. But does it have any effect on an employee's productivity?

For his subjects, Grant chose a group of university telemarketers tasked with raising alumni donations. They were not a particularly motivated bunch. At the time, turnover was at a staggeringly high 400 percent, meaning that the average employee remained on staff for about three months.

Grant's solution: a ten-minute intervention in which callers got to meet a student who had received a university scholarship and had therefore benefited from their work. During the meeting, employees had the opportunity to personally interview the recipient and were able to hear firsthand how his life had changed as a result of winning the award.

How much of an effect could a *ten-minute* meeting possibly have?

One month later, Grant returned to the call center and reviewed the numbers. The results were astonishing. Telemarketers in Grant's intervention doubled their calls per hour and generated 171 percent more in weekly revenue.

Their job was exactly the same as it had been a month earlier. The only thing that had changed was that they now had compelling evidence of the impact of their work.

The interesting implication for managers is that connecting employees with their end user can have a powerful motivating effect. In fact, Grant's research shows that building a direct personal connection between employees and their beneficiaries can, at times, be even more motivating than when a manager serves as the middle man and relays the very same information.

There's something unique about meeting the people whose lives we've affected that helps us see the value of our work.

WHY YOU SHOULD COMPLICATE YOUR WORKERS' LIVES

Some activities are more engaging than others. If we're lucky, at some point in our life we might find a hobby that captures our attention in ways we never thought possible. One in which we get fully immersed, losing track of time and place.

Psychologists have a term to describe these experiences: *flow*.
When people enter a state of flow, they are entirely absorbed in an
activity, concentrating fully on the present moment. Action feels
effortless. The world disappears. All that matters is the task. Video
game players encounter flow often, but they're not the only ones. Sur-
geons, athletes, and artists all report similar psychological experiences.

Pioneering researcher Mihaly Csikszentmihalyi has studied these
experiences and identified a number of factors that promote a state of
flow. They include having a clear understanding of the goal we're trying to achieve, and immediate feedback on our performance. Chess,
golf, and painting all fit this criteria and represent prototypical flow
experiences.

But there's one more element to flow that is just as vital. One that,
ironically, most workplaces try to minimize instead of promote: *progressive difficulty*.

According to Csikszentmihalyi, in order to experience flow, we
need to face challenges that either match or slightly exceed our current ability. If the tasks we're engaged in are too simple, we get bored.
And if we find ourselves in situations that are too far beyond our skill
level, we get overwhelmed.

In both cases the impact on our engagement is the same: We lose
interest.

One of the reasons video games are so good at sustaining our
attention is that they get harder with every level. At work, our experiences tend to take the opposite trajectory. Jobs tend to get easier the
longer we do them, making flow experiences all the more difficult to
achieve.

Compounding the problem is the fact that in most organizations,
the goal is to minimize the complexity of work. Efficiency is about
simplifying projects, creating replicable practices, and making output
more scalable. From a profit standpoint, it makes a lot of sense. But
from an engagement perspective, it's a path to ruin.

To create opportunities for flow in the workplace, we need to find the sweet spot that lies just beyond our current abilities. It's when we're stretching our skills and building our expertise that we are at our most engaged.

One way for managers to apply the lessons of flow is by deliberately looking for ways to challenge employees; for example, by assigning them projects that are just beyond their current skill level. Sure, doing the same tasks over and over might make your employees more efficient. But that's not the same thing as keeping them engaged. Flow comes through growth, not stagnation.

Another flow-promoting approach: asking employees to set a stretch goal every quarter and to develop a specific plan for achieving it. It's one thing for a manager to task employees with a difficult assignment. It's quite another for an employee to self-identify a challenge she wants to master. The more autonomous employees feel directing the course of their development, the more likely they are to show sustained engagement.

Finally, if you really want to promote flow experiences and intellectual curiosity in your company, consider making on-the-job learning a requirement. Offering a reading budget, encouraging employees to scan industry blogs during the day, and inviting employees to take courses that can help them build their skills are all ways of creating the experience of growth at work.

Our minds thrive on finding and integrating new information. When learning becomes part of our routine, we train ourselves to see new patterns and recognize important connections. Expanding our mental horizon primes us to think more creatively.

A labor force that's consistently acquiring new skills is also likely to be happier, more invested, and smarter about their work. Neurologically, learning is inherently rewarding. Acquiring new information increases our production of dopamine, which improves our mood and heightens our interest in related activities. It makes everything we do more interesting.

The moment employees stop growing, their enthusiasm sinks,

undermining their engagement and productivity. It's when our work becomes predictable that intellectual gridlock sets in and critical thinking stops.

By making it explicit that employees are expected to master new skills and by providing them with the time and resources to do so, organizations can prevent boredom, improve intellectual firepower, and enhance their competitive advantage. That may not guarantee that everyone at your company will experience flow. But it vastly improves the chances of it happening.

HOW TO BUILD A SOLUTIONS INCUBATOR

Encouraging employees to tackle new challenges fulfills their psychological needs for competence and autonomy. Now if only there was some way of achieving those objectives while also feeding their psychological need for interpersonal connections.

It turns out there is.

One thing all of the world's greatest athletes—Serena Williams, LeBron James, Tom Brady—have in common is their reliance on coaches to improve their performance. But it's not for the reasons we might expect. After an athlete reaches a certain level of expertise, the primary value of having a coach isn't in receiving explicit instructions or even the discipline that a coach can provide. It's in the coach's ability to observe the athletes' performance objectively and direct their attention to elements of their game that they are simply too close to appreciate.

The same line of thinking is behind the use of peer-to-peer coaching, a tool that many companies are now using to elevate employee performance.

For many people, the word "coaching" is an immediate turnoff. It implies ineptitude on the part of the learner, or a last resort for a manager considering letting someone go. It's a view we develop after years of schooling, where a tutor was brought in to fix underperformers.

But that model is all wrong.

Among top-level executives, coaching is viewed as something of a status symbol. The higher up you go, the more likely you are to be surrounded by advisers. Most CEOs don't run organizations by themselves. They have a senior leadership team that helps them think through big decisions. Even the president has access to a cabinet and a cadre of political campaign advisers.

To understand how peer-to-peer coaching works, and why it can be especially effective in the workplace, let's begin by first clearing up some common misconceptions about what it means to have a peer coach.

First, here are few things peer coaches *don't* do:

- Give advice
- Provide mentoring
- Rehabilitate problem employees

Next, here are some highlights of what peer coaching actually involves:

- Posing questions instead of providing answers
- Focusing on topics selected by the coachee, not the coach
- Having no vested interest in the outcomes of a coachee's decisions

Executive coaches tend to be expensive, costing hundreds of dollars an hour and up, which is why a number of organizations have begun offering coaching in-house. The process involves bringing in a professional trainer to teach employees how to use coaching techniques.

Generally speaking, a workplace coaching session unfolds in the following way. At the start of a session, the coachee identifies a challenge he is facing and would like to solve. Say, for example, trouble getting started on a difficult project. The coach's role is to ask a series of open-ended questions that are designed to help the coachee generate options for tackling the challenge:

- What would success look like on this project?
- What are some steps you're considering taking?
- Who could you talk to who's tackled a similar project?
- What can you do to chunk this project into manageable steps?

By the end of a successful session, the coachee has identified a direction in which he would like to go and created an implementation plan for putting that decision into action. When the two reconvene a week or two later, the coachee reports back on his progress, identifies his next challenge, and the cycle starts again.

In many peer-to-peer coaching programs, employees are assigned to three-person pods. Employee 1 coaches Employee 2, Employee 2 coaches Employee 3, and Employee 3 coaches Employee 1. It's an arrangement that prevents role confusion during conversations. To ensure that employees are comfortable speaking openly with their coach, teams are assigned according to department. Ideally, you want to group people who do not collaborate or interact frequently, so that they can be viewed as objective listeners.

Peer-to-peer coaching doesn't just benefit individuals. It helps organizations breed a consistently optimistic outlook for tackling their work. Instead of feeling stuck, everyone on the team has someone with whom they can discuss their next biggest challenge, without feeling pressured to have all the answers.

It's a process that also holds team members accountable for important decisions. Research shows that when we publicly announce our intentions to another person, we are more likely to follow through.

When Mihaly Csikszentmihalyi first became interested in studying flow, he conducted hundreds of interviews with those who experienced it most. His research included a fascinating list of subjects, from dancers and professional chess players to musicians and rock climbers. He was determined to find out what makes these individuals so much better at finding flow experiences than the rest of us.

Are they more adventurous? More comfortable with risk? Perhaps simply more aware of the present moment?

Surprisingly, he discovered that flow has less to do with the person than the nature of the task:

> In contrast to what happens in everyday life, on the job or at home, where often there are contradictory demands and our purpose is unsure, in flow we *always* know what needs to be done. The musician knows what notes to play next, the rock climber knows the next moves to make.

It's a critical point. To experience flow in our work we need clear objectives so that we know where to apply our energy. It's when we're missing a path forward that confusion sets in, stifling engagement and undermining performance.

It's yet another thing video games do so well: provide players with a clear path forward.

Knowing what to do next isn't as easy as it sounds, especially in the postindustrial workplace. Today, many of us are expected to chart new trails and craft innovative solutions on a daily basis. And this, ultimately, is why peer-to-peer coaching can be so valuable. By eliminating ambiguity and helping employees identify their next move, peer-to-peer coaching can help sustain the conditions that keep us at our most engaged.

WHAT ANGRY BIRDS CAN TEACH YOU ABOUT CREATING AN EXTRAORDINARY WORKPLACE

So yes, there's a lot we can learn from video games.

The same elements that keep us glued to our smartphones, computers, and video-game consoles are also the ones that can keep us enthusiastic about our work. When goal clarity, consistent feedback, a good narrative, and progressive difficulty are present, we can't help but become absorbed. It is, after all, our natural inclination to grow, connect, and master.

When video games can turn the adventures of an animated bird into an obsession, when they convince millions of us to pour our evenings and weekends into pursuing a fictional quest, they tell us something important about the human condition.

Engagement isn't about the task; it's about the conditions we build around it. When you fulfill people's psychological needs, any activity can become a passion.

The Lessons of Games
Action Items for Managers

If working for you is too easy, you're doing something wrong. While simplifying work and increasing efficiency may make financial sense, any activity that's devoid of challenge leads to boredom. To keep employees engaged, feed their need for competence by extending new challenges, rewarding learning, and increasing responsibility.

Make everyone a hero. For work to feel meaningful, we need to see a connection between our contributions and the well-being of others. Helping employees see the way their work has had a positive impact on other people—whether it be coworkers or customers—can be a strong motivator. Putting employees face to face with end users, sharing thank-you letters, and framing recognition within the context of how employees' work has impacted their clients make ordinary tasks feel more meaningful.

Use positive feedback strategically. Employees are dependent on positive feedback to guide their behavior and shape their focus. When you recognize an employee's actions, you tip the scales, increasing the perceived value of a particular behavior. Instead of simply offering positive feedback anytime an employee executes effectively, focus your comments on the elements you want to grow, feeding his need for competence while nudging him in the direction that will benefit the team's performance.

The Lessons of Games
Action Items for Emerging Leaders

Find optimal challenges by reading your mood. How you feel while doing an activity is useful information that can bring you closer to your next flow experience. Feeling bored? Look for ways to expand your responsibilities. Feeling anxious? Try slowing things down and focusing on less. We're most invigorated when we're tackling work that's just beyond our current skill set. Look for challenges that push you slightly out of your comfort zone.

Grow your influence by recognizing others. Receiving credit for a successful outcome can feel gratifying, but it's giving credit to others that builds our reputations as leaders. People like those who compliment them and view them as less selfish. Look around at the most successful leaders in your company. They're not the ones receiving compliments; they're the ones giving them.

Preempt your next performance review. If your manager is waiting for the end of the year to give you high-level feedback, he may be holding on to valuable information that is vital to your success. Don't let it happen. Instead of waiting for a year-end review, ask your manager for some time to discuss what you can be doing better. Taking the initiative is likely to impress, as is your focus on continuous improvement.

EIGHT

How Thinking Like a Hostage Negotiator Can Make You More Persuasive, Influential, and Motivating

Olivehurst, California
May 1, 1992

It's Friday, midafternoon.

A car approaches Lindhurst High School. Behind the wheel is a man in army fatigues, his face painted green and brown and black. Two belts of ammunition snake around his shoulders, circling the bulletproof vest on his chest.

He slips inside the school easily.

In one hand, he holds a semiautomatic rifle. In the other, a 12-gauge shotgun. There is no guard to see him coming, no security camera. In a rustic town of barely ten thousand, there has never been any need for protection. Until today.

The man's name is Eric Houston. He is twenty, unemployed, and angry. Later he will tell police that he never planned on coming here today. He will claim that he'd simply intended to head out for target practice, just as he'd done on the many afternoons since losing his job.

But now that he's back inside his old high school, he barely has to think about his next move.

He heads straight for Room C106.

Three years earlier, Eric Houston had been on the verge of graduating. That is, until he flunked out by a matter of points. It was economics that did him in. Or, if you asked Houston, a teacher by the name of Mr. Brens. Brens was the civics instructor who had refused to give him a passing grade, when all he needed was a lousy D- to earn a diploma.

Without the diploma, Houston had been barred from the school prom, which cost him his girlfriend. It infuriated his parents and alienated him from his friends. And now, years later, it had led to his losing his job on an assembly line when HR uncovered that he'd never graduated.

His life was in a tailspin. And he knew exactly why. It was all because of Mr. Brens.

The first thing Houston does when he enters Mr. Brens's classroom is smile. None of the students know who he is or why he is there. The room goes quiet. Then, without a word, Houston pulls the trigger, striking his old teacher with a shotgun blast to the chest.

Brens drops to the floor instantly, and for a split second, nothing happens. Ears are ringing. There is a smell of burned powder in the room.

Then one girl stands and lets out a panicked scream. Houston doesn't wait for her to finish. He points his gun and fires.

After that, things happen quickly. Houston leaves the classroom and walks into the frenzy of the hallway. Everywhere there is running. Shouting. In the rush to get out, some students are stumbling over each other. One of them nearly barrels into Houston. It sets him off.

He starts firing randomly. At students in the hallway. At those hiding beneath their desks. At the ones running for the exits, trying to escape. A burst of flame exits his gun with every blast, making it appear as if he is materializing out of smoke.

In a room down the hall, they try something different. Inside, they are barricading the doors, moving furniture around quietly. For a while, it seems this might work.

Until they hear a knock.

No one moves. Then a voice, trembling: "He knows you are in there, and if you don't open the door, he is going to shoot me in the back."

Finding a classroom full of students, Houston alters his approach. Instead of roaming the halls and shooting kids down, he begins collecting them. He grabs one of the boys and tells him to round up some of his friends. If he doesn't, Houston warns, he will begin executing the students he has, one by one.

By the time the police arrive, the room is full. Houston has in his possession eighty-five hostages.

And so began the standoff.

Houston had his hostages. The police had the building surrounded. It would be hours before the two sides would speak.

But then, at a little after ten that same evening, the inconceivable happened. Eric Houston put down his guns, removed his bulletproof vest, and placed his hands over his head. Not a single additional shot had been fired. Remarkably, after killing four people and wounding ten more, Houston had been persuaded to give himself up.

Houston's surrender was largely the work of Yuba County negotiator Chuck Tracy. A novice at the time of the Lindhurst crisis, Tracy had initially been instructed to simply stall Houston until the FBI's more experienced team of negotiators could arrive on the scene. Yet somehow, over the course of a few brief phone conversations, Tracy had managed to forge a powerful connection with Houston. To the surprise of everyone, the two men clicked. So much so, in fact, that by the time the FBI was ready to take the lead, Houston was refusing to speak with anyone else. There was only one man he would negotiate with and that man was Chuck Tracy.

So what did Tracy say?

How do you persuade a man who has just shot up a building full of children, a man who has no reasonable hope of ever walking free again, that it's in his best interest to turn himself in? And what exactly is it that hostage negotiators *do* to build a working relationship when collaboration seems entirely out of reach?

WHAT GOOD DOCTORS HAVE IN COMMON WITH THE WORLD'S BEST SALESPEOPLE

To fully appreciate why Chuck Tracy's techniques were effective (and more successfully incorporate them into the way you communicate), it helps to first have an understanding of why working relationships often deteriorate.

In 1994, a team of medical researchers began investigating precisely that, posing a question that had bewildered industry experts for years: Why do patients sue their doctors?

On the surface, the answer seems simple. Television legal dramas and newspaper headlines often portray malpractice as the result of physician error, prompted by misdiagnosis or the mishandling of a patient's treatment. But is that really the cause? After all, not every dissatisfied patient resorts to taking their doctor to court. So what separates the families that sue from the families that don't?

To find out, the researchers used an unusual approach. They went right to the source, analyzing nearly four thousand pages of plaintiff depositions that were filed during actual medical malpractice lawsuits. Of particular interest was the way plaintiffs answered a question that appeared near the start of each testimony: Why are you suing?

Plaintiffs could have mentioned any number of reasons for pursuing litigation, all of them legitimate. Excruciating pain. Loss of income. *Death.* (Not all medical lawsuits, of course, are filed by actual patients. Some are filed by siblings or other surviving family members.)

Instead, the one theme mentioned by nearly three quarters of all plaintiffs was this: The relationship between the doctor and patient had failed.

Families that sued tended to believe that their physician didn't understand them. They felt ignored, devalued, and, ultimately, deserted. Many had even tried taking their concerns directly to their doctor. It didn't work. Often all they got for their troubles was condescension. The lack of accessibility took a toll, and eventually, the family grew irate.

The results implied an interesting conclusion: The doctors hadn't necessarily failed as *physicians*. They had failed as *communicators*.

When we think about effective communication, we often focus on our choice of words or the manner in which we deliver them. To communicate, *Webster's* dictionary tells us, is "to convey knowledge" and "to cause to pass from one to another." But the realities of interpersonal dialogue—whether it's between a doctor and a patient, a husband and a wife, or a manager and an employee—are considerably more complex. Speaking represents just half of the communication equation, and research suggests that in many cases, it's *not* the more important half.

Take sales, for example. It's an area in which many of us assume speaking persuasively is vital. If I ask you to picture the prototypical salesperson, you're likely to think of an outgoing, gregarious personality, a walking infomercial who can't wait to tell you about the benefits that await you with the purchase of his product.

But research in a number of industries suggests that that's precisely the wrong approach to growing sales, especially when trust is a factor.

Consider the quandary faced by car salesmen, a profession that according to a 2012 Gallup poll is squarely at the bottom when it comes to perceived honesty and ethical standards. What can a car salesman say to make himself more convincing? The answer, according to one study, is quite literally *nothing*.

In a study conducted by marketing professors Rosemary Ramsey and Ravipreet Sohi, customers at a Florida Ford dealership were sent a survey a few months after purchasing a car. As part of the questionnaire, they were asked to report on their salesperson's behaviors, as well as to rate their willingness to buy from that salesperson again in the future. What Ramsey and Sohi found is that it's not simply the way a salesperson speaks to customers that matters. It's how he listens. The better a salesperson's listening skills, the more likely customers were to consider that salesperson trustworthy, which subsequently affected their willingness to buy.

Surprisingly, the relationship between listening ability and sales is even stronger in the financial services industry, in which advisers are often hired explicitly on the basis of their ability to provide guidance. In a 2008 study, seven hundred financial advisers were asked to invite their next four clients to complete a survey about their performance at work. (The researcher cleverly insisted on the *next* four clients so that the advisers would not be tempted to cherry-pick participants, thereby skewing the data.)

The results were eye-opening. The higher financial advisers scored as listeners, the better their clients rated them on quality, trust, and satisfaction. Effective listeners were also more successful at minimizing their customers' perceptions of financial risk, making them more likely to invest in the future.

And that's not all. Better listeners also reported greater sales. In fact, unbeknownst to them, their behaviors had sown the seeds for an upward cycle of selling. That's because the more an adviser listened, the more their clients wanted to recommend them to their friends.

Listeners had created a de facto sales force. They weren't the only ones focused on growing their business. So were their customers.

JUST HOW INFLUENTIAL ARE YOU?

Suppose while you were reading the previous section, I sent all of your coworkers a short survey asking them to rate you on the following items, using a scale of 1 ("never") to 7 ("always"):

- "He is able to persuade other people and change their opinions"
- "He is able to build coalitions to get things done"
- "He is able to build effective working relationships with others who have different opinions or interests"

How would you score? The results, according to a 2012 study, offer a reasonably good snapshot of your influence at work. The higher your rating, the more likely you are to be viewed as a leader in your organization.

Next I dig a bit deeper, asking a few questions about the way they view your work style:

- "He is able to use vivid images and compelling logic and fact to support an argument"
- "He is when making a point, is concise, clear, and brief"
- "as a listener, gets others to open up, elaborate, and share information"
- He is "listens effectively to criticism and alternate points of view"

Clearly, these are all positive behaviors that would be welcomed in just about any organization. But there's an important difference between these items, which you may have already noticed. The first two represent your *speaking abilities*, while the latter two represent your *listening abilities*.

When it comes to being influential in the workplace, which matter more?

Professors at Columbia University's Business School conducted a study to find out. What they discovered is that speaking abilities alone offer a surprisingly incomplete picture of an employee's influence in the workplace. That's because poor listeners tend to lack workplace influence, no matter how compelling their logic or concise their arguments. It's only when high verbal ability is *coupled* with strong listening skills that employees received high marks for being influential.

These findings heavily contradict much of the advice offered to managers. The image many of us implicitly hold of a competent leader is of one who possesses a strong sense of direction and seems to have all the answers. And yet, ironically, it appears there's a price for adopting an attitude of self-assuredness and demonstrating a lack of curiosity in what others have to say.

It can diminish our influence.

When it comes to effective management, underdeveloped listening skills can do more than just hurt a leader's ability to influence their team. It can also short-circuit their ability to maintain a group's loyalty.

Research conducted by the Gallup organization suggests that the strongest predictor of employee retention isn't salary or perks or confidence in a company's future—it's the quality of the employee–manager relationship. And a major component of that relationship is the way in which a manager communicates.

It's often said that employees join an organization because of a company's reputation but leave because they don't get along with their manager. Gallup's research suggests this assumption is largely accurate. Employees want to feel competent at work, and when their manager consistently fails to make them feel heard, their behavior sends a message—one that undermines trust and deteriorates long-term commitment.

That message? Your opinions are not valued.

THE ACTIVE LISTENER'S TOOLKIT

To be a good listener sounds easy enough. So why don't we do more of it? And more important: How do you know if you're doing it right?

One of the first things therapists are taught as part of their clinical training is that not all listening is the same. There's a fundamental difference between the sort of listening we're used to doing most of our lives and listening that motivates and persuades. The distinction is critical.

Passive listening is what you do when you're attending a conference or taking in a television show at the end of a long day. Then there's the type of listening you do when a colleague stops to tell you about the traffic jam he had to endure on the way to work. Here you might find yourself practicing some *selective listening*, tuning in and out just long enough to convince him that you're paying attention.

Both passive and selective listening are a far cry from the form good therapists use, which is called *active listening*.

Contrary to what most people assume, when therapists first meet a client, their goal is not to identify or solve a problem. It's simply to build rapport. Studies show that the client-therapist bond is the single best predictor of the treatment's success, which underscores why active listening is so important. Without a strong connection, the therapeutic approach is irrelevant. Progress will, at best, be negligible.

So what's different about active listening?

For one thing, **mental presence**: Your focus is placed *entirely* on what's being said—not what you'll say in response, or that important conference call you have in an hour, or what you're having for lunch.

If your day is stacked with meetings, you know achieving mental presence is a lot harder than it sounds. Workplace conversations often have two modes: talking and waiting to talk. But it's impossible to absorb the full meaning behind a speaker's words when you're mentally composing your next lines.

Another deceptively simple ingredient of active listening is **resisting the temptation to speak**. This aspect of active listening means that you don't finish the other person's sentences. Avoid making jokes. Never interrupt, even if it's to agree.

Power dynamics have an interesting way of revealing themselves during a conversational rhythm. The more dominant you consider yourself in a relationship, the more likely you are to do most of the talking and to cut in on another person's speaking time. Frequent interruptions—even if well intended—subtly communicate that your views are more important.

If you've ever sat across from a good listener, then you know that there's more to it than using your ears. Active listeners tend to adopt a **listening posture** that demonstrates that they care about what's being said. When people are eager to hear more, they lean forward. A tilt of the head is associated with interest and curiosity. Head nodding can be a powerful sign of encouragement, especially when the speaker is expressing a difficult emotional point.

It seems obvious that **eye contact** helps. What's surprising is how much. Simply holding someone's gaze heightens feelings of warmth, respect, and cooperation. Consider what happens to people's behavior when the possibility for eye contact is limited. On the sidewalk, it's rare for people to battle for position, cut each other off, or shout obscenities. Yet place them in the relative anonymity of a car and they become exponentially more likely to show aggression.

Paradoxically, when you're listening actively, you're not expected to remain entirely silent. In fact, if all you're doing is passively absorbing what the other person says, you're not connecting as well as you could be. So what should you do? The answer is, use your share of the dialogue to **flesh out and clarify what the other person has said**. In many ways, it's the opposite of what we're used to doing in a workplace conversation. Instead of maximizing our own speaking time, the focus shifts toward maximizing the speaking time of the other person.

It's an art with many instruments. Paraphrasing is one. Suppose a colleague tells you she's frustrated with the progress of a project you're collaborating on. One approach is to immediately defend your end of the work by saying, "I actually think the project is going fine." Alternatively, you can paraphrase to test your understanding of what you've heard. "So what you're saying is, We're not moving as fast as you hoped?"

Restating a complaint invites the other person to say more. You might be surprised to learn that what your colleague actually meant to convey is that she's been distracted by other deadlines and feels really guilty about not pulling her weight.

Repeating another person's words doesn't just help you ensure you've heard correctly—it allows the speaker to get a better sense of how he or she is coming across. It's why therapists use this method so often; simply hearing our sentiments reflected back at us gives us a sense of clarity we would not otherwise have.

Validation represents another important component of active listening. You don't want to brush aside your coworker's views, implying that she is wrong for feeling the way she does.

For example, if you say, "You worry too much. This project is a piece of cake," this dismisses your colleague's concern and is likely to hurt your relationship. No one wants to feel they've reached a foolish conclusion. Instead, try "Wow, it sounds like this is really eating you up." What's likely to happen is your colleague will reflect on her words and clarify what she meant, without your having devalued her perspective.

Ultimately, the best responses are the ones that simply communicate to the speaker that he or she has been heard. You don't have to agree with what's been said. You simply have to say enough to demonstrate that you've been listening.

HOW TO DEFUSE A WORKPLACE ARGUMENT

Not every workplace disagreement is as benign as a colleague discouraged about her productivity. Every now and then, we find ourselves immersed in a conversation so emotionally charged it seems to have nothing to do with the issues we're actually discussing.

What do you do when a conversation is spiraling out of control? When you've tried all the reflective listening you can muster and the other person still isn't willing to budge? How do you get the conversation back on track?

Anthony Suchman has invested a good portion of his career searching for an answer. A charming physician with a profound intellect, Suchman has been studying the dynamics of human relationships for more than three decades, publishing his results in some of the world's leading medical journals.

According to Suchman, every workplace conversation operates on two levels: a *task channel* and a *relationship channel*. Occasionally the two get fused, which is when disagreements intensify and collaborations break down.

Here's what he means: Suppose you and I are working together on a project. Along the way, we have a difference of opinion about our next steps. Perhaps I think we should use PowerPoint to deliver an important presentation and you see PowerPoint as a poor communication tool. When I express a point of view that's different from yours, you may take our disagreement at face value by saying, "Hmm, I guess Ron sees it differently." But if we're new to working together, or if we've had a few run-ins in the past, you're likely to read beyond my suggestion and perhaps use it to draw inferences about our relationship. For instance, you may misinterpret my suggestion as a lack of trust, a sign of disrespect, or even proof of competition.

It's at this point, Suchman argues, that our task-focused disagreement becomes contaminated with concerns about our relationship. And when that happens, things escalate. Fast.

Neurologically, what Suchman is describing is the activation of a fear response. When we perceive danger, our hypothalamus sends a signal that releases adrenaline and cortisol into our bloodstream. That triggers a fight-or-flight response that sends our bodies into overdrive, short-circuiting our ability to concentrate or think creatively. We experience tunnel vision.

In the evolutionary past, having an automatic reaction to fear was quite useful. It helped protect us from oncoming predators and kept us alive long enough to reproduce. But in today's workplace, an involuntary fear response can interfere with our ability to work collaboratively with others. It's one reason why the greater the emotional charge, the harder it is to get either side to listen.

How do you defuse an emotionally volatile situation?

Suchman believes the first step is to disentangle the task and relational channels. "When people disagree, it's often because one party misinterprets the feedback they've received as a personal attack," he says. "So it becomes: If you like my idea, you like me, and if you don't like my idea, you don't like me. That puts a huge encumbrance on the task channel and makes it really hard to speak openly."

Our mental capacity is limited, Suchman points out, which means we can attend *either* to the task channel *or* the relationship channel. It's when we get the two channels crossed that our ability to collaborate constructively suffers.

One approach to reducing tensions during disagreements involves deliberately attending to the relational channel and reaffirming your commitment to the relationship. This way, there's no confusion about what the argument is really about. By momentarily focusing on the relationship you disentangle the personal from the business.

Suchman recommends using a specific series of relationship-building statements to make the conversation more productive, which are represented in the acronym PEARLS.

Partnership	"I really want to work on this with you." "I bet we can figure this out together."
Empathy	"I can feel your enthusiasm as you talk." "I can hear your concern."
Acknowledgment	"You clearly put a lot of work into this." "You invested in this, and it shows."
Respect	"I've always appreciated your creativity." "There's no doubt you know a lot about this."

Legitimation   "This would be hard for anyone."
                      "Who wouldn't be worried about something
                      like this?"

Support   "I'd like to help you with this."
                      "I want to see you succeed."

Using relationship-building statements can feel unnatural at first, especially when you're not accustomed to complimenting others. I know they did for me when I first started using them in workplace conversations. The key, I've discovered, is to employ them sparingly at first, and to only say the ones that genuinely reflect how you feel.

Almost immediately, you'll notice that inserting a well-timed PEARLS statement can dramatically alter the tenor of a conversation. Because no matter how far up we climb on an organizational ladder, we are still stuck using an emotionally driven brain. When fear enters the equation, it's impossible to get people to do their best work, which is why restoring confidence in the relationship can be a powerful tool.

The value of relationship-building statements extends far beyond the workplace. They're as effective with spouses, children, and friends as they are with colleagues. The reason is simple: Anytime you attend to people's psychological need for connection, you have the potential of improving the quality of an exchange. The more heated the argument, the more vital they become.

Just ask Yuba County negotiator Chuck Tracy. Or better yet, let's listen in on some of his negotiations ourselves.

THE CLEVER NEGOTIATOR'S GUIDE TO PERSUASION

In the late 1990s, Laurie Charles, then a graduate student at Nova Southeastern University, was working to complete her doctorate in family therapy when she had an interesting idea for a study. As a therapist in training, Charles had been taught to manage the sort of intense family conflicts that often emerge during sessions. But what happens, she wondered, when a crisis develops *outside* the confines of a therapist's office? How do you motivate change during life-threatening conversations? What do you do when the stakes are high, time is short, and disagreement is not an option?

A typical psychologist might have designed an experiment. Charles contacted the FBI.

As a researcher, Charles wasn't interested in manufacturing a crisis situation. She wanted to see how they played out in real life. Her goal was to examine techniques used by actual negotiators and identify those that worked. With some ingenuity, Charles managed to gain access to recordings of actual hostage negotiations at the FBI Academy in Virginia. After listening to audiotapes of several incidents, one stood out: the Lindhurst High School shooting.

Charles analyzed all four hours of the negotiation, applying the principles of discourse analysis to identify unique themes that emerged over the course of the discussion. She then contacted the Yuba County Sheriff's Department and interviewed team members who had been involved in the Lindhurst High School negotiations, including its lead negotiator, Chuck Tracy.

What worked during the negotiation? Charles offers a glimpse of some of the highlights in a fascinating 2007 paper that appeared in the *Journal of Marital and Family Therapy*:

- **Avoiding judgment.** Negotiator Chuck Tracy could have opened the exchange by laying out some sobering facts. For example, by telling hostage-taker Eric Houston that the police had the building surrounded, or noting that snipers had a lock on his position. But doing so would have only raised the emotional temperature.

  Instead, he began the negotiation by encouraging Houston to share his side of the story, asking numerous questions that allowed him to explain his point of view. Tracy was applying the first principle of effective negotiation: *Listen more than you speak.*

Hearing Houston out gave Tracy an advantage: He had demonstrated an interest in understanding the situation from the hostage taker's perspective. By showing that he wasn't there to lecture or threaten, Tracy established his credibility as an objective party. This made him more persuasive down the line.

- **Taking a go slow approach.** When tensions are running high, trying to reach a quick resolution can backfire. Tracy discovered this the hard way when a few of his early attempts to reach an agreement resulted in Houston losing his temper and cursing indiscriminately.

It was only when Tracy stopped trying to solve things too quickly, allowing Houston to flesh out his perspective, that he was able to defuse the tension and establish a working relationship.

- **Expressing empathy.** Once Houston had revealed his frustrations at failing out of high school, Tracy had the opening he needed. "When he said this, the lights went on," Tracy said, recounting the negotiation. "The bells rang. It was like *here* is the handle. It was handed to me. Just as big as could be."

Once Tracy had insight into Houston's experience he had an opportunity to strengthen their relationship using empathy.

TRACY: I'm here trying to help you.
HOUSTON: Yeah . . .
TRACY: Okay?
HOUSTON: [You] know, Mr. Brens tried to fuckin' help me too.
TRACY: Who's Mr. Berns?
HOUSTON: Mr. Brens.

TRACY: I'm sorry, Mr. Brens.

HOUSTON: Yeah he tried to help me. He tried to help me fucking pass. And he fuckin' flunked my ass with one fucking grade. Fucking knocked everything down. All my fucking dreams. *[Disclosing emotional pain]*

At this point negotiator Chuck Tracy had a few options. He could:

1. Promise Houston that he's nothing like Mr. Brens.
2. Gently remind Houston that Mr. Brens has nothing to do with their negotiation.
3. Warn Houston that if he doesn't release the hostages soon the police would have no choice but to storm the building.

But all of these options would have kept the two parties on opposing sides. So instead, Tracy chose to mirror Houston's emotions, to build rapport.

TRACY: Okay, it seems like . . . it's very apparent to me that this upsets you. And I'd like to . . . I'd like to—*[Empathizing]*

HOUSTON: Upsets me!? It ruined my fucking life! *[Disclosing further]*

- **Joining.** In most negotiations, the relationship between opposing parties is inherently adversarial. What benefits one side hurts the other. To overcome this mind-set, Tracy emphasized common interests, focusing on what he and Houston could *both* gain from a peaceful resolution.

Over the course of several conversations, Tracy began working in use of the word "we" while highlighting the hard work he and Houston were doing together to find a solution. From time to time, he would even check in with Houston to see how he felt about their progress.

TRACY: Listen, if you see something out there that upsets you, you tell me, and I'll make sure that they're not there to upset you. Do you understand that?

HOUSTON: I'm serious. I don't want no fucking snipers, and I don't want no SWAT tactical units. I don't want no helicopters going above, fucking landing 'em on the top and you pulling down. I don't want nunna that shit. I know your guys' tactics. I know how you fuckin' work. Alright?

TRACY: Okay. I understand that. And we want to work with you. So if you see something that makes you uncomfortable, I'm the guy that you talk to and the guy that helps you, okay?

By using a blend of active listening and relationship-building statements, Tracy was able to tame Houston's fury and alter the tone of their negotiation. He used the rapport he'd established early on to convince Houston that releasing a small group of the students would make the remaining hostages easier to manage. Later, he would strike a deal that led to the release of even more hostages in exchange for pizza, soft drinks, and, at Houston's request, a bottle of Advil.

At about 10:20 that evening, Tracy persuaded Houston to give himself up.

What did he offer in return? A lighter jail sentence and educational opportunities that would allow Houston to earn a diploma during his years in prison. (Unfortunately for Houston, police are not bound by the concessions they make during hostage negotiations. Today, Houston sits on death row awaiting execution.)

There's an unmistakable irony in a school shooter turning himself over to the police in exchange for the opportunity to attend more classes. But in the end, that is what Houston really wanted: a path forward.

It was Tracy who figured it out. And he did it by listening.

THE SECRET TO BETTER WORKPLACE RELATIONSHIPS

The conclusion of the Lindhurst High School shooting offers more than a fascinating look into a well-executed hostage negotiation. It also tells us something important about human nature and offers a number of useful lessons on building a better workplace.

Let's begin with the lessons.

The first is that listening is a motivational tool. It's not just something you do when you're trying to be polite or mentally reloading another argument. It's when you're at your most influential.

We often sell listening short because it appears so passive, but therapists and negotiators know it's actually one of the most effective arrows in their quiver. When people feel heard, their resistance dissolves. They feel valued and respected, which simultaneously motivates them and makes them more open to new ideas.

While executives are often encouraged to take public speaking courses that promote one-way communication, research suggests they would be far better off developing their listening skills instead.

The second lesson: No matter how much you differ with another person, your disagreements don't need to be disagreeable. It's hard to find two parties whose interests are further apart than a murderer holding a room full of hostages and the SWAT team outside his door. And yet Tracy was able to use active listening and relationship-building statements to keep his discussions with Houston from escalating into an emotional melee.

Marriage therapists often say that the prospects for a long-term relationship are hard to judge until a couple experiences their first fight. The same can be said for workplace relationships.

If a conversation between you and a colleague turns unpleasant, there's a good chance you're no longer talking about the work. And when that happens, it's a signal that your relationship needs some attention. Attending to your relationship with a colleague or employee is not something you do *in addition* to the work. In times of disagreement, it can be the work itself.

Research on successful marriages shows that the number of arguments a couple has is rarely indicative of the quality of their relationship. Far more important is the way the spouses fight. The best relationships distinguish themselves not by a lack of disagreements but by what happens after one has broken out.

But the biggest takeaway from the Lindhurst negotiation? The one that every manager who wants a motivated team needs to appreciate?

When you're trying to change behavior, the more you dominate the conversation, the less you persuade.

There's a reason why therapists don't lecture their clients. And it's not because they don't have the right answers. It's because they know that being told what to do is not an effective strategy to sustaining long-term motivation. Remember the negotiator's rule of thumb: *Listen twice as much as you speak.*

Which brings us to that insight on human nature. One that's at the core of most modern approaches to therapy. Here it is: People only change when they are accepted for who they are. And listening is the universal language of acceptance.

The Lessons of Listening

Action Items for Managers

Shrink your talking-to-listening ratio. Athletes know that aiming to play well is too broad a goal to improve performance, so they create a set of minigoals that serve as guideposts along the way. A useful metric for measuring your conversational performance is monitoring your talking-to-listening ratio. Talking too much? Ask questions to restore the conversational balance. Finding it hard not to cut in? Practice mentally counting to two after the other person has finished speaking.

Free the "task channel." Good management involves creating an environment that allows employees to focus on their work. Quieting the relational channel by attending to it from time to time is a valuable tool for getting the most out of the people on your team. If your employees are constantly worried about whether or not they have your respect, they're devoting valuable mental energy that could be better applied to their work.

Ask more, answer less. Having all the answers may make you an expert, but it won't make you an inspiring leader. Asking questions that challenge those around you shows you value their opinions, trains them to find their own solutions, and results in a more motivated team.

The Lessons of Listening
Action Items for Emerging Leaders

Win fewer arguments. If you find yourself locking horns in a workplace power struggle, beware. Winning arguments is often predictive of losing long-term relationships. Instead of thinking in terms of winners and losers, change the paradigm. Look for *joining* opportunities, and ask your coworkers to tell you more about their opinions. Winning in the workplace is not about getting your way. It's about finding ways of making others feel like they've contributed.

Beware the shift response. Want to be a better listener? Then you'll need to avoid one of listening's more menacing pitfalls, which is highlighted in the works of sociologist

Charles Derber. When a colleague tells you he's having a hard day, do you ask him to tell you more, or do you say, "I know what you mean—my day has been a disaster!"

The former is a *support response*, one that allows your colleague to open up and positions you as an active listener. But the latter is a sneaky conversational tactic that transfers the spotlight away from your colleague and onto you. It's called the *shift response*, and it often hurts the quality of interpersonal connections. You might think it shows that you're listening, but your colleague won't experience it that way.

Make relationship-building statements a habit. Another minigoal that can help you better connect with others is striving to incorporate a single PEARLS (a statement of partnership, empathy, acknowledgment, respect, legitimation, or support) into every workplace conversation. If you fear complimenting others will appear inconsistent with your past behavior, starting with one PEARLS per conversation will allow you to test the waters and see for yourself whether it softens your colleagues' receptiveness to your ideas.

NINE

Why the Best Managers Focus on Themselves

It is set point and Monica Seles is pacing.

She has just buried a two-fisted backhand into the net. It's an unforced error, one that hands her opponent a remarkable opportunity. Four points to win the opening set.

The year is 1990 and we are in Paris. Sixteen-year-old Monica Seles is vying to become the youngest player in tennis history to win the French Open. At the moment, her prospects are looking grim.

It was not always this way. A few games back, Seles had appeared invincible. To the surprise of everyone, she had come out focused and aggressive, taking a commanding 3-to-0 lead against the world's number one player, Steffi Graf. But the lead would not hold. Graf has battled back relentlessly, first tying the score at 6 to 6, and now grabbing a 6-to-2 tiebreaker lead.

Seles's inexperience is starting to show. It's her first time at a Grand Slam final, and Graf knows it. One more mistake and the set will be over.

Seles circles the baseline and draws in a breath. She scans the strings of her racket, blows on her fingers. Knees bent, she prepares to weather Graf's 110-mile-an-hour serve.

The first serve sails wide, and for the moment, Seles earns a reprieve. She wastes no time returning to ready position, resuming her customary dance. Her legs hop from side to side, as if she is barefoot on a bed of burning coals.

When the serve finally arrives, Seles is ready. If you watch the play in slow motion, you'll notice Seles lunge to her right immediately, the instant the ball propels off Graf's racket. She takes a short step and turns her body, unleashing everything she has.

"Haaaa-Eeeeh!!!"

Graf can do little more than watch. Seles has struck a cross-court winner.

When the point is over, the crowd cheers. Seles casually turns her attention back to her racket. Not an eyebrow is raised at the strange, guttural shriek that accompanied Seles's backhand. After all, anyone watching the match will have heard that cry more than a hundred times already. It's simply the sound of Monica Seles playing tennis.

At 6 to 3, it is now Seles's turn to serve. She lifts the ball high into the air and growls on contact.

"Beeeeehhh!!!"

Graf's return sails long.

6 to 4.

On the next exchange, Seles has her opponent on the run, forcing a defensive Graf to lob the ball weakly.

"Eeeeehhh!!!"

Seles puts away the overhead decisively, erasing a third set point.

6 to 5.

The serve reverts back to Graf, who uncharacteristically double faults, squandering the last of her set points.

6 to 6.

From there, Seles is unstoppable. With one *"Haaa-Eeeh!!!"* she retakes the lead. A *"Beeeeehhh!!!"* and three *"Haaa-Eeeh!!!"*s later and the comeback is complete.

The first set is hers. Final score: 8 to 6.

Strutting back to her chair, Seles pumps her fist. The ovation is thunderous. In the stands, her father covers his mouth in disbelief.

The rest of the match progresses quickly. Graf makes a valiant effort but can never quite reestablish her footing. Her shots come off a little flat and her shot selection has turned questionable. A little more than thirty minutes later, Seles will launch her racket into the air, in a moment that will be replayed millions of times on television sets around the world.

Seles's 1990 French Open performance set the tennis world on fire. At just sixteen years of age she had become the youngest player in history to win a grand slam tournament, an achievement made all the more remarkable by the fact that she had been playing professionally for only a single year. Her rise from complete unknown to athletic sensation was as rapid as it was astounding.

But that's not all that happened that day in Paris. Although she didn't know it, Seles had managed to accomplish something far more significant than simply winning a trophy. Something no one watching that match could have predicted or even realized until decades had passed.

In one afternoon of tennis, Monica Seles had altered a social norm.

THE SOUND OF VICTORY

In the years following Monica Seles's French Open victory, something strange happened to the sport of tennis. It grew a lot louder.

Before Seles defeated Graf in Paris, the number of players who regularly grunted could be counted on a single hand. Chris Evert and Jimmy Connors were known to sound the occasional groan in the 1970s and 1980s, but neither came close to the aural fireworks of a Seles solo.

Yet today grunting is routine.

Take a look at the top ten tennis players at the start of the 1990 tennis season, the same year Seles defeated Graf. Consistent grunters— those who grunt on the majority of their forehands, backhands, and serves—are marked in bold.

MEN'S TENNIS	WOMEN'S TENNIS
1. Ivan Lendl	1. Steffi Graf
2. Boris Becker	2. Martina Navratilova
3. Stefan Edberg	3. Gabriela Sabatini
4. Brad Gilbert	4. Zina Garrison
5. John McEnroe	5. Arantxa Sánchez Vicario

You'll notice that not a single nineties' star qualifies. Now take a look at the top ten players at the start of the 2013 tour:

MEN'S TENNIS	WOMEN'S TENNIS
1. **Novak Djokovic**	1. **Victoria Azarenka**
2. Roger Federer	2. **Maria Sharapova**
3. Andy Murray	3. **Serena Williams**
4. **Rafael Nadal**	4. **Agnieszka Radwanska**
5. **David Ferrer**	5. **Angelique Kerber**

Quite a change.

And it's not just the sheer number of players who are grunting. It's their volume. The past two decades have witnessed the emergence of a vocal arms race in the world of tennis. What was once a rare spectacle has now become so familiar that fans in thousand-dollar seats have been sighted using earplugs and, on at least one occasion, wearing earmuffs suitable for a snowstorm.

Who could blame them? Guidelines issued by the Occupational Safety and Health Administration (OSHA) mandate that sound levels be kept below 90 decibels to avoid inflicting long-term damage on the human ear. If that's the case, going to a tennis match today is a risky endeavor. Stars like Maria Sharapova (recorded at 101 decibels) and Serena Williams (88.9 decibels) rival the clamor of a lawn mower (90 decibels), a subway car (95 decibels), and a motorcycle engine (100 decibels).

Grunting in tennis has gotten so loud that in the summer of 2012, the Women's Tennis Association formally declared it had heard enough. Announcing that it was determined to silence "excessive grunting," the tour outlined plans to arm umpires with portable devices that read players' on-court sound levels and penalize those who exceed acceptable limits.

Which is pretty extraordinary: In a span of just over two decades, tennis had gone from a sport in which competitors rarely mouthed a peep to one in which the governing authority felt compelled to institute a formal ban restricting the practice of grunting.

So, what happened?

FROM CENTER COURT TO THE BOARDROOM

Tennis's grunting epidemic reveals something important about human behavior: It's contagious.

Although we like to think of ourselves as independent decision makers, the truth is that we've inherited a brain that's designed to mimic. From the moment we're born, we show a tendency to imitate. As infants, we open our mouths, stick out our tongues, and smile after seeing Mom and Dad do so. As toddlers, we learn to speak by mimicking the sounds made by those around us and gradually absorbing their meaning. As teenagers, we internalize our friends' fashion sense, copy their hairstyles, and adopt their slang.

Mimicry is quite noticeable when it occurs in children. And as adults, many of us dupe ourselves into thinking we're immune to its effects. But studies show we're prone to mimicry throughout our lives, in ways we rarely detect.

Consider the last time you visited a restaurant. How much did you eat? Research suggests the answer depends, in part, on who you were with. We unconsciously match the pace of our partners when sharing a meal. When they chew slowly, we chew slowly. When they take a few extra bites, we do the same. And the more people we're with, the more eating there is to mimic, which is one reason, on average, people consume 35 percent more food dining with another person, 75 percent more in a group of four, and 96 percent more when in groups of eight or more.

We're programmed to imitate a whole host of behaviors, and for the most part, we do so unconsciously. And it's not just the people we know. We often copy the behaviors of people we've never met. Consider the way you maintain your home. Your lawn care habits, recycling behaviors, and energy usage are largely influenced by the people in your neighborhood. We take our cues from those around us, particularly those we're near.

Romantic partners are especially susceptible to behavioral contagion. Over time, couples adopt similar diets, synchronize exercise regimens, and visit doctors with comparable frequency. They even begin using similar patterns of speech. It's easier to notice the change when a close friend begins dating someone new. Every now and then, you'll startle at hearing them use a phrase that seems completely out of character. Some researchers believe mimicking one another over the course of so many years is the reason married couples begin to look alike. When you and your significant other exercise the same facial muscles again and again, it's bound to have an effect on your appearance.

Given how much time we spend with our colleagues, it's natural that the people we work with also have a powerful impact on our behavior.

Have a colleague sidle over and conspiratorially whisper, "Did you hear?" and chances are, you'll respond in a hushed tone that is equally discreet. Spot a coworker scanning their iPhone, and without thinking, you'll find your fingers itching to do the same. Officemate yawning? Watch out. You're likely to be next.

And it's not just *behaviors* that spread from person to person within companies—it's *emotions* like happiness, excitement, and fear. When we mimic the postures, facial expressions, and vocal tones of those around us, we tend to "catch" their emotions. The reason is simple: Our minds spend a lifetime associating certain physical movements with specific patterns of thought. We smile when we're happy. We scowl when we're mad. Over time, the link between movement and mental state becomes so strong that doing the physical movement alone is enough to trigger the emotion.

Sit straight and you're likely to feel a little prouder. Droop your shoulders and you're likely to feel a bit more depressed. Read this sentence aloud in a high-pitched tone and you'll feel yourself getting excited (!!!).

The consequences of workplace contagion are even more profound when you consider the impact it can have on employees' job performance. Take, for example, research I conducted with motivational experts at the University of Rochester. In a series of experiments we invited volunteers to do a set of word puzzles in the lab. Before they started, we arranged for participants to "accidentally" overhear either a highly motivated or highly unmotivated participant discuss their experience in an unrelated experiment. In reality, this "fellow participant" was a trained actor playing the role of a volunteer.

Half of our participants overheard a highly motivated actor describe a task he had worked on—an exercise completely different from the word puzzle participants were about to do—and mentioned how energized he felt doing his work. The other half of our participants overheard a highly unmotivated actor describe his task, noting that he was only doing the experiment in order to receive extra credit.

Then it came time for our participants to do the word puzzle. How would they perform?

Our results were compelling. Among those who had overheard a highly unmotivated participant, the average number of puzzles solved was 12.8. But among those who had overheard a highly motivated participant, performance was 37.5 percent better, with an average of 17.6 solved puzzles.

Surprisingly, when we asked participants if they could think of anything that might have affected their performance on the puzzles, not a single person mentioned the overheard volunteer. The effect appeared to have occurred unconsciously. And all it took was a few minutes of being in the same room.

The findings of this and other studies on mimicry offer up some fascinating implications for the workplace, where colleagues sit in close quarters, and behaviors, emotions, and motivations reverberate from person to person.

One conclusion we can draw is that the behavior of our colleagues often matters more than we think. How *you* feel at work is not just a reflection of your attitude or job responsibilities. It's also a reflection of the people on your team. If you're surrounded by people who are passionate and inspired, that's likely to influence your experience. The same goes for working alongside those who are burned out and disengaged.

Second, we're often unconscious of the ways in which our motivation is influenced by those around us. We live in an individualistic society in which we're encouraged to believe that everything we do is solely a consequence of personal choice. It's a comforting theory; it's just not true. As social beings, we are constantly affected by others, especially those with whom we're close.

And finally, our colleagues don't just have an impact on our emotional experience. They influence how successful we are at doing our job. Motivation is about more than just feeling. It's about goals, effort, and persistence. Catching someone's positive motivation changes our approach, which often leads to better results.

If you're lucky enough to find yourself working with the right group of people, you enjoy the many benefits of mimicry. However, mimicry can also work in the other direction, making bad habits more common and negative viewpoints more pervasive.

So why do it? Why are we so quick to adopt the behaviors, emotions, and motivation levels of those around us? What good does it do us to mimic?

HOW MIMICRY SAVED YOUR LIFE

To understand the value of mimicry, you must first appreciate that for most of human history, life was quite different than it is today.

Not too long ago, our species lived in small, tightly knit tribes. Conditions were harsh, and staying alive was difficult. Belonging to a group provided tremendous advantages, especially when it came to promoting our survival. Not only do groups afford members greater resources for finding food and fending off predators, they also offer access to the holy grail of evolutionary success: potential mates.

The rare few who tried going it alone rarely survived. Those who did were unlikely to reproduce.

So where does mimicry fit in?

Mimicry binds individuals into groups by signaling *similarity*. When we find others who share our views, we connect. If, while passing me in the office corridor, you nod in my direction and I do the same, we both feel an automatic sense of kinship. It's because few things communicate "we're on the same team" more effectively than when those around us feel and act the way we do.

But there's more to mimicry than simply shared connection. There's also value in automatically catching emotions by imitating facial expressions and body language.

Suppose the two of us passed each other *not* in the hall but back in the plains of the savanna. By noticing that your eyes have widened and that your nostrils have flared, the fear I suddenly feel better prepares me to deal with an imminent danger in our shared environment. After all, you may have spotted a lion that I have missed. Having that information immediately—without having to wait for you to communicate a single word—is a significant advantage.

And when you consider, as cognitive psychologists do, that the development of emotion is likely to have preceded the arrival of language, contagion no longer seems like a quirk at all. Quite the opposite: It starts to seem pretty essential.

Today, of course, the value of emotional and behavioral contagion is considerably more limited. If you're anxious about this afternoon's client presentation, it does me little good to go into high alert.

But thousands of years ago it may have been the very thing that kept me alive.

Scientists believe that mimicry is so essential to our survival that we've evolved specific neurological structures that predispose us to copy one another. They're called "mirror neurons," and they're located in regions throughout the brain.

When we see someone perform a behavior—whether it's sipping a glass of wine, lifting a heavy bag, or flashing a wide smile—mirror neurons in our brain light up *as if we are doing the exact same thing.* Mirror neurons enable us to empathize and relate to one another's experiences. When you get a paper cut, I automatically wince. It's because the mirror neurons in my mind simulate your experience and prod me to sympathize with your feelings. Part of me quite literally experiences your pain.

The existence of mirror neurons offers a compelling biological explanation for why mimicry happens in the presence of others. Our brains reenact everything we see. But what about when no one's around? How do we account for the spread of behaviors when no one is watching?

That, psychologists argue, is where *social norms* come into play.

Consider the last time you rode an elevator with a group of strangers. If you are like most people, you entered quietly, moved to a location maximizing the amount of space between you and your fellow passengers, and faced the front to watch the floor numbers change. No one provided you with explicit instructions on how to behave, and you certainly didn't need to wait for your mirror neurons to kick in to tell you what to do.

As group members, we all carry with us a set of beliefs about behavior that is appropriate in a given situation. Social norms are those unspoken rules that tell us how to act in a way that is consistent with others in our group.

Every group has norms—your colleagues at work, your buddies at the gym, fellow fans at a football game—and we are all motivated to stay within the bounds of what our group finds acceptable. Which is why when we see those around us behaving in a certain way, we tend to unconsciously mimic their behavior.

We are quietly signaling our allegiance to our group.

MIRROR NEURONS, SOCIAL NORMS, AND THE ROOTS OF COMPANY CULTURE

When it comes to setting social norms, some group members are more influential than others. High-status group members are watched more closely and carry more credibility, which is why their behaviors and attitudes often set the tone.

When Monica Seles won the French Open in 1990, she instantly became a leader in the world of tennis. That made her behaviors "stickier" than those of the average player, including her unusual habit of grunting with every swing. Lower-status group members often copy the behaviors of those in leadership positions, because it helps align them with individuals who hold more influence in the group. That's one reason *established* tennis stars like Martina Navratilova and

Ivan Lendl didn't develop a spontaneous grunt. But newer players—those who were not yet part of professional tennis in 1990 and wouldn't come into their prime for another generation—took their cue from Seles, especially in the ensuing years, when she ascended to the tennis world's number one spot.

A similar pattern unfolds in the workplace. While every colleague has some degree of influence over another employee's experiences, it is the company leaders who hold the greatest sway. Research on mimicry shows that while both people in a relationship tend to copy some aspects of each other's behaviors, on average, it is the person with the lower status who tends to change the most.

It's something the best managers recognize intuitively. As leaders, *their* behaviors, emotions, and motivations unleash a ripple effect that shapes the employee experience.

MIT management professor Edgar Schein sees even broader implications for managerial behaviors, arguing that "culture and leadership are two sides of the same coin." Schein, an organizational expert who has studied corporations for over half a century, makes a persuasive case that company culture is not created through mission statements, slogans, or a set of written values. It is a product of leaders' interactions with their team. Those at the top provide a model that establishes group norms. Over time, these norms come to define the culture of an organization.

Which behaviors matter most when it comes to shaping company culture? In his landmark book, *Organizational Culture and Leadership*, Schein identifies a number of specific actions by which leaders (often unconsciously) influence the culture of a workplace:

- **What leaders pay attention to (and what they ignore).** Leaders signal what is important to an organization by paying more attention to some issues than others. The more focus a leader places on particular areas of the business—by personally controlling them, measuring them, or regularly commenting on them—the more they become priorities for their teams. For example, if a CEO devotes most of his energy to acquiring new customers, growth becomes an organizational priority. To the extent that he does so while paying little attention to the execution of existing projects, their quality is likely to drop, due to employee inferences about what is more important.

- **Emotional outbursts.** When a leader's mood swings abruptly employees take notice. In particular, negative emotions, like anger, reveal which issues a leader deems especially crucial. Strong emotional reactions, even when unintentional, direct team members to a leader's priorities.

- **Reactions to incidents and crises.** At any workplace things occasionally go awry. When this happens, a sense of anxiety tends to come over employees, heightening their sensitivity to a leader's response. It's at these moments that leaders are watched especially closely. The way in which a leader reacts to unexpected negative developments communicates their core values and contributes to organizational norms about how adverse situations are to be handled.

- **How leaders allocate rewards and status.** Employee behaviors that win a leader's praise or admiration are likely to be repeated, while those that are ignored tend to fizzle out. Over time, organizational culture tends to reinforce actions that leaders consistently reward. For example, a CEO may publicly state that she wants work-life balance in her company. But when all the acclaim goes to employees who pull all-nighters and toil through the weekend it contributes to the creation of a 24/7 work culture.

Managers are often told that paying close attention to their employees is the key to doing their job effectively. But what this research suggests is that there are times when managers would be better off focusing a little more closely on their own behaviors. It's because the actions of those in leadership positions have long-term implications that shape the evolution of a workplace culture.

From Schein's perspective, even the most casual remark or benign question from a leader can have extraordinary consequences.

"Leaders do not have a choice about *whether or not* to communicate," he says. "They only have a choice about how much to manage what they communicate."

WHEN COMPANIES ADOPT THE PERSONALITY OF THEIR LEADER

Sometimes the influence of a single leader is so strong it can hijack an entire organization. That's one of the many fascinating implications of a 2007 study, in which two Penn State economists examined how a CEO's level of narcissism impacts organizational performance.

Narcissism, psychologists argue, has two main features: the belief that one's abilities are superior to others, and a continuous, unquenchable thirst for admiration. What effect does having a narcissistic leader have on the way a company does business?

To find out, researchers Arijit Chatterjee and Donald Hambrick needed a creative methodology. CEOs are not the easiest people to get a hold of, and even if they were, the chances of getting one to submit to a battery of personality assessments were—to put it optimistically—slim. Chatterjee and Hambrick were facing a serious roadblock. How do you measure the personality of someone you've never met?

Their solution was clever. Instead of relying on a direct measure of narcissism that could only be collected with CEO interviews, they devised an indirect measure, using data on publicly traded high-tech companies and their chief executives.

Among the metrics they collected:

1. The size of the CEOs' photograph on their company's website
2. The length of the CEOs' biography in *Who's Who*

3. The frequency with which the CEOs' name was mentioned in company press releases

4. The number of times the CEOs referred to themselves during interviews

5. The CEOs' salary, relative to that of the second-highest-paid executive in their company (a figure that, as everyone knows, they influence heavily)

All told, Chatterjee and Hambrick analyzed the narcissism of 111 CEOs.

Next, they looked at operational decisions made by each company, using shareholder reports. How often did these companies change directions from year to year? What was their strategy for pursuing growth? Did they favor incremental progress or dramatic power grabs?

CEOs can be expected to have *some* influence over these decisions, of course, but they also operate within significant constraints. After all, these are large, publicly held firms with board members, shareholders, and bureaucracies. As leaders, however, CEOs do wield extraordinary influence over organizational culture by rewarding certain actions with more attention and modeling behaviors that, over time, become company norms.

Chatterjee and Hambrick wanted to know: Do companies with narcissistic leaders conduct themselves any differently?

Here's what they found: Companies with narcissistic leaders make significantly more volatile business decisions. They pursue more bold, attention-grabbing strategic shifts than their competitors and make more optimistic (and occasionally deluded) attempts to take over large companies. In a word, they behave narcissistically.

Now, to be fair, having a narcissistic leader wasn't all bad for organizations. Overall, companies with narcissistic leaders didn't fare any better or worse than those with selfless leaders. But they did behave more erratically, because they took so many attention-seeking risks. When those risks paid off, their organizations were rewarded handsomely. But when they backfired, the consequences were dire.

While having a narcissistic CEO can yield mixed results for a company's bottom line, other features of a CEO's personality have been found to hold more reliable consequences on firm performance.

In 2003, a research team led by London Business School's Randall Peterson used biographies, interviews, and company documents to gauge CEO personality. They also read through archival sources to assess the decision-making dynamics within each CEO's top management team.

The results provide a fascinating glimpse at the extent to which a single leader's personality can sway organizational dynamics. Among the findings: Warm and trusting CEOs have more cohesive senior leadership teams. Intellectually curious CEOs have teams that are flexible and tolerant of risk. Anxious CEOs have teams that are generally unwilling to change their attitudes and beliefs, even in response to new evidence.

Management teams, in other words, come to adopt the personality of their leader.

And critically, these dynamics don't simply reflect the way a leadership team communicates. They also have serious implications for a firm's financial performance. In Peterson's 2003 study, the more cohesive, optimistic, and intellectually flexible the management team, the more money their company tended to make.

WHEN WHO YOU KNOW DETERMINES WHO YOU ARE

Few of us enjoy the elevated status of a CEO, which might lead us to infer that our ability to influence those around us is quite minimal. But according to social network researchers Nicholas Christakis and James Fowler, that assumption is wrong.

Suppose you and I meet up for an early-morning espresso. On the basis of what you've read so far, you might assume that if you're in a good mood when the two of us meet, I might leave slightly happier than when I arrived. And that's where your influence ends, right?

Not quite.

A number of researchers believe that our capacity for mimicry can have implications that extend well beyond our immediate reach. Christakis and Fowler have studied the ways people's social networks influence their experiences. Using decades of data on thousands of Massachusetts residents, Christakis and Fowler were able to analyze how changes in the life of a *single individual* affect their broader network of family, friends, and neighbors. Their findings reveal the magnitude to which we unconsciously influence one another. In a series of papers published in top academic journals, Christakis and Fowler show that attitudes, emotions, and behaviors don't just spread from person to person. They infect *entire networks.*

Among their conclusions: happiness, loneliness, obesity, smoking, depression, illegal drug use, and suicide are all contagious. So are voting behaviors, charitable contributions, and fashion decisions. And in most cases, the influence of any one person tends to reverberate for up to *three* degrees of separation.

What does that mean in practical terms? It means that how happy you are at this very moment is significantly related to the happiness of your colleague's friend's spouse. At the same time, Christakis and Fowler argue, the reverse is also true. *Your* actions echo well beyond the people you know and affect networks of people you may never even meet.

Epidemiologist Gary Slutkin sees a similar dynamic in the spread of violence. After spending ten years fighting infectious diseases in Africa, Slutkin founded an organization that stifles violence in inner-city Chicago by applying the same methods a physician might use to combat disease. The goal of Slutkin's group, CureViolence, is to reduce the *transmission* of violence from person to person by targeting "infected spreaders."

How do you keep violence from spreading in a community where crime and retribution is the norm? By giving people a new model to mimic. CureViolence community activists, called Interrupters, are recruited from the streets and prisons of Chicago. The organization specifically aims to hire reformed gangbangers and trains them in deescalation methods. Slutkin has found that, as spokespeople, this demographic is especially persuasive because of their inherent similarity to their target audiences.

CureViolence leverages mimicry and social norms as tools for social change.

"Punishment doesn't drive behavior," Slutkin told the *New York Times*. "Copying and modeling and the social expectation of your peers [are] what drives your behavior."

Slutkin wasn't talking about managers and employees, but he may as well have been. Because the same principles hold true for organizational culture. It is our nature to mimic one another, whether we're on the streets of Chicago, the courts of Roland Garros, or simply sitting at our desks.

Every human organization is an ecosystem. All it takes is a single spreader to start a virus.

The Lessons of Mimicry
Action Items for Managers

Manage your mood, not just your employees. Managers influence employees in more ways than they realize. Excited about a project? Your team is likely to feel it. Flooded with stress? Take a good look: So are your direct reports. Emotions are contagious, especially those of a team's leader. Maintaining a positive emotional tone, by exercising, getting enough sleep, and taking time to emotionally disconnect, won't just help sustain your psychological health. It will also help you get the most out of your team.

Know when to *recognize publicly* versus *thank privately*. Acknowledging employees for their hard work is vital to keeping them engaged, but that doesn't mean that every positive behavior should be recognized the same way. As a leader, you can use public recognition to draw attention to behaviors that are consistent with the culture that you are trying to promote, and that you'd like others to mimic. For behaviors that are worthy of acknowledgment but are inconsistent with the ideal workplace culture, use private recognition.

Facing an employee with a bad attitude? Shake up his network. The company we keep has a powerful influence on the way we think. Changing the people with whom an employee spends the majority of his time can alter his impression of organizational norms and lead him to recalibrate his approach at work. Instead of criticizing underperformers, try adjusting their social networks by pairing them with a new officemate or assigning them to a new work group, moving them closer to employees you'd like to see them mimic.

The Lessons of Mimicry
Action Items for Emerging Leaders

Model the behaviors you wish to see. People's tendency to mimic means you can influence their actions by setting an example. A former colleague of mine wanted her coworkers to send out agendas prior to group meetings. She could have pleaded with them, inviting defensiveness, but she preferred to avoid confrontation. Then she had an idea. One day she began sending agendas ahead of her meetings, without imposing on anyone else. Before she knew it, others began copying her behavior, and soon a new social norm was born.

Distance yourself from colleagues with a negative influence. Finding yourself unusually gloomy or stressed at work? Look around. It may not be you. We take our emotional cues by reading the body language, facial expressions, and emotional tone of those around us. A nightclub bouncer keeps out the riffraff to maintain a positive vibe. Try doing the same. Keep negative influences at a distance (e-mail, phone) while saving personal interactions for those who bring out your best.

Look for projects that involve leaders you wish to emulate. You can turn mimicry to your advantage by surrounding yourself with the right people. Start by taking a hard look at your current colleagues. Chances are, you and your team are becoming more similar by the day. If that sounds like welcome news, you're in the right place. If not, seek out collaborative opportunities that allow you to work closely with leaders who can bring you closer to the person you'd like to be.

PART THREE

Attracting and Retaining Top Performers

TEN

Seeing What Others Don't

How to Eliminate Interview Blind Spots That Prevent You from Reading People's True Potential

Moments before auditioning for the Buffalo Philharmonic Orchestra, classical violinist Megan Prokes closes her eyes and draws a deep breath. Her body is tense. In the last few days, she has been taking a little longer to settle into her practice routine, her concentration drifting.

"It's just an audition!" she wrote in her journal the night before, chiding herself to stay calm.

At twenty-eight, Prokes is something of a veteran on the auditioning circuit. Over the past four years, she has traveled the country, performing in front of interviewing committees nearly thirty times. Yet there is something different about this position.

She can't help it. She wants this one badly.

All morning, candidates have been summoned to the stage and instructed to perform one of fifteen preselected pieces. A perfect rendition meant playing for a full ten minutes. More often than not, however, auditions were cut short. At any point, the beauty of a Bach sonata would be ravaged with a curt "thank you," the player dismissed without another word. It's an outcome most applicants had come to expect. By Prokes's estimate, for every ten auditions a professional musician gives, she advances to the second round only once.

When her turn arrives, Prokes appears on stage but resists saying hello to the judges. She is not allowed to speak. She walks on a rug set down for the express purpose of masking her footsteps and takes a seat. Her violin on her shoulder, she looks out at the audience. The theater is empty with the exception of one section. There are no faces looking back at her. The judges are hidden behind a screen.

There's a lot for classical musicians to worry about during auditions like this: the steadiness of their fingers, the level of their volume, the consistency of their speed. But there is one anxiety-provoking element they can scratch off their list of concerns: their appearance.

Unlike most organizations, professional orchestras are keenly aware of the way a candidate's looks can skew observers' assessments. And they've got the data to prove it.

Back in the 1950s, many conductors openly opposed the hiring of female musicians, claiming that women did not possess the musical abilities of men, or that the female temperament was too volatile for an orchestra. But then, slowly, opinions began to shift. The bigotry that had prevailed for generations was steadily being challenged, especially after World War II, when female performers proved themselves perfectly capable of filling in for men who had been called off to fight.

Something, many believed, had to change. Yet finding a solution wasn't going to be easy. With so many conductors vehemently opposed to the inclusion of women, it wasn't clear what—if anything—could be done.

Then, in 1952, the Boston Symphony Orchestra (BSO) happened upon a solution. To provide applicants with an impartial tryout, the BSO introduced several steps to ensure that a musician's identity was concealed. Numbers were assigned in place of names. A rug was laid down on the stage so that listeners could not pick up on gender clues from the sound of an applicant's shoes. A screen prevented judges from seeing musicians as they played.

The goal was to create a "blind" interview process that hired musicians not on the basis of their looks, but on the quality of their performance.

As blind auditions grew more common in the decades that followed, a remarkable thing happened—orchestra rosters underwent a conspicuous change. In the 1970s, fewer than 10 percent of the musicians in major orchestras were women. Today, that number is closer to 35 percent. Economists at Harvard and Princeton have even quantified the impact of shielding a musician's identity: It improves the chances of women advancing by an astounding 50 percent.

When Megan Prokes performed that day in Buffalo, not a single member of the selection committee had any idea who she was. They did not know her name, because she had received a preassigned number to go by during the day's audition; they did not hear her voice, because a proctor was used to relay messages between the two sides; and they could not see her face, because they were seated behind a cloth screen.

So you can understand why it is that when, after several grueling rounds, the decision was made to hire Megan, and her name was revealed to the committee, an audible gasp filled the hall. Megan Prokes was no stranger to the Buffalo Philharmonic Orchestra. In fact, she had been an extended member of the family her entire life. Her father, Robert Prokes, had been performing with the orchestra for over thirty years.

Would Prokes have been hired if the committee had known her identity? We can't say for sure. On the one hand, her personal connections might have given her an inside track. But on the other, it could also have had the reverse effect, leading the committee to judge her more harshly in an attempt to appear objective.

What's less uncertain about Prokes's success is that her selection was based on her abilities rather than the preconceived notions of her listeners.

"No one could have known that it was me," she said, reflecting on her audition. "That makes me feel as if this job is really legitimately mine, and it had nothing to do with anything except my playing that day. And to me that's really, really important. I don't want a job I don't deserve."

How many employees can make a similar claim about their performance being the reason they were hired? And how many managers can say with absolute certainty that their hiring decisions are based solely on job-relevant criteria?

As we'll discover in this chapter, in almost every industry with the exception of classical music, the answer is just about none.

WHY YOU ARE WORSE AT INTERVIEWING
THAN YOU THINK

Imagine that you are facing a hiring decision. Your division has been authorized to bring on a midlevel manager with about ten years of experience. Fortunately, your HR department has done most of the heavy lifting, winnowing down hundreds of applicants to two qualified candidates. They've even put time on your calendar so that you can interview them both over the phone.

Just before your first call, you scan the résumés and note their relative strengths. You've got a few minutes to spare, so you turn to your computer and search for their LinkedIn profiles to put a face with each name. Both applicants appear to be in their late thirties, but one is considerably better looking than the other.

Would it make a difference? Or, to ask a slightly more provocative question, is the attractive candidate likely to give a better interview simply because you find his looks appealing?

In a classic experiment conducted in the late 1970s, psychologists at the University of Minnesota examined this very question. A group of men were shown a picture of either an attractive or an unattractive woman and told they would be speaking with her over the phone for ten minutes. In reality, the women in the photos had nothing to do with the study. The men were actually speaking to a randomly assigned participant whom they had never seen.

After the chat ended, the experimenters asked the men to rate their impression of their conversation partner. Not surprisingly, those who thought they were speaking with an attractive woman rated their partner as more likable than the men who were led to believe they were speaking with an unattractive partner.

But what is surprising is what happened next. The psychologists then took recordings of the conversations and asked a group of independent raters to listen in. Importantly, the experimenters neglected to tell raters which photo the men had seen. How did the judges view the women? As it turns out, they agreed with the men. They too found the women who were initially perceived as better looking as more likable, friendly, and sociable.

How did this happen? The answer lies in the behavior of the male interviewers. When the men thought they were speaking to an attractive woman, they behaved in ways that brought out their partner's best qualities. They acted more friendly and demonstrated considerably more warmth, which in turn drew out a more positive response.

Their first impression had created a self-fulfilling prophecy.

A similar process unfolds when we interview job applicants. Our initial expectations lead us down a path that influences the information we attend to, as well as the questions we pose. A candidate who appears outgoing may receive a question about whether she "has experience leading groups," while a candidate who we take to be more introverted may be asked if she is "comfortable in group settings." The variation in wording is subtle, but the responses they prompt are likely to differ, leading us to believe that our initial impressions were right all along.

Our opinions of a candidate can also affect our behavior in other, less obvious ways. When we like those we're interviewing, we tend to use their name more often, offer more encouragement while they are speaking (with head nodding and the occasional "uh-huh"), and transition between questions more positively (think "Ok, great" versus complete silence). The more encouraging our responses, the more confident they grow, and the better they perform.

The trouble with first impressions, however, is that we can't help overestimating their value.

The first piece of data we learn about an individual tends to hold a disproportionally large influence on the way we interpret information revealed later on, despite the fact that it is not necessarily more representative. It's the interview equivalent of what Nobel Prize–winning psychologist Daniel Kahneman refers to as a *cognitive anchor.*

To illustrate how anchors work, Kahneman often uses this example, taken from a study he conducted in 1974. If you ask a group of people to quickly guess the value of $1 \times 2 \times 3 \times 4 \times 5 \times 6 \times 7 \times 8$, their average estimate is likely to be close to 500. But if you ask a comparable group to guess the value of $8 \times 7 \times 6 \times 5 \times 4 \times 3 \times 2 \times 1$, their average estimate will be closer to 2,000. The equation is functionally identical. But our minds don't read it that way. We pay more attention to the *first* number in a sequence than we do to the rest, which misdirects our calculation of the final product.

What's the first piece of information we draw on when we meet someone new? More often than not, it's their physical appearance. And looks are a veritable minefield for interpersonal assessment, producing snap judgments that are often wrong.

Studies show, for example, that our preference for beauty distorts our view of people's abilities. Psychologists call it the *halo effect,* arguing that a single positive characteristic (like a winning smile) can color our impressions of unrelated qualities (like an applicant's abilities). Within an interview setting, the halo effect can wreak havoc. We like looking at attractive people and often confuse the positive feelings we experience when we're around them for a judgment of their actual skills.

Good-looking people are perceived as more intelligent, competent, and qualified than their less attractive colleagues, despite not being objectively better at any of these things. The more attractive the employees, the more likely they are to be hired, promoted, and retained when someone needs to be let go.

And it's not just looks. We also draw erroneous assumptions about people's abilities by observing their height. A 2013 study, for example, asked people to rate the leadership potential of a job candidate and included a photo of the applicant standing in the park. The images were identical, with the exception of the candidate's height, which had been Photoshopped to make him appear either short or tall. The impact of height was striking. Participants rated a six-feet-four-inch version of the man as having 25 percent more leadership ability than a five-feet-four-inch version of the same person. (The same results also held for women, though the effect was not as large.)

If the results of a single lab experiment strike you as too far removed from the complexities of the real world, consider a study that tracked over 8,500 American and British workers from their youth through late adulthood. Decades of data revealed a clear relationship between height and salary, and the effect held at every age.

Of course, the business world isn't the only setting where height contributes to success. As numerous historians have noted, presidential candidates with a height advantage are about twice as likely to win the popular vote.

Another extraneous feature that sways our assessments of people's abilities is the sound of their voice. We unconsciously associate lower-pitched speakers with greater strength, integrity, and leadership. Think Morgan Freeman or James Earl Jones. There's a reason they, and not Pee-wee Herman, are narrating powerful dramas. We instinctively use a person's voice to reach conclusions about his character.

It should go without saying that we rarely enter an interview intending to hire candidates based on their attractiveness, height, or voice quality. Yet the research suggests that we can't help being swayed by these factors. The obvious question, of course, is why. Why are we so heavily influenced by criteria that are often far removed from the qualities we're looking for in an employee?

Psychologists argue that it's because many of the cues we unconsciously use to size people up contained valuable information in the evolutionary past.

We are drawn to good-looking people, for example, because attractiveness is a proxy for health. Beautiful faces tend to be more symmetrical, and symmetry is a sign of good genes. When there is a gross imbalance in a person's features, it may signal that he has experienced an illness or is carrying a parasite. In either case, it's best to stay away. Feeling attracted to symmetrical faces while being repelled by the deformed is part of what helped us avoid illness and reproduce with healthy partners.

Genetically speaking, height is also a good marker of physical fitness. When we're raised in a nourishing environment, free from injury, disease, and excessive stress, we are more likely to grow strong and reach our full physical potential. On average, taller people truly are healthier.

In the past, height also signaled leadership ability. Over the course of evolutionary history, many of the leadership challenges faced by our ancestors were physical (for example, fighting off predators), and brute strength provided an important advantage. Paying attention to physical indicators of strength (such as size) helped our distant relatives identify leaders who could help promote their survival.

A similar logic explains why we ascribe greater leadership ability to deep-voiced speakers. Men with lower voices actually *are* bigger and stronger (as well as higher in testosterone) than their high-pitched counterparts. Their voices convey an audible cue of their size.

Taken together, the research paints an alarming picture. No matter how closely we might be attending to a candidate's abilities, our unconscious is ever present, filtering our impressions using an outdated set of criteria that have little to do with an applicant's actual potential. It's not just an inconvenience. It clouds our judgments, prejudices our reactions, and sways the behavior of the very candidates themselves.

INSIDE THE MIND OF AN INTERVIEWER

But wait. It gets worse.

Research shows that a candidate's physical characteristics represent just one of the many cognitive pitfalls that lead to inaccurate evaluations. The human mind is susceptible to a range of interview biases that make finding the right candidate far more difficult than it appears.

The first: We can't help but favor those who remind us of ourselves. In Chapter 5, we saw how similarity can draw coworkers closer together. And while similarity can provide a valuable tool when we're looking to grow relationships, it introduces a troublesome blind spot when we're evaluating others. If a candidate attended your alma mater, follows the same sports as you, or shares a similar interest in books, it's easy to misread that job-irrelevant data as evidence that he will be a good fit.

A second interview bias involves the order in which we meet the candidates. Research indicates that *when* a candidate is evaluated has a significant impact on their ratings. The reason is that interviewers don't assess applicants simply on the merits of the candidate's performance; they also take into account the scores they've awarded previous candidates that day. If an interviewer has already awarded several positive assessments, they are less likely to recommend a candidate who appears later on. It's because, as interviewers, we like to have balance in our evaluations. On average, high interview scores in the morning beget lower scores in the afternoon, irrespective of the candidates' actual performances.

Yet another interview bias highlights an unusual quirk in the way we gauge people's personalities. Harvard Business School professor Amy Cuddy argues that when we meet someone new, we instinctively evaluate them along two dimensions: first warmth, and then competence.

Both judgments are rooted in our evolutionary need to make quick survival decisions. In the past, identifying immediate threats was vital to staying alive, which is why, to this day, the moment we encounter a stranger, our mind is laser-focused on answering two questions:

1. Is this person a friend or a foe? (i.e., How *warm* are they?)
2. Is he or she capable of following through on their intentions toward me? (i.e., How *competent* are they?)

That seems straightforward enough. Now here's the twist.

Studies suggest that when we meet someone who is high along one dimension (say, an interviewee who is especially friendly) we mistakenly infer that they are low on the other ("He must be inept!"). That is, we tend to assume that warmth and competence are *inversely* related. And, as a consequence, we see friendly candidates as less capable and view capable candidates as interpersonally cold.

Warmth and competence are not inherent opposites, of course, yet we tend to form biased impressions that treat them as if they were. Research conducted at the University of Colorado shows that people draw inferences about one dimension from the other, especially when they lack sufficient information to adjust their views.

On some level, it appears we're aware of the trade-off between warmth and competence, and in certain cases, even use this knowledge to our advantage. Studies show that people strategically act less competent when their goal is to appear warm, and act less warm when they want to appear more competent.

Consider your own behavior at meetings. If your goal is to connect with those around you and exhibit warmth, you may be more likely to agree, offer compliments, and let others take the lead. On the other hand, if your focus is on appearing competent, you're likely to use a different approach. You may try to direct the conversation, emphasize your personal experience, and more firmly stand your ground.

With all of these psychological pitfalls, you'd assume we'd develop some pretty sophisticated tools to guide us through the process of selecting candidates.

Not quite.

Most managers today continue to rely on the same evaluation technique their grandparents used nearly a century ago: the job interview. As we've just seen, it's an approach that's rife with interviewer biases. And as we'll discover in this next section, it's also one that often turns even the most well-intentioned candidates into outright liars.

HOW TO LIE DURING A JOB INTERVIEW

As any experienced professional well knows, job interviews are a sort of game. Interviewers attempt to pick out the best candidate from a field of applicants, each determined to show that he or she provides the perfect fit.

In many interviews the following situation eventually unfolds. A candidate encounters a question about an experience or skill he doesn't quite have, something the interviewer clearly believes would be valuable. The room goes quiet. For the candidate, the calculus is simple: admit you are underqualified and flunk the interview or stretch the truth and potentially win the job.

It's at this point in the interview that lying maximizes the chances of being hired.

Research suggests that outright lying generates too much psychological discomfort for people to do it very often. More common during interviews are more nuanced forms of deception, which include embellishment (in which we take credit for things we haven't done), tailoring (in which we adapt our answers to fit the job requirements), and constructing (in which we piece together elements from different experiences to provide better answers).

Just how frequently do job hunters bend the truth during interviews? Eighty-one percent of the time, according to one eye-opening experiment conducted at the University of Massachusetts.

Within the study, psychologists led a group of job applicants to believe that they were interviewing for a tutoring position. After each interview was over, the researchers sheepishly admitted that there was, in fact, no job to be had. It had all been part of a study. They then asked the participants to watch a recording of their interviews, adding one request: Please identify every instance in which you deliberately misled the interviewer.

The results were depressing. Not just because four out of every five applicants admitted lying, or that they each did so, on average, more than twice. It's that the interviews had been brief—only ten questions long.

It's also not very reassuring to note that participants in the study had every reason to be conservative in their lying estimates. If you were seated next to a psychologist who had recorded your interview, how many lies would you voluntarily admit to telling before asking if you could please go home now?

We like to think that we're good at spotting liars. As interviewers, we watch a candidate's eyes, observe his posture, listen for changes in the tone of his voice. We want to believe, as Freud once said, that "no mortal can keep a secret. If his lips are silent, he chatters with his fingertips; betrayal oozes out of him at every pore."

The unfortunate truth is this: We're rarely effective at picking out dishonesty. In fact, we're only slightly better at determining if someone has lied to our face than we are at predicting whether a flipped coin will land on its head. Seasoned interviewers are no better than novices. They are, however, significantly different in one respect: Although they are just as bad as everyone else at recognizing deception, they feel significantly more confident in their conclusions.

But the problem with job interviews extends well beyond the issue of honesty. Even if we were able to magically root out lying in all its forms, how predictive would giving a good interview really be of later job performance? In many cases, job interviews are entirely disconnected from the reality of people's day-to-day work. Some candidates excel at interpersonal communications. That's useful data if you're looking to fill a position that involves sales or customer service. But when that's not the case, basing your decision on a standard job interview may actually do more harm than good.

We rely on job interviews because we believe they help us find the right applicant. But as we've seen, the picture they provide is often misleading, and occasionally, downright false.

If that weren't bad enough, add to it the fact that we seldom receive comprehensive feedback on our hiring decisions. We pluck a single individual out of a pool of applicants and dismiss the rest, without ever learning how the others would have performed. We lack the data to determine if we've made the right choice.

It's rare for managers to think back on the employees they didn't hire. But what if we've been choosing the wrong people all along?

THE SINGLE BEST WAY OF IMPROVING YOUR HIRING DECISIONS

One morning in 2004, a series of mysterious banners appeared in the subway station at Harvard Square. They hung down from the ceiling, each fifty feet wide and dangling above the heads of thousands of commuters, many of whom were on their way to the country's top universities.

The banners did not reveal a sponsor. Nor did they ask viewers to actually *do* anything.

All they said was this:

> { first 10-digit prime found in consecutive digits of e } .com

Most people can identify this as some type of math problem. Beyond that, however, they are at a loss. And this was exactly the point. The signs were not intended for everyone—they were designed to reach commuters with mathematical expertise and a passion for solving problems.

The correct answer (www.7427466391.com) led users to yet another complex puzzle, just to be sure they were sufficiently motivated. Then the reveal . . .

Congratulations. Nice work. Well done. Mazel tov. You've made it to Google Labs and we are glad you are here.

One thing we learned while building Google is that it's easier to find what you're looking for if it comes looking for you. What we're looking for are the best engineers in the world. And here you are.

The banners, which appeared in other carefully selected locations, represented the launch of an atypical recruitment effort from one of the world's most atypical companies. When Google needs an employee, they don't simply post an ad on Monster. They look for like-minded people, and this is the result: a job ad written in Geek.

Google's recruitment campaign offers a number of lessons, not the least of which is that introducing excitement and intrigue into the hiring process can garner extraordinary press. What often gets lost, however, is that the real genius of the ad lies not in its provocative execution but in its strategic approach.

Generally speaking, there are two ways of finding extraordinary employees. The first is to get better at choosing between candidates, which, as we've seen, is tricky. The other is improving the quality of your applicant pool before starting your evaluation. It's a lot easier to reach smart hiring decisions when the vast majority of your applicants are a good choice.

One way of improving a candidate pool is by turning outstanding employees into recruiters. Research shows that people tend to socialize with those with similar personalities. This means that if you have hard workers with an optimistic mind-set, chances are they know a number of people who share those characteristics.

Studies indicate that on the whole, referred hires outperform those who get their jobs through more formal channels. In part, it's because they enter a company with a preestablished bond to a coworker, which translates into higher organizational loyalty and greater effort. An internal study comparing accountants at Ernst & Young found that referred hires also stay longer and are quicker to integrate into teams.

How do you get top performers to make more referrals? A growing number of companies have begun rewarding employees with a range of giveaways. Deloitte incentivizes employees with prizes like iPads and big-screen TVs. The Everett Clinic in Washington offers its physicians a $10,000 bonus for referring a former classmate or colleague to its practice.

The use of rewards may not be ideal for every organization. Not only is putting a focus on extrinsic rewards likely to reduce employees' intrinsic motivation for making a referral, it's also likely to diminish the quality of the candidates, especially when there are no repercussions for referring a subpar candidate. The best scenario from an organizational standpoint is one in which employees recruit others because they want to work with great teammates and believe that their company would genuinely benefit from bringing that particular employee onboard.

A wiser investment of resources involves streamlining the referral process and helping recommenders look good to those they refer. At the fiberglass manufacturing company Owens Corning, referred candidates receive expedited interviews, which helps demonstrate the value of a recommender's opinion. Consulting firm Accenture allows referrers to monitor the status of the people they recommend via intranet, enabling them to update their friends and stay current on the latest developments. Diageo, a producer of alcoholic beverages, has begun announcing job openings internally first, so that employees can give the people in their network advance notice.

An active referral program can find better candidates at a fraction of the cost of a professional recruiter. And it does something the classifieds won't do: *reach qualified candidates who are happily employed.* The best candidates are not searching the Internet for a job. More often than not, they are perfectly satisfied in their current position. Which is why job postings can be a crapshoot. The chances of a truly superb candidate looking for a job at the very moment you have an opening are remarkably slim.

But no matter how satisfied you are with your job, the moment someone you respect compliments your skills and says he'd like to work with you, you can't help it. You listen.

HOW TO SHRINK YOUR INTERVIEW BLIND SPOTS

Getting the right candidates in your applicant pool is half the battle. But once you do, how do you select among them? After all, you're still stuck using the same faulty software that makes interviews so problematic in the first place.

Fortunately, there are a number of steps you can take to improve your chances of making the right choice.

The first involves tearing a page out of the orchestra interviewing playbook and using a modified version of the blind audition. Blind auditions direct a selection committee's attention to the criteria that matter most: the way a musician plays. There is a workplace equivalent to this approach, and it involves creating an interview that's centered on a work assignment.

What assignment should you ask applicants to complete? The answer depends on the position you're looking to fill. Ask an analyst to write an action memo, a Web designer to mock up a landing page, and a business development candidate to present to you as if you were a client. Better yet, ask applicants to solve a problem you're facing so that you can evaluate their approach and potentially evolve your own thinking. The important thing is to create an assignment that is job relevant, allowing your impressions to form around skills that are pertinent to the role.

Extraneous data, such as a candidate's appearance or charisma, lose their influence when you can see the way an applicant actually performs. It's also a better predictor of their future contributions, because unlike traditional in-person interviews, it evaluates job-relevant criteria.

Including an assignment can help you better identify the true winners in your applicant pool while simultaneously making them more invested in the position. Research shows that when we make a personal sacrifice to get something we want (for example, by investing our time), we value it more once we get it. Just ask anyone who's been in a fraternity. The more difficult the rite of passage, the more pride they're likely to take in their membership.

At the same time, the required investment is likely to discourage window shoppers, which is a benefit in its own right. It's a great way of exposing candidates who are not serious about the position before they take up too much of your time.

Another step to help minimize your interviewing blind spots: Include multiple interviewers and give them each specific criteria upon which to evaluate the candidate. Without a predefined framework for evaluating applicants—which may include relevant experience, communication skills, attention to detail—it's hard for interviewers to know where to focus. And when this happens, fuzzy interpersonal factors hold greater weight, biasing assessments. Far better to channel interviewers' attention in specific ways, so that the feedback they provide is precise.

If possible, assign individual interviewers to judge candidates on *different* dimensions, allowing them to hone in on a specific aspect of the candidate's responses (for example, interpersonal skill *or* work-related abilities). Earlier we saw the inherent challenge in simultaneously judging people's warmth and competence. By separating these dimensions and having interviewers evaluate one or the other, you're more likely to get an accurate read.

It's also worth having interviewers develop questions ahead of time so that: (1) each candidate receives the same questions, and (2) they are worded the same way. The more you do to standardize your interviews, providing the same experience to every candidate, the less influence you wield on their performance.

Two types of questions can be especially useful: *behavioral interview questions* and *situational judgment questions*. Behavioral interview questions are focused on an applicant's *past* behavior within specific work situations. Here are some examples:

- Tell me about a time when you had a conflict with a supervisor. What steps did you take to resolve the conflict?
- Tell me about a time when you led a group. Describe what you did and how that reflects your leadership style.

The value of behavioral interview questions is that they are focused not on a candidate's intentions or philosophical approach but on their actions. Past behavior is a strong predictor of future behavior, which is why learning how a candidate handled a particular situation can be useful. The interviewer can then follow up with a series of how or why questions to drill down and unearth the candidate's decision-making process.

A related line of inquiry—called situational judgment questions—involves asking candidates how they would handle a hypothetical situation in the *future*. The goal here is to get a sense of how they will behave within your organization. Some examples of situational judgment questions include:

- Suppose we land Project X and I assign you as the lead. How would you go about approaching the project?
- Say you're about to go on a sales presentation for Company Y. What sort of research would you do to prepare for your meeting?

Encourage your interviewers to take notes during their discussions with the candidate. The more we record our observations, the less likely we are to be swayed by our memories, which place too much weight on the beginning and the end of an interview. Note taking during interviews also draws our attention to a candidate's actual performance, minimizing the influence of false expectations.

Depending on the status and function of the role you're trying to fill, you might also consider placing a candidate in more than a single situation. Excelling in a one-on-one setting is obviously important for most positions. But in many cases, so is performing well in a group, and in social settings outside of the workplace. That's one reason management consulting firm Grant Thornton evaluates applicants not just in the office but over a cooking class, after traditional interviews are through. The company's leadership correctly recognizes that the more settings you use to evaluate a candidate, the more accurately you can assess their true personality.

What you do with the data after an interview is over can be just as critical as your handling of the interview itself. It's important, for example, to ask team members to share their impressions with you first, and one at a time rather than in a group setting, where pressure to agree can shift people's views. Only after impressions are shared privately should you enter into a group discussion.

Finally, follow up with team members by offering them feedback on their assessments, so they can improve. If an employee spent an hour with a candidate only to return with a superficial evaluation ("I like her!"), show him a sample of the sort of detailed feedback you find especially helpful.

Each of these steps can minimize the impact of interview biases and help us reach better hiring decisions. And yet they are not foolproof. Every once in a while you will encounter a well-prepared candidate who offers a terrific work sample and aces every behavioral and situational judgment question. But six months after hiring him, you can't help noticing that he is not a good fit.

So what went wrong?

WHAT TO LISTEN FOR DURING AN INTERVIEW

If hiring the right employee were simply a matter of identifying the most competent candidate, we would not need interviews. We could administer a series of tests—complete with a battery of behavioral and situational judgment questions—and have computers grade responses and send the applicant with the highest score an automated offer letter.

But we don't. And the reason we don't is that there's more to finding the right candidate than technical ability. There's their personality, their attitude, and the feeling we get when we're in their company.

Given the myriad of ways interviews are lacking, it's easy to question what use they provide. But there is one thing a well-conducted interview can reveal that no résumé, referral, and sample projects can offer: an inside look into a candidate's emotional tone.

In most conversations, our attention is naturally drawn to an exchange of facts. We listen for who, what, where, and when. Unless something unusual happens, we rarely go into depth and analyze the communications beneath the surface.

Therapists, however, make it a habit to listen differently. They focus on the emotion behind the story. Years of training have taught them that people's outlooks follow a pattern—one that's reflected in the way they describe events. How we have experienced the past is predictive of how we will experience the future.

Consider how a candidate responds to the following open-ended question: *What can you tell me about your experience at your current (or previous) job?* It's a question they can take in many directions. Do they focus on ways in which their position enhanced their development, or do they talk about all the ways their role was not a good fit?

How candidates view their professional life is not simply about the work they've done. It's a reflection of who they are. Research shows that candidates who have had positive workplace experiences in the past are likely to continue to have positive experiences in the future, while candidates who have been disgruntled in previous jobs are likely to continue to find fault in their next position.

Asking candidates to describe past experiences is one way of uncovering their emotional outlook. Another is asking open-ended questions that reveal more about a candidate than how he or she operates at the office. One example is a question Google founder Sergey Brin likes to ask during his interviews: *Teach me something I don't know.* How candidates respond to this unanticipated question can tell you how they handle unexpected situations, as well as provide a window into topics they are passionate about and confident enough to explain.

The same rationale applies to projective questions that require candidates to reveal aspects of their personality as part of their response. Seemingly innocuous questions that appear to have very little to do with the job can reveal a lot about a candidate.

While interviewing for a medical residency position, my wife was asked, "If you were a fabric, what type of fabric would you be and why?" Needless to say, this is not a question she had come prepared to answer. But her response—"velvet, because I'm warm on the inside and smooth on the outside"—helped communicate that she was committed to being a team player.

When you listen for emotion, you become better at picking out highly skilled candidates who may be hampered in their careers by negative outlooks. One marker of a challenging personality is the tendency to describe oneself as a victim. The more people view themselves as victims, the easier it is for them to shirk personal responsibility for their circumstances. To be fair, victimized candidates may be accurate in their assessments. Incompetent bosses and backstabbing colleagues are a reality in the corporate world. But blaming others is a difficult habit to break.

Another emotional red flag: sarcasm. While the occasional biting comment can spark a good laugh, frequent sarcasm tends to reflect dissatisfaction, which may be rooted in what some psychologists believe is anger and hostility.

Why read so much into a candidate's use of humor? Researchers argue that there is a fundamental difference between positive humor (which is good-natured and friendly) and negative humor (which can be aggressive or self-defeating). While both types can lift our mood temporarily, negative humor is often used to help people feel superior in situations where they perceive they have little control.

When candidates are often sarcastic, it suggests that they feel disempowered, which reflects poorly on their potential for leadership. It also means that a year from now you may find them teasing coworkers in a way that allows them to veil their criticisms while claiming that they were simply joking all along. Worse still, by the time you uncover it, you might find that the practice has already spread to others on your team.

THE BENEFITS AND DRAWBACKS OF HIRING FOR
CULTURAL FIT

Suppose that over the course of your interviews you meet a candidate who has all the right skills but has a personality and background that differ considerably from your existing employees.

Your team is easygoing and upbeat. This candidate is introverted and reserved. Your team is process-oriented and collaborative. This candidate has worked independently for years. Most of the people on your team have spent their entire careers working inside your industry. This candidate comes from a different background entirely but appears qualified to do the work.

She aced her interview and everyone seems to like her just fine. Should you offer her the job?

For a growing number of organizations, cultural fit has become an important priority when reaching hiring decisions. Rather than simply selecting employees who have the necessary skills, companies like Zappos are now looking to ensure that new hires share common values before bringing them onboard.

The idea holds intuitive appeal. When employees have similar norms and attitudes, they're more likely to get along. And the better they get along, the more likely they are to produce. Right?

As it turns out, the equation is not always so simple.

While similarity among coworkers can foster smoother interactions and better working relationships, there's a point at which too much similarity can actually stifle certain elements of performance. The reasons are several. For one, similarity fosters complacency. When we're surrounded by others who share our viewpoint, there's little reason for us to do additional thinking. We get stuck doing things the way we've always done them because no one is challenging us to think differently.

Similarity also breeds overconfidence. When everyone around us sees the world exactly as we do, we overestimate the accuracy of our opinions. That unfounded self-assurance leads us to invest less effort in our decisions, making errors more common.

And finally, the more we have in common with our colleagues, the less likely we are to encounter a fresh perspective. This can be especially problematic when the work we do requires innovative thinking.

A fascinating 2009 study looked at the way too much similarity can derail a team's decision-making. Within the study, teams of three were asked to solve a problem with the help of a new team member who was either similar or dissimilar to the existing group. The results were clear: While homogenous teams felt more confident in their decisions, it was the diverse teams that performed best.

How exactly did the mismatched newcomers elevate their team's performance? Not in the way we might suspect. It wasn't, for example, by introducing new ways of seeing old problems. Rather it was by motivating veteran team members to reexamine their assumptions and process data more carefully. Which is the very thing they neglected to do when everyone in their group was similar.

The mere presence of an outsider led insiders to think harder.

What's the right degree of cultural fit for a job candidate? The answer can be complex.

When the work itself is simple and creative thinking is rarely required, establishing a homogenous workforce has its advantages. But the same can't be said for organizations looking to be on the forefront of innovation. Here, exposing people to different viewpoints can generate more value than ensuring that they gel.

Another factor to consider: the company's place in its corporate lifecycle. When an organization is small or just getting off the ground, shared values and a common outlook are vital. Taking a four-person company to a five-person team increases its workforce by 20 percent—a considerable change. It's at this early stage that cohesion is too important to overlook.

But as an organization matures, too much similarity can actually backfire. Replicating employees isn't ideal—especially in industries where the work revolves around complex thinking. Without diversity of opinion, there is also a lack of innovative tension. Ideas grind to a halt. The glue that keeps the pieces together can also keep them stuck in place.

THE HARD TRUTH ABOUT HIRING

To create a great workplace you need to excel at hiring. It's because no matter how well you manage, how often you recognize, or how generously you reward, there's simply no substitute for selecting talented people and placing them in the right roles.

If we've learned anything in this chapter, it is this: Finding great employees is a lot harder than it seems.

Our minds evolved to survive on the savanna—not to discern among hundreds of applicants. That's why it's critical that we think intelligently about the information we collect, taking steps to correct for the cognitive biases that muddy our perceptions. Ultimately, hiring is a gamble. And with every gamble, there is uncertainty and risk. The better we get at minimizing the ambiguity, the more we improve our odds.

The Lessons of Hiring
Action Items for Managers

Create your own blind audition. Instead of relying primarily on in-person interviews to select among candidates, invite applicants to complete an assignment that is directly relevant to the work they will do at your organization. If possible, use this deliverable as the basis for introducing the candidate to your team, so that their first impression is grounded in ability rather than appearance.

Leverage your employees to recruit top talent. It's axiomatic in the business world to say: "A players attract A players, while B players attract C players." Yet it's rare for organizations to put that insight to good use. The reality of the job market is that the best employees are rarely searching for a new job. That's why your best opportunity for reaching top performers—other than paying thousands of dollars to a recruiter—is actively engaging your best employees to identify and recruit future coworkers.

Beware the lure of cultural fit. Hiring on the basis of similarity can be a useful strategy, especially for budding teams for which the top priority is getting along. What it doesn't mean, however, is that uniformity is always the best approach. When everyone in an organization has the same personality, it can lead to a narrowed perspective and weaker decision-making. Rather than assuming similarity is always best, remember the benefits of diversity.

The Lessons of Hiring
Action Items for Emerging Leaders

Mine your network. You can wait for your manager to find your next colleague or you can recommend someone you'd like to work with for the position instead. The benefits of moonlighting as your company's HR representative are many. Your friends will appreciate your thinking of them. Your manager will notice your investment in the company's success. The chances of you working with someone you respect improve exponentially. Also worth considering: The better the candidate looks, the smarter you appear. It's because we tend to assume people are similar to their friends, which makes recommending an outstanding candidate a shrewd career move.

Open with warmth. Earlier in the chapter, we learned of a cognitive blind spot that leads people to assume that there is an inverse relationship between our level of warmth and our level of competence. When making a first impression with a colleague or a client, many of us focus on emphasizing our competence in an effort to demonstrate that we are valuable contributors. However, research suggests that this is precisely the wrong approach to creating a lasting connection. Highlighting our strengths can diminish perceptions of our warmth, making trust more difficult to establish. To lead effectively in the workplace, try connecting with others first, by showing interest in their views and establishing common ground. Only then, after you've projected warmth, can you build on the foundation without risking coming across as cold.

Plan your first impressions. When you meet a new client or colleague, the first few minutes of an exchange can have a dramatic impact on your relationship. Instead of leaving those critical moments to chance, consider scripting out what you plan to say, so that your first impression is a strong one. If you're interviewing for a job, for example, memorize an opening you can use if your interviewers start with a blanket question like, "Tell me about yourself." If that's not the first question you receive, try addressing their query and then work back to your preplanned response. You can generally recover from a mistake made in the middle of a meeting; coming back from a shaky opening is considerably more difficult.

ELEVEN

What Sports, Politics, and Religion Teach Us About Fostering Pride

The elevator doors slide open. You enter the apartment, hearing Miles Davis accompanied by the gentle clinks of champagne flutes. There are more people here than you expected. Most of them in suits and gowns. Even the waiters are immaculately dressed.

On your way up, you received a text.

Traffic is terrible. Will be another 45 minutes.

Perfect, you think. Here you are, arriving at a cocktail party knowing absolutely no one.

Fortunately there is a woman here to greet you. She is in her early fifties and has the look of someone who summers in the south of France. She welcomes you into her home.

"You have a lovely place," you say, wondering why you ever agreed to meet *inside* the party instead of in the lobby. Now, of course, it is too late to escape. Not after you have given her your coat and told her your name.

"So tell me," she says, handing you a glass of wine, "where do you work?"

Let's pause here for a moment. Imagine yourself in this exact situation, standing in a room full of strangers, on the verge of answering. Now direct your attention inward. How does it feel in that split second, when you're about to reveal the name of your workplace?

The question isn't simply rhetorical—it's diagnostic. The way we experience telling others where we work provides a valuable assessment of our workplace pride.

Consider your reaction to telling people the name of your company. Do you find yourself standing a bit taller, or does your posture subtly shrink? Do you expect a boost in your listener's admiration, or a look of polite confusion instead? Are you secretly hoping for a change in topic or a series of follow-up questions?

It's rare for organizations to give much thought to whether their employees are proud of their workplace, yet the implications can be profound. Research indicates that pride is associated with greater employee loyalty and reduced interest in looking for other jobs. In many industries, keeping turnover to a minimum is vital. The longer employees work for a company, the better they know the business, and the more valuable their contributions.

Pride also influences people's willingness to tell their friends and neighbors about where they work. And those conversations add up. The more glowingly employees describe their company to people around them, the stronger the organization's reputation with future hires and prospective clients.

Studies suggest that pride can also contribute to on-the-job performance in several ways. Researchers have found that the experience of pride is energizing and leads people to persevere longer on challenging tasks. Salespeople who report workplace pride are more motivated, put in more effort, and show better results. And it's not just profits. Studies show proud employees are also more likely to help their colleagues, as well as engage in behaviors that improve the functioning of their organization as a whole.

A 2009 experiment looked at the impact of *making* people feel proud in the lab. After completing a bogus exam purportedly designed to test spatial reasoning, participants were told that they scored in the 94th percentile, which, the experimenter added, was among the highest scores she'd ever seen.

Participants were then asked to solve a three-dimensional puzzle—this time alongside a partner.

How would experiencing pride influence people's performance on a team? To find out, the experimenters compared participants who received positive feedback on their exam with others who took the test but were never told how they did. The results underscore the subtle ways pride can affect behavior in a workplace setting. Proud participants took more initiative on the problem-solving task and exhibited greater leadership within their team, though not in ways that might be experienced by colleagues as overbearing. They were assertive without being pushy. In fact, compared to those who received no feedback on their test, proud participants were considered more likable by their teammates.

Leaders often assume that so long as employees are happy with their job, organizational pride will naturally follow. But it's not clear that this is actually the case. It's one thing to enjoy working at a company and quite another to feel proud of it.

Take Craig Sherman, who, at thirty-six years of age, finds his role as a manager immensely gratifying. Every day Craig helps a growing team of employees build new skills, meet a variety of challenging deadlines, and delight hundreds of customers.

Craig loves his job. But that doesn't mean he's proud of the fact that he works at McDonald's.

So what do you do when you want the Craigs of the world to feel proud of their workplace? How do you get employees genuinely excited to talk about their company the next time someone asks?

We know that pride can elevate an organization's performance. But what's the formula for growing pride?

WHERE PRIDE COMES FROM

Social psychologists who study the science of human emotion argue that, at its core, pride is fundamentally about *status*. Pride is the pleasurable feeling we get when we reflect upon achieving a socially desirable outcome, one that elevates our standing within our group.

As social animals, we long to be viewed positively. It's because being valued by others brings with it significant evolutionary advantages: more attention, greater influence, access to important resources.

One way we determine whether we're valued is by comparing our social rank with the rank of those around us. When our status rises, we feel good about ourselves and experience pride. But the moment our status sinks, we tend to experience the opposite emotion: shame.

The idea that pride and shame are intricately linked to social status explains why losing a job and winning a competition can affect us so strongly. Changes in our perceived standing are directly tied to our emotional experiences. Pride and shame serve as emotional guideposts that tell us whether we're succeeding at socially valued objectives.

We take pride in achievements that elevate our status in the eyes of others: an impressive job title, a fancy car, an attractive family. These are the things we advertise to our friends and neighbors—not our financial struggles or marital discord.

We use similar criteria for determining whether to put our group affiliations on display. When we're associated with a group that enhances our social status—a prestigious golf club, an academic institution, Mensa—we express a great deal of pride in our affiliation. But if a group confers minimal advantage or diminishes our perceived status, we're generally prone to keeping it to ourselves.

Studies suggest we're quite strategic in signaling our affiliations. The behavior of sports fans provides a useful illustration. Research shows that fans are significantly more likely to wear a team's paraphernalia the day *after* a team is victorious, promoting their connection with a proven winner. But the moment a team hits a losing streak, the caps and jerseys mysteriously disappear. Psychologists call it BIRGing, an acronym that stands for *basking in reflected glory*. In many cases, it's an unconscious impulse, and one that is not limited to sports.

In the days following the 2008 general election, psychologists wondered how long it would take supporters of Barack Obama and John McCain to remove the lawn signs displayed in their yards. To find out, researchers drove by hundreds of homes every day for a week, recording if the signs were still up. On average, McCain signs vanished relatively quickly. Obama supporters, on the other hand, saw no rush, keeping signs displayed for nearly five extra days.

The psychological basis of pride raises an unusually thorny problem from a workplace perspective. If pride is rooted in status, what can an organization possibly do to lift its employees' social standing?

As we'll discover in this next section, the answer is more than you might initially think.

THE BUILDING BLOCKS OF PRIDE

Not every organization is equally adept at fostering group pride. Driving down the highway, you're a lot more likely to find a bumper sticker expressing pride in an ethnic group or a minor league baseball team than you are to see one communicating passion for a workplace.

It's a curious disconnect. We spend almost half our waking hours working in companies that finance our livelihood, grow our skills, and bind us to many of our closest friends. Yet we rarely display even a fraction of the enthusiasm for our organizations as we do for groups that often play far less prominent roles in our lives.

What is it that makes some groups—particularly religious institutions, political parties, and sports teams—so effective at sparking pride among their members?

Let's take a look at some of the characteristics that *pride-inducing* groups often have in common and examine how each element can be used to build pride in the workplace.

BUILDING BLOCK #1: A GRAND NARRATIVE

The first feature of pride-inducing groups: a compelling story about the group's future, as well as about its past.

Let's begin with the future first. Religious institutions, political parties, and sports teams all unify their members around an inspirational vision. By providing members with a shared vision of a success (e.g., entering into heaven, reforming the tax system, winning a championship) each group offers its followers a reason to view their membership as an investment—one in which their status will be elevated.

Leadership experts Jim Collins and Jerry Porras argue that successful organizations need more than a corporate mission; they also need a "big hairy audacious goal" to keep their teams energized. Religions, political parties, and sports teams have used this approach for generations, painting an emotionally compelling picture of a future that group members can achieve by working collaboratively. The more energized people are around the objectives of their group, the more pride they can take in being part of it.

Focusing on the future offers an added benefit: It makes people more willing to sacrifice in the present. This is one reason dieters are willing to forgo the lure of delicious, albeit fattening, foods. By envisioning their future self in a bathing suit, they're better able to summon the willpower to resist temptation in the present.

To paraphrase Friedrich Nietzsche, "He who has a why, can bear almost any how."

But when it comes to fostering group pride, an inspiring vision of the future is often only half the equation. In many cases, it's a company's *history* that represents its greatest untapped resource for growing employee pride. The reason is simple: The more team members know about their organization's past achievements, the more pride they can take in belonging to the group. There's a difference between pitching for the Tampa Bay Rays and the New York Yankees—and it's not just geographic location. When we feel like we belong to an organization with a storied tradition, it boosts our perceived status and elevates our connection to the team.

Political and religious leaders often weave historical events into major speeches, building a sense of connection to the past before laying out their vision for the future. It's an effective rhetorical technique. Invoking a group's history gives listeners the sense that they are part of something bigger and makes membership feel more meaningful.

Contrast that with the reality in many organizations, where employees are thrown into positions without any sense of how their contributions fit in with their company's history. A lack of context keeps them from fully appreciating and taking pride in their role.

It's not uncommon for leaders to become so consumed with meeting the demands of the present that they neglect presenting a vision of the future or celebrating the successes of the past. From a pride-building perspective, doing so squanders an important opportunity. Which is why it makes sense to invest in educating new employees about a company's history, to install visual displays in the workspace that highlight past achievements, and to use the occasional speech to remind existing team members of how far they've come.

The more attuned employees are to their organization's story—past and future—the easier it is for them to take pride in playing a role.

BUILDING BLOCK #2: GROUP DISTINCTIVENESS

Another characteristic of pride-inducing groups: a clear point of difference.

In the past, rituals, language, and clothing served to distinguish tribal members from outsiders. Visual and behavioral reminders of a group's distinctiveness helped facilitate bonding between members while making outsiders more noticeably different.

Today, identifying differences between our "tribe" and outsiders can be more challenging.

When nearly everything about a company is similar to its competitors—from its product offerings to its workspace design to the look and feel of its brand—it's hard for employees to find something to take pride in. It's not enough to know what your organization does well. In order for workplace pride to emerge, you need a clear understanding of what makes it distinctive.

Whether it's an unconventional company mission, a unique workplace culture, or an exceptional workspace, organizations that have an explicit point of differentiation are at an advantage when it comes to fostering group pride.

Ultimately, how a company goes about defining its distinctiveness is less important than the fact that it has one that its members find meaningful. It's when we view every group as similar ("Republicans, Democrats . . . they're all the same!") that we stop taking pride in our membership.

BUILDING BLOCK #3: A COMMITMENT
TO THE GREATER GOOD

A third feature of pride-inducing groups: a devotion to improving the lives of others.

It's common for religious groups and political parties to trumpet the way their work benefits society. Even sports teams often frame their desire for winning around the implications their success will have for their schools, their fans, or their cities.

Organizational altruism can make membership more appealing. When a group's contributions benefit the broader community, its members' social standing improves. Not only do employees take pride in their affiliation, they also want others to know that they're part of a company that does socially valued work.

Psychologists believe that while we are motivated to maximize our self-interest, we're also hardwired to collaborate and act selflessly in certain circumstances. Helping others is intrinsically rewarding and makes us feel good about ourselves. It also lends the work we do greater value by allowing us to see that our sacrifices have meaning.

One way organizations often highlight their commitment to the greater good is by making charitable contributions to important causes. It's a laudable endeavor. But in many cases, it's done in a way that fails to take full advantage of the opportunity for building company pride.

In most organizations, contribution decisions are reached at the executive level, leaving employees surprisingly disconnected from the process. Donations are simply announced in an e-mail or a newsletter. And while employees may be genuinely appreciative of their company's involvement, their participation is minimal.

The trouble with this approach is that it's missing an important psychological component of pride: personal responsibility. It's hard to feel proud of an outcome to which we barely contributed.

Organizations like Allianz Life, an insurance company in Minnesota, are attempting to address this issue by inviting employees to nominate nonprofits and allowing them to vote on the organization's charitable giving as a group. Others, like Charles Schwab, match employees' personal contributions to nonprofits, multiplying the impact of their individual gifts.

Another way of using organizational giving to build pride is by allowing employees to take time off from work to volunteer. Outdoor clothing company Patagonia, for example, has made volunteering a cornerstone of its corporate strategy. Each year it organizes a series of internships for employees, enabling them to volunteer at conservation groups for up to sixty days.

At many companies, offering employees extended time away from the office isn't a realistic option. Microsoft's Dollars for Doers program offers an interesting alternative. The computer software giant asks employees to report the amount of time they spent volunteering at charitable organizations and matches their efforts with a charitable contribution of seventeen dollars for every hour worked. It's a way of demonstrating a company's commitment to the greater good while putting employees in charge of leading the way.

BUILDING BLOCK #4: THE CONVICTION THAT EVERY MEMBER COUNTS

A final ingredient of pride-inducing groups: making each member feel like their contributions are valued.

Religions and political parties often emphasize that every member can make a difference. Whether it's spreading God's word or going out to the polls on Election Day, the underlying message is the same: Each one of us matters.

One way of making employees feel like their contributions matter at work is by helping them develop a sense of ownership. The more ownership we feel in our group, the easier it is for us to take pride in being a member.

Involvement in organizational decisions—like choosing which charities receive a contribution—is one way of growing employee ownership. So is putting their name on client-facing deliverables and featuring their biographies on the company website.

Seeing our names connected to our work enables us to take pride in our achievements. It also eliminates the anonymity that can contribute to subpar performance. When there's a visible link between our identity and our work product, our performances become reflective of who we are.

If you've visited an upscale restaurant in recent years, you've probably noticed a growing trend of chefs' names appearing on menus. It's hard to know whether this does more to elevate the amount of effort the chefs put into preparing their dishes or simply enhances diners' expectations, but in my experience, it's predictive of a good meal.

Another way of helping employees feel like their contributions matter is by expressing appreciation directly to their families. Families are a major arbiter of our perceived status. When an organization makes an employee look good in front of a spouse or their children, it affects them in ways that are a lot more powerful than a simple pat on the back at work.

Here are some of the more innovative ways organizations have begun elevating employees' status at home at various points of their tenure with the company:

For New Hires

- Sending flowers or cookies to the home of a new hire after an offer is accepted (McMurry, a marketing agency)
- A letter to the new hire's spouse welcoming him or her to the family (Acuity, an insurance provider)
- Inviting family members for a tour of the company on the first day of work (Talent Plus, a recruitment company)

For Hardworking and Long-serving Employees

- Gift baskets to loved ones when an employee has put in extra hours (Kimpton Hotels & Restaurants)
- A weekend getaway at a Lake Tahoe cabin owned by the company (DPR Construction)
- A thank-you note and $100 gift card to spouses at the end of a busy tax season (accounting firm EKS&H)
- After five years of tenure, an additional week off and $5,000 toward a vacation (staffing provider Akraya Inc.)

For New Parents

- Chef-prepared meals for a week after a new baby arrives (employment website Snagajob)
- Teddy bears for the new arrival's siblings so that they don't feel left out (Holder Construction)

- "Babycash" to help pay for nursery furniture, diapers, and onesies (Facebook)
- A new car seat to bring the baby home safely (Integrated Project Management)
- An added bonus to parents whose child is adopted (Deloitte)

For Parents with Older Kids
- A gift certificate on every child's birthday (Studer Group)
- Time off for first day of kindergarten and first grade, as well as for Parent-teacher conferences (Spokane Teachers Credit Union)
- A wall at the office dedicated to the artwork of employees' children (Alston & Bird)
- An annual scholarship to high-achieving students (Badger Mining Corporation)
- Inviting employees' children to design the company holiday card (Integrity Applications Incorporated)

Employees want to feel proud of their organization. When a company goes out of its way to recognize their efforts while helping them look good in front of loved ones, the experience of pride is a natural outcome.

And, as many companies that apply these family-oriented techniques are discovering, the value these benefits provide often extends beyond growing employee pride. In many cases, they also prompt employees' spouses, family, and friends to speak glowingly about a company, elevating an organization's reputation within the community and paving the way for it to attract future talent.

THE WRONG WAY TO BUILD PRIDE

Not everything a company can do to elevate employees' status is worth doing. In fact, some steps are surprisingly counterproductive.

Take job titles, for example.

Suppose you've set aside funding for a new sales position at your company. You've got the perfect candidate in mind and call to offer her the job. After you've finished describing the position, she asks you a question you haven't quite considered: What will be her title?

You take a moment to think through the options. On the one hand, "sales associate" is technically accurate, though not particularly glamorous. Then there's "director of sales," which is far more distinguished, but also something of a stretch. This is your company's first full-time sales position, meaning the only person your new employee will be directing is herself.

Still, you can't help but wonder whether the pride she'll experience at having a director-level position might motivate her to work harder, turning her into a better salesperson.

It's a reasonable assumption. Unfortunately, the research suggests it's also wrong.

Studies show that when employees receive an unearned job title, they do experience an immediate boost in satisfaction—exactly as we would expect. Their elevated status even leads to a brief uptick in performance. But it doesn't last. After a short interval, something funny happens. They grow dissatisfied and their job performance slides.

The reason? They start feeling underpaid.

"Job title inflation," as it's termed by human resource experts, is everywhere—from the "director of first impressions" greeting you at reception to the countless vice presidents occupying corner offices on every floor. Management professor Arthur Martinez argues that job inflation comes in two major varieties: *covert deception* and *overt flouts*.

Covert deceptions are often used by businesses looking to elevate the status of their employees in the eyes of their clients. The higher the title of an organization's representative, the thinking goes, the more attention their client feels they are receiving. It's a risky strategy. Some clients fall for it. Others eventually come to wonder about an organization's integrity. (As do, one would imagine, the employees themselves.)

Another reason organizations use covert title inflation: as a substitute for compensation. When a company can't afford (or decides against) paying its employees the salaries they deserve, it can attempt to mollify them with fancy titles.

It tends to backfire. As we've seen, inflating job titles can sow the seeds for later dissatisfaction—especially in the Internet age, when anyone with a smartphone can access the average salary for their position within seconds. The moment employees discover that they're being underpaid is the moment their trust begins to waver. Ironically, the lasting impact of an inflated job title is that it enhances the appeal of an employee's résumé when he enters the job market, making him more likely to find an alternative position.

Unlike covert deceptions, overt flouts are far more benign. They involve creative and occasionally sarcastic representations of the employee's role. Starbucks has baristas, Apple has geniuses, and Subway has sandwich artists. Technically they're all customer service workers—but that's not the way their organizations want employees or customers viewing these roles. The titles highlight that these positions require knowledge and specialized skills.

It's an approach that's not limited to the service industry. Over the years, *Fast Company* has run several features on the emergence of unorthodox corporate job titles. The list includes:

- Idea ambassador (for an account executive at a marketing firm)
- Chief detonator (for a public relations specialist)
- Minister of comedy (for a liaison tasked with helping executives prepare PowerPoint presentations)

Are these titles effective?

Creative job titles can certainly attract attention and build enthusiasm for a role, particularly among younger, less experienced employees. When you're entering the labor market fresh out of school, a new job represents more than just a paycheck—it signifies a new identity. To the extent that unusual job titles help newer employees better understand their roles within a company, they are likely to help.

But among seasoned employees whose credibility is already established, unusual titles are unlikely to foster the same degree of pride. It's one thing to be a few months out of college and carrying a business card that says "Marketing Rockstar." It's another to be on the verge of retirement and introducing yourself at cocktail parties and networking events as the "VP of awesome."

WHEN PRIDE MAKES YOU *LESS* SUCCESSFUL

I have a confession to make. So far in this chapter, I've presented pride in a uniformly positive light, implying that it can do nothing but good for an organization.

That's not entirely true.

Psychologists argue that pride comes in two forms: the positive, achievement-oriented pride we've discussed until this point, known as *authentic pride*; and a darker, more narcissistic version, called *hubristic pride*. It's this latter version that Dante referred to as the most lethal of the seven deadly sins. Chinese philosopher Lao Tzu put it this way: "Those who glorify themselves have no merit; those who are proud of themselves do not last."

Is pride good or bad for us? The answer depends on the type of pride we're experiencing.

When our pride is authentic, we don't feel the need to boast, act cocky, or show off. We become more confident and altruistic, growing our status not by dominating others but by sharing our knowledge and earning others' respect.

Hubristic pride, on the other hand, leads to an entirely different set of outcomes. Instead of acting humble, we do the opposite, shouting our pride from the rooftops. Research shows that people who score higher on measures of hubristic pride tend to be less cooperative, more aggressive, and ironically, more prone to experiencing shame. They are also more likely to rely on force and intimidation as strategies for building their status, which complicates their relationships and causes them to be disliked.

What leads people to experience authentic versus hubristic pride? Much of it has to do with the way they interpret the causes for their success.

When something good happens to you—say, winning a promotion at work—there are a number of explanations you can give for that achievement. On the one hand, you might think, "I got promoted because I am talented." Or you might say, "I got promoted because I've worked hard to keep up on the latest industry trends."

There's a subtle difference in these explanations that can have a profound impact on our experience.

Here's why. The first interpretation—*I am talented*—implies that success is a matter of ability rather than effort. You received a promotion because of who you are, not because of what you did. The second interpretation—*I've worked hard*—implies the opposite: Namely, that success is a matter of effort, not ability. Here, you've earned that promotion because of a specific course of action that you chose to implement. From this perspective, your success is a direct result of your hard work.

Studies indicate that it's this latter interpretation—the one that's grounded in the belief that success is about what you do, not who you are—that fosters genuine pride. Conversely, when we view getting ahead as a matter of ability, we're more likely to experience the less assured, hubristic pride.

It's because the belief that success is a matter of talent can actually feel quite threatening. It means that you possess limited control over outcomes in life. Either you have what it takes, or you don't. No wonder hubristic pride leads to bombastic displays of self-promotion—it's as if by convincing others of our virtues we hope to simultaneously diminish our own insecurity.

There's an important lesson here about fostering the right kind of pride in the workplace. When good news reaches an organization, it's often the leaders at the top who hear it first. What this research suggests is that the way they talk about their team's victory can have a powerful impact on the type of pride that's experienced.

Highlighting the specific actions that precipitated a major achievement ("We really did our homework before heading into this presentation") is likely to foster more genuine pride than boasting about a group's ability ("This proves we've got more talent in this building than any other firm").

This approach can be a lot more difficult than it seems. When good things happen, we want to express pride in our team and recognize how much talent they have. But the research indicates that emphasizing ability at the expense of effort can come with a price.

The more pride people take in who they are, the less focused they are on the behaviors that actually help them succeed.

The Lessons of Pride
Action Items for Managers

Elevate their status. We take pride in groups that enhance our perceived standing compared to others. For employees to feel pride in their workplace, they need to believe that their organization makes them look smart, accomplished, or giving. Emphasizing past achievements, having an ambitious vision for the future, and delivering tangible benefits to the community can all foster pride by helping employees view their affiliation with a company as a boon to their social status.

Look to the past, not just the future. While a "big hairy audacious goal" can inspire hard work, so too can a deeper understanding of an organization's past achievements. In the world of business, it's tempting to focus all of your attention on what's next. But research suggests that by helping your team reflect on how you got here can boost their motivation and make them more successful.

Publicize ownership. Rather than allowing employees to hide behind the anonymity of their company, put them front and center by advertising their role as contributors. Some managers believe that highlighting employees fosters egotism and diverts attention away from the company brand. Taken to extremes, it can. But anonymity is worse. Requiring people to attach their name to their work leads them to feel more connected to their product, and enables them to experience a greater sense of pride when they succeed.

The Lessons of Pride
Action Items for Emerging Leaders

Ask about your company history. Learning your organizational history can help you better understand your current role and reveal a great deal about the perspectives of the people running your company. I've worked with several companies where no one knew precisely how the organization had come to exist, with the exception of the person who happened to be running it. Asking leaders to share your company's history doesn't just provide you with good information. It also strengthens the bond between you and those at the top.

Plant the seed for pride-boosting narratives in the minds of your coworkers. Instead of complimenting colleagues the next time they score a big win, ask them how they managed to be so effective. Your question will direct their attention to the work they did and the sacrifices they made. At the same time, when praise is framed as a question, it makes it easier for people to accept your compliment without the awkwardness of appearing conceited.

Build a bridge between your workplace and the greater good. Many organizations make financial contributions to charitable causes without involving their employees. Often, it's not that they don't want the input. It just never occurred to them to ask. Consider asking your management team if they would accept nominations from you and your coworkers, and perhaps be open to a vote. If it works, you might suggest using the same process for pro bono work. When decisions on group giving are reached collectively, it's easier for everyone to take pride in the outcome, knowing that they've all played a role.

Three Keys to Creating an Extraordinary Workplace

Every year or so, the Gallup organization releases a poll on employee engagement that inspires the collective hand-wringing of news anchors and editorial writers around the country.

The results are as predictable as they are bleak. The latest figures indicate that a full 70 percent of American employees feel disengaged at their jobs. Of these, 18 percent are "actively disengaged," meaning that they're not simply failing to meet their potential—they're acting out in ways that measurably damage their company. Some are more flagrant than others. They call in sick regularly or voice negative attitudes with colleagues. Then there are those who take out their frustrations on customers. According to Gallup's estimates, disengaged employees cost American businesses a striking amount: up to $550 billion each year.

Even more alarming, America's workforce is nowhere near the bottom when it comes to workplace engagement. A 2010 study spanning 120 countries found that, internationally, 84 percent of employees are disengaged at work.

You would think Gallup's data would incite a major workplace overhaul—that business leaders would laser in on employee engagement with all the urgency and resolve they'd devote to a manufacturing flaw. Except that's not what's happened. Gallup's data suggest that practically nothing has changed since it began tracking employee engagement near the turn of the twenty-first century. In 2012, 30 percent of American employees were engaged at their job. A decade prior, that number was *exactly* the same.

What are we to make of the lack of progress when it comes to raising employee engagement?

One possibility is that there still exist many businesses that don't recognize the value of engaged employees. Certain industries—like technology, for instance—are more attuned to the connection between engagement and performance. But they're the exceptions. Others still lag far behind.

While it's true that some sectors place greater value on employee engagement than others, this is unlikely to be the reason Gallup's numbers have remained flat. Awareness that engaged employees are more productive is growing, and no one is promoting the opposite view. Even if only a small percentage of businesses were focused on lifting employee engagement, we should still see some increase in the overall figures, especially over the lengthy span of a full decade.

A second possibility is that turbulent economic factors have made it difficult to increase employee engagement over the last decade. We have, after all, just experienced a deep recession that left many businesses financially strapped. It is challenging for organizations to devote resources to their workplace experience when they are doing all they can just to stay afloat.

But this explanation is also not very satisfying. After all, the economy was performing admirably before the housing bubble burst. Yet Gallup's data show that in 2007—the same year the stock market reached its highest level in six years—employee engagement remained stuck at 30 percent.

At the same time, if businesses viewed employee engagement as an investment in future earnings, wouldn't they do everything possible to build engagement, regardless of economic conditions?

The better answer is that organizational leaders *have* tried to increase employee engagement but that they've gone about it the wrong way. In part, it's because of the continued overreliance on salaries, titles, corner offices, and many of the other short-term boosts we've examined in this book that make long-term engagement so difficult to sustain. As Jim Harter, Gallup's chief scientist for workplace management and well-being, put it, "There is a gap between knowing about engagement and doing something about it in most American workplaces."

This is where the science can help.

As we've seen throughout this book, research is now shedding light on practical methods that any organization can use to improve its workplace. We now have a rich and growing understanding of the conditions that promote intrinsic motivation, spark creativity, and enhance performance. No longer do we need to guess about ways of fostering colleague relationships, building a positive emotional climate, or instilling a sense of pride.

At the beginning of this book, I mentioned that I don't think there exists a one-size-fits-all recipe for a great workplace. And, after wading through thousands of journal articles and academic books, that's a conclusion I continue to support. There's no *one* right way of operating an organization. Managing a law practice is not the same thing as running a bakery. Even within the same industry, the challenges facing a small business differ vastly from those of a multinational corporation. The workplace is just too complex to be reduced to a simple formula.

That is why this book has not offered a single, homogenous approach. Instead it has provided a framework for understanding the needs of employees and options for experimenting with proven techniques.

That said, if you step back and take a broader view of the suggestions in this book, you may notice that certain themes emerge. These are not simply a random blend of research findings. There is a pattern to the recommendations.

Here are the three overarching lessons of *The Best Place to Work*:

LESSON 1: PSYCHOLOGICAL NEEDS ARE AT THE HEART OF EMPLOYEE ENGAGEMENT

How do you get employees engaged in their work? By providing opportunities for them to experience autonomy, competence, and relatedness on a daily basis.

Here's a quick recap of how to make that happen. Employees experience autonomy when they have a sense of choice on the job. To promote autonomy, provide a rationale when tasks are presented, offer flexibility on how and when a task is performed, and minimize the focus on rewards. You can also grow autonomy by providing employees with options on where to do their work. That can mean creating a variety of settings within an office, or it can mean allowing them the option of occasionally working from home, a coffee shop, or the beach.

How do you help employees feel competent? By creating a workplace that provides them with immediate feedback, meaningful recognition, and opportunities for growth. Ensuring that employees experience competence at work is critical to sustaining their interest, but it's not necessarily enough. Also important is empowering them to find new challenges to master. This is one reason why allowing for the occasional failure is so important. When we're terrified of making mistakes, we stop searching for new ways of developing our competence. And when our workplace no longer satisfies our need for competence, it's just a matter of time before our engagement drops.

Within the business world, relatedness has long been the most underappreciated of the three psychological needs. But as we saw in Chapter 5, connecting employees to one another doesn't just help them enjoy being at work, it leads to quantifiable gains in their performance.

To build employee connections, it's important to create interactions that harness the natural catalysts of close relationships: *proximity*, *familiarity*, *similarity*, and *self-disclosure*. You can do that by designing an extended onboarding process with an eye toward sparking friendships, by offering nonwork activities that allow colleagues to collaborate on superordinate goals, and by building communal spaces that create opportunities for coworkers to bond, even when they're not talking about work.

LESSON 2: ORGANIZATIONS ARE MORE SUCCESSFUL WHEN THEY ADDRESS THE LIMITS OF THE MIND AND BODY

Throughout this book we encountered many limitations of the human condition. We learned that our concentration dips every afternoon, that it takes us a long time to regain our focus after even a brief interruption, and that our problem-solving skills decline when we're overloaded with stress.

Our brains have limited mental bandwidth, and when the cognitive resources we have are depleted—whether because we're surrounded by a hectic office environment, inundated with too many requests, or working continuously without a break—our mood sours and our performance slumps.

Instead of ignoring the body's limitations and insisting that employees power through periods of low energy, organizations are far better off designing workspaces that allow employees to conserve their existing mental resources and offering them opportunities for restocking their energy supply when they are running low.

Depending on the type of work an organization does, for some workplaces that can mean creating a range of "caves and campfires" that empower employees to choose an environment best suited to the nature of their task. For others, it can mean allowing employees to exercise, play, and occasionally nap, even on company time. In all cases, access to natural sunlight, a personalized workspace, healthy snacks, and restorative experiences can help.

As we saw in Chapter 3, in the past the amount of time employees spent on the factory floor was directly tied to their level of productivity. Today, sitting in front of our computers is no longer predictive of quality work. Some of our best contributions come when we're away from our desks, distracting ourselves and allowing disparate ideas to meld.

A related observation can be made for client-facing employees. When we're low on energy, we have a harder time connecting with customers and risk spreading negative emotions. Regardless of whether your work involves thinking up big ideas or answering phones at reception, having more mental energy can help.

The nature of work is changing. What might have once appeared to traditional managers as wasted time can today be an important key to delivering high-level performance.

LESSON 3: INTEGRATING WORK AND FAMILY LIFE IMPROVES THE QUALITY OF BOTH

Back when I was looking to enter the corporate world, a number of organizations I interviewed with highlighted their commitment to "work-life balance" as a selling point. It sounded nice. It just never materialized.

At most organizations, the idea of work-life balance is a myth. Over the past two decades, our personal lives have come under siege. It began with the advent of e-mail in the mid-1990s and accelerated rapidly with the explosion of smartphones a decade later. Today, home is rarely off-limits from the office. In a growing number of work-places, it has become an unspoken expectation that employees remain connected and on call during evenings and weekends.

The reality, of course, is that standout employees are working around the clock, even when they're not corresponding after hours. They're continuously plotting ahead and thinking up new ideas while showering, driving their kids to gymnastics, or drifting off to sleep.

Instead of pretending that work and personal time are separate, one of the lessons of this book is that organizations are better off when they actively seek to blend the two worlds. Earlier we saw the merits of including employees' significant others in after-work activities as a means of deepening workplace friendships. We examined the value of using the workplace as a vehicle for connecting employees to nonprofits in their communities. And we looked at how expressing appreciation directly to an employee's family can influence their company pride.

We live in a world in which it is acceptable for work to interrupt personal time. And yet we're not as comfortable when personal time interrupts work. Why? When organizations trust employees to manage their time responsibly, making it acceptable for a worker to take an hour during the day to watch his daughter's soccer game, they create loyalty and commitment that ends up *saving* them money in the long term.

The future of great workplaces lies in helping employees fuse their personal and professional lives in ways that position them to deliver their best work.

CREATING AN EXTRAORDINARY WORKPLACE

While writing this book, I've often wondered what the modern workplace would look like if the factory had never been invented. If we were building a workplace today from scratch, would we still demand that all employees "clock in" at the same time, or insist they "man their stations" for eight-hour shifts, or promote the notion that good employees take their orders from a manager?

And yet we do.

We now have striking proof that many aspects of the modern workplace are outdated, counterproductive, and even psychologically harmful. Which is why it should surprise no one when Gallup reports that over 80 percent of employees worldwide are disengaged. They're working within structures that make it nearly impossible to thrive.

Fortunately, we now have evidence-based techniques for creating a better workplace. As I hope this book has demonstrated, there are practical steps any organization can take to elevate their workplace experience.

When we fulfill employees' needs for autonomy, competence, and relatedness, when we allow them to leverage the full breadth of their mental capacity, when we provide them with the flexibility to succeed in both their personal and professional lives, we achieve more than an extraordinary workplace.

We create an organization that performs at its very best.

ACKNOWLEDGMENTS

A little while after my wife and I had our first child, a political consultant I know shared this gem of an insight: "The only reason people agree to have children," he declared with unwavering certainty, "is that they're too naive to appreciate what they're really getting themselves into."

While some of us might argue that he was selling parenthood short, I'm pretty sure his analysis was dead on when it comes to writing your first book. Fortunately, I've also discovered that writing a book and raising a child bear one other similarity. In both cases, good friends and a forgiving spouse can help see you through.

Over the years, I've been fortunate to have met a number of outstanding educators whose passion, generosity, and authenticity have been a steady source of inspiration. For that I'd like to thank Brooklyn College's Dr. Benzion Chanowitz, Skidmore College's Dr. Sheldon Solomon, and the University of Rochester's Dr. Andrew Elliot, Dr. Edward Deci, Dr. Richard Ryan, Dr. Harry Reis, and Dr. Miron Zuckerman.

Many friends, researchers, and executives generously reviewed portions of this book, providing suggestions that improved the final product exponentially: Dr. Art Aron, Dr. Peter Caprariello, Dr. Cheryl Carmichael, Dr. Edward Deci, Dr. Andrew Elliot, Dr. Jim Fryer, Timothy Harrington, Craig Herman, Jon Iuzzini, Dr. Karen Jehn, James Masciale, Mike Ofsowitz, Paul Nunes, Dr. Harry Reis, Nikil Saval, Dr. Dean Simonton, and Dr. Marina Tasopoulous-Chan. Dr. Susan Thompson deserves her own line because her comments were so comprehensive and insightful that she practically served as a freelance editor.

Thank you to Tufts University's Dr. Laurie Charles, Jacob Illustration's

Gary Jacobs, Northeastern University's Dr. Dinesh John, Buffalo Philharmonic Orchestra's Megan Prokes, and Relationship Centered Health Care's Dr. Anthony Suchman for agreeing to be interviewed. I hope I have done your insights justice; they were invaluable.

I am grateful to FullContact's Bart Lorang, Google's Katelin Jabbari, Harvard Medical School's Dr. John Ratey, London Business School's Dr. Julian Birkinshaw, UCLA's Dr. J. David Craswell, and Wright State University's Dr. Rosemary Ramsey for taking the time to contribute via e-mail.

Authors Charles Benoit, Dr. David Burkus, and Dr. Art Markman were kind enough to tell me about their experiences writing their books. These conversations were profoundly helpful. A special thanks to psychologist Sonja Lyubomirsky for sharing her prospectus for *The How of Happiness*, giving me my first glimpse of a successful book proposal.

Alia Macrina and Sahil Koul assisted in transforming an intimidating stack of books, articles, and printouts into a reference section. Thank you for your help.

Thank you to Joel Benenson, Larry and Judy Katzman, Matthew McKeveny, Tina Olechowski, soon-to-be Dr. Suzanne Piotrowski, Kevin Ryan, Alan Sclar, Anthony Weiner, and Miranda Wilcox for being some of the smartest people I know.

Thank you to Sean Blanda, Erin Collier, Jocelyn Glei, Sarah Green, Lybi Ma, and Jennifer Rooney for featuring my work on your websites before the publication of this book.

If you are scanning this section for the name of a sensational literary agent specializing in books on business or psychology, look no further. His name is Giles Anderson. You can visit him at andersonliteraryagency .com. He is an extraordinary resource who does so much more for his authors than simply place their books that the title of literary agent fails to do him justice.

Giles introduced me to John Duff, a brilliant editor who heads Perigee Books, a division of Penguin Random House. John's advice before I began writing ("people will read the statistics, but they'll remember the stories" and "perhaps you could mention a few action items at the end of each chapter") shaped my plan for this book. Later on his feedback and suggestions elevated the final product in every way. Thank you, John. And thank you to members of John's remarkable team, especially art director Lisa Amoroso, senior publicist Lindsey Ruthen, executive director of publicity Brianna Yamashita, and editorial assistant Amanda Shih.

I am forever grateful to my family. To my parents, who don't quite understand what I do, but have remained quiet anyway; to my children, Madeleine, seven, and Henry, two, who endured subpar parenting for over a year and pretended not to notice; and to my implausibly supportive wife, Anna, whose inspirational mantra of "finish already" helped steer this work to its conclusion.

NOTES

Introduction: A Tale of Two Menus

ix **Story of Irfan Dama:** I am grateful to Google's Global Communications and Public Affairs manager Katelin Jabbari for helping me flesh out the details of this story. For photos of Chef Dama's dishes and a sample menu, see Trevor Fletch, "Lunch at Google HQ Is as Insanely Awesome as You Thought," *Serious Eats*, January 8, 2014, available at: www.seriouseats.com/2014/01/lunch-at-google -insanely-awesome-as-you-thought.html.

x **The employee benefits at Google:** See Adam Lashinsky, "The Perks of Being a Googler," *Fortune* (CNNMoney.com), accessed May 23, 2014, available at: http:// money.cnn.com/galleries/2007/fortune/0701/gallery.Google_perks; "Inside Google's Kitchens," *Gourmet*, March 7, 2012, available at: www.gourmet.com/food/gour metlive/2012/030712/inside-googles-kitchens; "Inside the Googleplex," *Economist*, August 30, 2007; Jonathan Strickland, "How the Googleplex Works," HowStuffWorks.com, accessed May 9, 2014, available at: http://computer.how stuffworks.com/googleplex.htm; Rob Waugh, "Putting Greens, Basketball Courts and Private Gardens; Google Offers Rare Glimpse Inside Its Californian 'Google- plex' HQ," *Daily Mail*, February 12, 2012, available at: www.dailymail.co.uk/ sciencetech/article-2100879/Google-offers-rare-glimpse-inside-California -Googleplex-headquarters.html; Olivia Wu, "How Google's Cooking / Internet Giant's Free, Gourmet Global Cuisine Powers Its Workforce While Offering Chefs and Producers a Place to Shine," *San Francisco Chronicle*, March 1, 2006, available at: www.sfgate.com/recipes/article/Now-Google-s-cooking-Internet-giant-s-free -2502994.php.

x **The employee benefits at SAS:** See Marc C. Crowley, "How SAS Became the World's Best Place to Work," *Fast Company*, January 22, 2013, available at: www .fastcompany.com/3004953/how-sas-became-worlds-best-place-work; David A. Kaplan, "SAS: A New No. 1 Best Employer," *Fortune* (CNNMoney.com), January 22, 2010, available at: http://money.cnn.com/2010/01/21/technology/sas_best_companies .fortune.

x The employee benefits at Facebook: See Luke Stangel, "Facebook's 12 Most Fantastic Employee Perks," *Silicon Valley Business Journal*, April 8, 2013, available at: www.bizjournals.com/sanjose/news/2013/04/03/facebooks-12-most-fantastic-employee.html?page=all.

xi The employee benefits at Wegmans: See Jillian Berman, "Wegmans Improves Its Bottom Line by Helping Employees Shrink Their Waistlines," *Huffington Post*, August 5, 2013, available at: www.huffingtonpost.com/2013/08/05/wegmans-wellness_n_3696411.html; Wegmans also provides a compressive list of benefits at: www.wegmans.com/webapp/wcs/stores/servlet/CategoryDisplay?categoryId=284278&storeId=10052&langId=-1.

xi Happiness doesn't cost their company money—it ensures they stay on top: Within the workplace literature a distinction is made among the phrases "employee happiness," "employee satisfaction," and "employee engagement." They are not one and the same. However, for the sake of simplicity I use the term "happiness" in this chapter because satisfied and engaged employees tend to be happy.

xi The advantages of having happy employees: See Stephane Cote, "Affect and Performance in Organizational Settings," *Current Directions in Psychological Science* 8, no. 2 (1999): 65–68; James K. Harter, Frank L. Schmidt, and Corey L. Keyes, "Well-Being in the Workplace and Its Relationship to Business Outcomes: A Review of the Gallup Studies," in *Flourishing: The Positive Person and the Good Life*, eds. Corey. L. Keyes and Jonathan Haidt (Washington, DC: American Psychological Association, 2002), 205–224; Sonja Lyubomirsky, Laura King, and Ed Diener, "The Benefits of Frequent Positive Affect: Does Happiness Lead to Success?" *Psychological Bulletin* 131, no. 6 (2005): 803–855.

xi Research conducted by the Great Place to Work Institute: See "What Are the Benefits?" *GreatPlaceToWork.com*, accessed May 9, 2014, available at: www.greatplacetowork.com/our-approach/what-are-the-benefits-great-workplaces.

xi Parnassus Investments: See Mark C. Crowley, "The Proof Is in the Profits: America's Happiest Companies Make More Money," *Fast Company*, February 22, 2013, available at: www.fastcompany.com/3006150/proof-profits-americas-happiest-companies-also-fare-best-financially.

Chapter 1: Success Is Overrated

3 The story of Silas Johnson: See Angela Accomando, "HOMETOWNS: Si Street—Major-Leaguer Johnson Still a Prominent Sheridan Name," *The Times* (blog), July 30, 2010, available at: www.mywebtimes.com/life/hometowns-si-street—major-leaguer-johnson-still/article_10dedb2a-f2ff-56b2-9f7e-6b5eb1741124.html; David Craft, "Silas 'Si' Johnson: Pitcher, Coach, Fan," *Sports Collectors Digest*, January 19, 1990, 210; Mike Cunniff, "Area Native Played Ball with the Babe," *Ottawa Daily Times*, June 9, 1992; Mal Florence, "Striking Out the

Babe Wasn't as Big by Then," *Los Angeles Times*, April 22, 1992, available at: http://articles.latimes.com/1992-04-22/sports/sp-354_1_babe-ruth; Mark Mandernach, "The Day the Bambino Bombed," *SI Vault*, June 14, 1993, available at: http://si.com/vault/article/magazine/MAG1138666/index.htm.

5 The story of Albert Ellis: See *The Albert Ellis Reader: A Guide to Well-Being Using Rational Emotive Behavior Therapy*, eds. Shawn Blau and Albert Ellis (Secaucus, NJ: Carol Publishing Group, 1998); Matt Dobkin, "Behaviorists Behaving Badly," *New York* magazine, October 31, 2005, available at: http://nymag.com/nymetro/news/people/features/14947/; Michael T. Kaufman, "Albert Ellis, 93, Influential Psychotherapist, Dies," *New York Times*, July 25, 2007, available at: www.nytimes.com/2007/07/25/nyregion/25ellis.html?pagewanted=all&_r=0; Anthony Ramirez, "Despite Illness and Lawsuits, a Famed Psychotherapist Is Temporarily Back in Session," *New York Times*, December 9, 2006, available at: www.nytimes.com/2006/12/10/nyregion/10ellis.html?_r=0.

8 The work of Dean Keith Simonton: See Dean Keith Simonton, "Career Landmarks in Science: Individual Differences and Interdisciplinary Contrasts," *Developmental Psychology* 27, no. 1 (1991): 23119–130; Dean Keith Simonton, "Creative Productivity: A Predictive and Explanatory Model of Career Trajectories and Landmarks," *Psychological Review* 104, no. 1 (1997): 66–89; Dean Keith Simonton, "Developments as Acquired Expertise: Theoretical Issues and an Empirical Test," *Developmental Review* 20 (2000): 238–318; Dean Keith Simonton, *Origins of Genius: Darwinian Perspectives on Creativity* (New York: Oxford University Press, 1999).

10 Thomas Edison: See Paul Israel, *Edison: A Life of Invention* (New York: John Wiley, 1998); Michael Peterson, "Thomas Edison, Failure," *American Heritage of Invention and Technology* 6 (Winter 1991): 8–14.

10 Steve Jobs: See Walter Isaacson, *Steve Jobs* (New York: Simon & Schuster, 2011); Nick Schulz, "Steve Jobs: America's Greatest Failure," *National Review Online*, August 25, 2011, available at: www.nationalreview.com/articles/275528/steve-jobs-america-s-greatest-failure-nick-schulz; Peter Sims, "Five of Steve Jobs's Biggest Mistakes," *Harvard Business Review Blog*, January 21, 2013, available at: http://blogs.hbr.org/2013/01/five-of-steve-jobss-biggest-mi/.

10 Babe Ruth on batting .600: Quoted in Russell Roberts, *Stolen!: A History of Base Stealing* (Jefferson, NC: McFarland, 1999), 71.

10 Career strikeout mark: See "Career Leaders & Records for Strikeouts," Baseball-Reference.com, accessed May 19, 2014, available at: www.baseball-reference.com/leaders/SO_career.shtml.

11 Kobe Bryant: See "Lakers News: Kobe Sets NBA Record for Most Career Misses," LakersNation.com, January 10, 2013, available at: www.lakersnation.com/lakers-news-kobe-sets-nba-record-for-most-career-misses/2013/01/10/.

11 **Brett Favre:** See "NFL Career Passes Intercepted Leaders," Pro-Football-Reference
.com, accessed May 19, 2014, available at: www.pro-football-reference.com/lead
ers/pass_int_career.htm.

11 **Wayne Gretzky:** See Daniel Coyle, *The Little Book of Talent: 52 Tips for Improving
Skills* (New York: Bantam Books, 2012). Also see Daniel Coyle, *The Talent Code:
Greatness Isn't Born: It's Grown, Here's How* (New York: Bantam Books, 2009).

11 **Eric Schmidt on Google Wave:** See Ina Fried, "Eric Schmidt on the Demise of
Google Wave," CNET News, August 4, 2010, available at: www.cnet.com/news/
eric-schmidt-on-the-demise-of-google-wave/.

12 **The story of Sara Blakely:** See Alexandra Jacobs, "Smooth Moves: How Sara
Blakely Rehabilitated the Girdle," *New Yorker*, March 28, 2011, available at: www.
newyorker.com/reporting/2011/03/28/110328fa_fact_jacobs?currentPage=all;
Stacy Perman, "How Failure Molded Spanx's Founder," *BusinessWeek*, November
21, 2007, available at: www.businessweek.com/stories/2007-11-21/how-failure-
molded-spanxs-founderbusinessweek-business-news-stock-market-and-financial-
advice; Beth Silcox, "Success Stories—Sara Blakely, Improving Her Assets," *Success*
magazine, March 30, 2009, available at: www.success.com/article/success-stories-
sara-blakely. An outtake of Sara Blakely's interview with Anderson Cooper is
available at: www.youtube.com/watch?v=DT-5Ni-jtHY and her keynote at *Inc.*
magazine's 2011 Women Summit is available at: www.inc.com/sara-blakely/the
-spanx-story-how-sara-blakely-turned-footless-pantyhose-into-a-business.html.

14 **Edward Burger:** See Edward Burger, "Teaching to Fail," *Inside Higher Ed*, August
12, 2012, available at: www.insidehighered.com/views/2012/08/21/essay-importance
-teaching-failure#sthash.uWRzlyUz.dpbs; Stephen Spencer Davis, "Star Math
Teacher Applies the Power of Failure, Squared," *Globe and Mail*, August 31, 2012,
available at: www.theglobeandmail.com/life/parenting/back-to-school/star-math
-teacher-applies-the-power-of-failure-squared/article4513390/.

16 **Remote Associates Test:** The items included in this book represent a modified
version of the original RAT, which is now a bit outdated. To learn more about the
original RAT, see Sarnoff Mednick, "The Associative Basis of the Creative Process," *Psychological Review* 69, no. 3 (1962): 220–32; and Sarnoff A. Mednick and
Martha T. Mednick, *Examiner's Manual, Remote Associates Test: College and Adult
Forms 1 and 2* (Boston: Houghton Mifflin, 1967).

16 **Approach and avoidance motivation:** Worth noting, while the influence of
avoidance on creativity tends to be negative, at times, there can be moderators of
this effect. For a comprehensive review, see Andrew J. Elliot, *Handbook of Approach
and Avoidance Motivation* (New York: Psychology Press, 2008).

17 **Pychologist Mark Seery:** Because Seery's experiment was not hypothetical and
involved many subjects, a five-dollar reward for every correct response would have
been costly. He therefore used the more modest amount of fifty cents, which in

some ways makes his results all the more compelling. The study is reported in Mark D. Seery, Max Weisbuch, and Jim Blascovich, "Something to Gain, Something to Lose: The Cardiovascular Consequences of Outcome Framing," *International Journal of Psychophysiology* 73, no. 3 (2009): 308–12.

18 **Robert Sapolsky:** See Robert M. Sapolsky, *Why Zebras Don't Get Ulcers: A Guide to Stress, Stress Related Diseases, and Coping* (New York: W. H. Freeman, 1994).

18 **"Necessity Is the Mother of Invention":** See Marieke Roskes, Carsten K. W. De Dreu, and Bernard A. Nijstad, "Necessity Is the Mother of Invention: Avoidance Motivation Stimulates Creativity Through Cognitive Effort," *Journal of Personality and Social Psychology* 103, no. 2 (2012): 242–56. For more on the relationship between psychological states and creativity, see Kris Byron and Shalini Khazanchi, "Rewards and Creative Performance: A Meta-Analytic Test of Theoretically Derived Hypotheses," *Psychological Bulletin* 138, no. 4 (2012): 809–30; Kristin Byron, Shalini Khazanchi, and Deborah Nazarian, "The Relationship Between Stressor and Creativity: A Meta-Analysis Examining Competing Theoretical Models," *Journal of Applied Psychology* 95, no. 1 (2010): 201–12; Ronald S. Friedman and Jens Forster, "The Influence of Approach and Avoidance Motor Actions on Creative Cognition," *Journal of Experimental Social Psychology* 38 (2002): 41–55; Jens Forster, Nira Liberman, and Oren Shapira, "Preparing for Novel Versus Familiar Events: Shifts in Global and Local Processing," *Journal of Experimental Psychology: General* 138, no. 3 (2012): 383–99; Karen Gasper, "When Necessity Is the Mother of Invention: Mood and Problem Solving," *Journal of Experimental Social Psychology* 39, no. 3 (2003): 248–62; Klodiana Lanaj, Chu-Hsiang Chang, and Russell Johnson, "Regulatory Focus and Work-related Outcomes: A Review and Meta-Analysis," *Psychological Bulletin* 138, no. 5 (2012): 998–1034.

19 **Amy Edmondson:** See Amy C. Edmondson, "Learning from Mistakes Is Easier Said Than Done: Group and Organizational Influences on the Detection and Correction of Human Error," *Journal of Applied Behavioral Science* 32, no. 1 (1996): 5–28; Amy C. Edmondson, "Teamwork on the Fly," *Harvard Business Review* 90, no. 4 (April 2012): 72–80; Amy C. Edmondson, "Strategies for Learning from Failure," *Harvard Business Review* 89, no. 4 (April 2011): 48–55; Anita L. Tucker and Amy Edmondson, "Why Hospitals Don't Learn from Failures: Organizational and Psychological Dynamics That Inhibit System Change," *California Management Review* 45, no. 2 (2003): 1–18.

20 **The story of Amanda Zolten:** Adapted from Sue Shellenbarger, "Better Ideas Through Failure," *Wall Street Journal*, September 27, 2011, available at: http://on line.wsj.com/news/articles/SB10001424052970204010604576594671572584158.

21 **Rewarding employee failure:** See Leigh Buchanan, "Rethinking Employee Awards," *Inc.com* (July 2011), available at: www.inc.com/magazine/201107/rethink ing-employee-awards.html; Arlene Weintraub, "Is Merck's Medicine Working?"

BusinessWeek, July 29, 2007, available at: www.businessweek.com/stories/2007-07-29/ is-mercks-medicine-working; "Cultivating Business-Led Innovation," *Economist Intelligence Unit*, October 17, 2012, available at: www.oracle.com/us/products/ applications/eiu-oracle-bus-innovation-1867915.pdf.

22 **Failure CV:** See Julian Birkinshaw, "Taming Your Company's Most Elusive Beast," *Harvard Business Review Blog*, November 7, 2012, http://blogs.hbr.org/ 2012/11/three-rules-for-making-innovat/. In an e-mail exchange with Dr. Birkinshaw I learned that the source of this fascinating tidbit was former HCL Technologies CEO Vineet Nayar.

Chapter 2: The Power of Place

26 **Google, Intel, and Cisco:** See Adam Alter, "How to Build a Collaborative Office Space Like Pixar and Google," 99U.com, May 20, 2014, available at: http://99u .com/articles/16408/how-to-build-a-collaborative-office-space-like-pixar-and -google; Andrew Laing,"What Will the Future Workplace Look Like?" CNNMoney.com, January 19, 2011, available at: http://management.fortune.cnn .com/2011/01/19/what-will-the-future-workplace-look-like/; "Office Design Case Study: How Cisco Designed the Collaborative Connected Workplace Environment—Cisco on Cisco," Cisco.com, May 20, 2014, available at: www.cisco .com/web/about/ciscoitatwork/collaboration/connected_workplace_web.html; "Google Was Cubicle Land When We Started Designing Offices for Them," *Dezeen* magazine, March 17, 2014, available at: www.dezeen.com/2014/03/17/ office-design-google-clive-wilkinson-interview/; Kristina Shevory, "Office Work Space Is Shrinking, but That's Not All Bad," *New York Times*, January 19, 2011, available at: www.nytimes.com/2011/01/19/realestate/commercial/19space.html?_ r=0. For more on the history of office redesigns in the high tech industry, see John Markoff, "Where the Cubicle Is Dead," *New York Times*, April 25, 1993, available at: http://www.nytimes.com/1993/04/25/business/where-the-cubicle-is -dead.html.

26 **Consider a 2007 study:** See Joan Meyers Levy and Rui (Juliet) Zhu, "The Influence of Ceiling Height: The Effect of Priming on the Type of Processing That People Use," *Journal of Consumer Research* 34, no. 2 (2007): 174–86.

27 **Influence of color:** See Pam Belluck, "Reinvent Wheel? Blue Room. Defusing a Bomb? Red Room," *New York Times*, February 5, 2009, available at: www.nytimes .com/2009/02/06/science/06color.html; Andrew J. Elliot, Markus A. Maier, Arlen C. Moller, Ron Friedman, and Jörg Meinhardt, "Color and Psychological Functioning: The Effect of Red on Performance Attainment," *Journal of Experimental Psychology: General* 136, no. 1 (2007): 154–68; Ravi Mehta and Rui (Juliet) Zhu, "Blue or Red? Exploring the Effect of Color on Cognitive Task Performances," *Science* 323, no. 5918 (2009): 1226–29.

28 **Influence of sound:** See Ravi Mehta, Rui (Juliet) Zhu, and Amar Cheema, "Is Noise Always Bad? Exploring the Effects of Ambient Noise on Creative Cognition," *Journal of Consumer Research* 39, no. 4 (2012): 784–99; George Prochnik, "I'm Thinking. Please. Be Quiet," *New York Times*, August 24, 2013, available at: www.nytimes .com/2013/08/25/opinion/sunday/im-thinking-please-be-quiet.html?_r=0.

28 **Influence of furniture:** See Rui (Juliet) Zhu and Jennifer J. Argo, "Exploring the Impact of Various Shaped Seating Arrangements on Persuasion," *Journal of Consumer Research* 40, no. 2 (2013): 336–49.

29 **The story of Robert Propst:** See Yvonne Abraham, "The Man Behind the Cubicle," *Metropolis* (November 1998), available at: http://tds.ic.polyu.edu.hk/digital_ design/case_action_office/Metropolis%20Feature_%20The%20Man%20Behind% 20 the%20Cubicle.pdf; David Franz, "The Moral Life of Cubicles," *New Atlantis* (Winter 2008), available at: www.thenewatlantis.com/publications/the-moral -life-of-cubicles.; Marc Kristal, "An Idea Whose Time Has Come," *Metropolis* (June 2013), available at: www.metropolismag.com/June-2013/An-Idea-Whose-Time -Has-Come/; Robert Propst, *The Office, A Facility Based on Change* (Elmhurst, IL: Business Press, 1968); Julie Schlosser, "Trapped in Cubicles," *Fortune* (CNNMoney .com), March 22, 2006, available at: http://money.cnn.com/2006/03/09/magazines/ fortune/cubicle_howiwork_fortune/; Tim Sullivan, "Where Your Cubicle Came From," *Harvard Business Review Blog*, January 24, 2013, available at: http://blogs .hbr.org/2013/01/where-your-cubicle-came-from/. Finally, if you're interested in learning more about the history of office design, I highly recommend Nikil Saval's impressively comprehensive book *Cubed: A Secret History of the Workplace* (New York: Doubleday, 2014).

31 **Working in a cubicle:** See Matthew C. Davis, Desmond J. Leach, and Chris W. Clegg, "The Physical Environment of the Office: Contemporary and Emerging Issues," in *International Review of Industrial and Organizational Psychology*, Volume 26, eds. Gerald P. Hodgkinson and J. Kevin Ford (Chichester: Wiley-Blackwell, 2011), 193–235; Helena Jahncke, Staffan Hygge, Niklas Halin, Anne Marie Green, and Kenth Dimberg, "Open-Plan Office Noise: Cognitive Performance and Restoration," *Journal of Environmental Psychology* 31, no. 4 (2011): 373–82; Guy Newsham, Jay Brand, Cara Donnelly, Jennifer Veitch, Myriam Aries, and Kate Charles, "Linking Indoor Environment Conditions to Job Satisfaction: A Field Study," *Building Research and Information* 37, no. 2 (2009): 129–47; Jennifer Veitch, "Workplace Design Contributions to Mental Health and Well-Being," *Healthcare-Papers* 11 (2011): 38–46; Jacqueline C. Vischer, "The Effects of the Physical Environment on Job Performance: Towards a Theoretical Model of Workplace Stress," *Stress and Health* 23, issue 3 (2007): 175–84; Jacqueline C. Vischer, "Towards an Environmental Psychology of Workspace: How People Are Affected by Environments for Work," *Architectural Science Review* 51, no. 2 (2008): 97–108.

33 **Management Professor Anne-Laure Fayard:** See John Tierney, "From Cubi-
    cles, Cry for Quiet Pierces Office Buzz," *New York Times*, May 19, 2012, available
    at: www.nytimes.com/2012/05/20/science/when-buzz-at-your-cubicle-is-too-loud
    -for-work.html?pagewanted=all.

34 **Evolutionary psychology and design preferences:** See Sally Augustin, *Place
    Advantage: Applied Psychology for Interior Architecture* (Hoboken, NJ: John Wiley &
    Sons, 2009); Marc G. Berman, John Jonides, and Stephen Kaplan, "The Cogni-
    tive Benefits of Interacting with Nature," *Psychological Science* 19, no. 12 (2008):
    1207–212; Irving Biederman and Edward Vessel, "Perceptual Pleasure and the
    Brain," *American Scientist* 94 (2006): 249–55; Grant Hildebrand, *Origins of
    rchitectural Pleasure* (Berkeley: University of California Press, 1999); Rachel
    Kaplan, "The Nature of the View from Home: Psychological Benefits," *Environ-
    ment and Behavior* 33, no. 4 (2001): 507–42; Rachel Kaplan and Stephen Kaplan,
    The Experience of Nature: A Psychological Perspective (Cambridge: Cambridge Univer-
    sity Press, 1989).

35 **Benefits of sunlight and exposure to nature:** See Ruth Ann Atchley, David L.
    Strayer, and Paul Atchley, "Creativity in the Wild: Improving Creative Rea-
    soning Through Immersion in Natural Settings," *PLoS ONE* 7, no. 12 (2012);
    Amanda L. Chan, "Windows in the Workplace Linked with Better Sleep,"
    Huffington Post, June 12, 2013, available at: www.huffingtonpost.com/2013/06/12/
    windows-workplace-sleep-sunlight-exposure_n_3415797.html; Mary M. DeSchriver
    and Carol C. Riddick, "Effects of Watching Aquariums on Elders' Stress,"
    Anthrozoös 4, no. 1 (1992): 44–48; Phil Leather, Mike Pyrgas, Di Beale, and
    Claire Lawrence, "Windows in the Workplace: Sunlight, View, and Occupa-
    tional Stress," *Environment and Behavior* 30, no. 6 (1998): 739–62; American
    Academy of Sleep Medicine, "Study Links Workplace Daylight Exposure to
    Sleep, Activity and Quality of Life," *ScienceDaily*, June 3, 2013, available at:
    www.sciencedaily.com/releases/2013/06/130603114000.htm; Stephanie Lichten-
    feld, Andrew Elliot, Marcus Maier, and Reinhard Pekrun, "Fertile Green: Green
    Facilitates Creative Performance," *Personality and Social Psychology Bulletin* 38, no. 6
    (2012): 784–97; Donald Liu, Bernadette O. Fernandez, Alistair Hamilton, et al.,
    "UVA Lowers Blood Pressure and Vasodilates the Systemic Arterial Vasculature
    by Mobilization of Cutaneous Nitric Oxide Stores," *Journal of Investigative Derma-
    tology* 133 (2013): S209–29; Ravi Mehta and Rui (Juliet) Zhu, "Blue or Red?
    Exploring the Effect of Color on Cognitive Task Performances," *Science* 323, no.
    5918 (2009): 1226–29; Ruth K. Raanaas, Katinka Horgen Evensen, Debra Rich
    et al., "Benefits of Indoor Plants on Attention Capacity in an Office Setting,"
    Journal of Environmental Psychology 31, no. 1 (2011): 99–105; Roger Ulrich, "View
    Through a Window May Influence Recovery from Surgery," *Science* 224, no. 4647
    (1984): 420–21.

37 **Cornell University management professor Franklin Becker:** See Franklin Becker, *Offices at Work: Uncommon Work Space Strategies That Add Value and Improve Performance* (San Francisco: John Wiley & Sons, 2004).

37 **Employees use the quality of an office environment to draw inferences:** See Craig Knight and S. Alexander Haslam, "The Relative Merits of Lean, Enriched, and Empowered Offices: An Experimental Examination of the Impact of Work Space Management Strategies on Well-Being and Productivity," *Journal of Experimental Psychology: Applied* 16, no. 2 (2010): 158–72.

38 **The value of using organizational touchpoints:** To read more about the design of this lobby exhibit and see images of the display, visit www.ferrettidesigns.com/branding.html.

39 **Created a "favorites wall:"** See Clint Chapple, "Daxko's Double Helix," Daxko.com, December 27, 2012, available at: http://daxko.com/blog/2012/12/daxkos-double-helix.

39 **Getting [employees] personally involved in the design:** See Lambeth Hochwald, "Encouraging Employees to Put Their Personal Stamp on the Workplace," *Entrepreneur*, August 1, 2012, available at: www.entrepreneur.com/article/224070.

40 **Committed to delivering memorable nightlife experiences:** See "The Most Creative Meeting Room Names in the U.S," *eVenues Blog*, accessed May 23, 2014, available at: http://blog.evenues.com/2011/11/19/the-most-creative-meeting-room-names-in-the-u-s/.

40 **Physical composition of furniture:** See Josh M. Ackerman, Chistopher C. Nocera, and John A. Bargh, "Incidental Haptic Sensations Influence Social Judgments and Decisions," *Science* 328, no. 5986 (2010): 1715.

41 **Bathroom learning at Google:** See Bharat Mediratta, "The Google Way: Give Engineers Room," *New York Times*, October 20, 2007, available at: www.nytimes.com/2007/10/21/jobs/21pre.html.

41 **Organizations that neglect to build gathering spaces have *half* the number of employees with a best friend at work:** See Tom Rath, "Wanted: More Conversations in the Workplace," *Gallup Business Journal*, July 13, 2006, available at: http://businessjournal.gallup.com/content/23596/wanted-more-conversations-in-the-workplace.aspx.

42 **Creativity and innovation thrive on serendipitous encounters:** See Malcolm Gladwell, "Designs for Working," *New Yorker*, December 11, 2000, available at: www.newyorker.com/archive/2000/12/11/2000_12_11_060_TNY_LIBRY_000022275.

42 **Sociologist Jennifer Glass:** See Jennifer Glass, "It's About the Work, Not the Office," *New York Times*, March 7, 2013, available at: www.nytimes.com/2013/03/08/opinion/in-defense-of-telecommuting.html.

42 **U.S. News & World Report columnist Susan Milligan:** See Susan Milligan, "In Defense of Marissa Mayer's Telecommuting Ban," *U.S. News & World Report*,

February 28, 2013, available at: www.usnews.com/opinion/blogs/susan-milligan/
2013/02/28/in-defense-of-yahoo-and-marissa-mayers-telecommut
ing-ban.

43 **The benefits of telecommuting:** While the following studies present evidence
that telecommuting can be beneficial to employee health and output, we should
not take them to mean that telecommuting is an unmitigated good. Gallup data
indicate that employees who work remotely for *some* portion of the week tend to be
more engaged than those who spend all of their work hours at the office. However,
the data also show that employees who telecommute *more* than 20 percent of the
time are less engaged than those who telecommute less frequently. It therefore
appears that having some flexibility around telecommuting is beneficial but that
too much time out of the office can have a deleterious effect on engagement and,
consequently, performance. For more on the benefits of telecommuting, see Nicholas Bloom, James Liang, John Roberts, and Jenny Ying, "Does Working from
Home Work? Evidence from a Chinese Experiment," *Quarterly Journal of Economics*,
available at: www.stanford.edu/~nbloom/WFH.pdf; Steve Crabtree, "Can People
Collaborate Effectively While Working Remotely?" *Gallup Business Journal*, March
13, 2014, available at: http://businessjournal.gallup.com/content/167573/people
-collaborate-effectively-working-remotely.aspx; Andrew DuBrin, "Comparison of
the Job Satisfaction and Productivity of Telecommuters versus In-House Employees: A Research Note on Work in Progress," *Psychological Reports* 68, no. 4 (1991):
1223–34; Edwin Glenn Dutcher, "The Effects of Telecommuting on Productivity:
An Experimental Examination. The Role of Dull and Creative Tasks," *Journal of
Economic Behavior and Organization* 84, no. 1 (2012): 355–63; Edward J. Hill, Jenet
J. Erickson, Erin K. Holmes, and Maria Ferris, "Workplace Flexibility, Work
Hours, and Work-Life Conflict: An Extra Day or Two," *Journal of Family Psychology*
24, no. 3 (2010): 349–58; Apgar Mahlon, "The Alternative Workplace: Changing
Where and How People Work," *Harvard Business Review* 76, no. 3 (May–June
1998): 121–36.

43 **The cost of multitasking:** See Mark W. Becker, Reem Alzahabi, and Christopher J. Hopwood, "Media Multitasking Is Associated with Symptoms of Depression and Social Anxiety," *Cyberpsychology, Behavior, and Social Networking* 16, no. 2
(2013): 132–35; Gloria Mark, Victor M. Gonzalez, and Justin Harris, "No Task
Left Behind? Examining the Nature of Fragmented Work," *Conference on Human
Factors in Computing Systems* (2005): 321–30; Rachel E. Silverman, "Workplace Distractions: Here's Why You Won't Finish This Article," *Wall Street Journal*, December
11, 2012, available at: http://online.wsj.com/news/articles/SB100014241278873243
39204578173252223022388; "Too Many Interruptions at Work?" *Gallup Business
Journal*, June 8, 2006, available at: http://businessjournal.gallup.com/content/
23146/too-many-interruptions-work.aspx#2.

44 **Organizations that encourage employees to customize their workspace:** See Craig Knight and Alexander Haslam, "Your Place or Mine? Organizational Identification and Comfort as Mediators of Relationships Between the Managerial Control of Workspace and Employees' Satisfaction and Well-Being," *British Journal of Management* 21, no. 3 (2010): 717–35.

44 **Providing new hires with a modest budget for decorating:** See Nadia Goodman, "What Your Desk Says About You," *Entrepreneur*, January 13, 2013, available at: www.entrepreneur.com/blog/225512; Tim Henneman, "DreamWorks Animation Etches Out a Creative Culture Through Connectivity," *Workforce.com*, July 25, 2012, available at: www.workforce.com/articles/dreamworks-animation-etches-out -a-creative-culture-through-connectivity.

47 **Gary Jacobs:** Gary was kind enough to sit down with me for an interview on August 21, 2013. To learn more about Gary's work visit www.jacobsillustration.com. Worth noting, while Gary uses the distinction "caves and campfires," others prefer "caves and commons." The words are different but the ideas are generally the same.

47 **Sounds and creativity:** See Anahad O'Connor, "How the Hum of a Coffee Shop Can Boost Creativity," *New York Times Blog*, June 21, 2013, available at: http://well.blogs.nytimes.com/2013/06/21/how-the-hum-of-a-coffee-shop-can -boost-creativity.

Chapter 3: Why You Should Be Paid to Play

51 **Obama's decision:** See Mark Bowden, *The Finish: The Killing of Osama Bin Laden* (New York: Atlantic Monthly Press, 2012); Mark Bowden, "Inside Osama Bin Laden's Final Hours—and How the White House Chose Their Assassination Plot," *Vanity Fair*, November 2012, available at: www.vanityfair.com/politics/2012/11/in side-osama-bin-laden-assassination-plot; John A. Gans Jr., "'This Is 50-50': Behind Obama's Decision to Kill Bin Laden," *Atlantic*, October 10, 2012, available at: www.theatlantic.com/international/archive/2012/10/this-is-50-50-behind-obamas -decision-to-kill-bin-laden/263449/.

53 **Research on unconscious thinking:** See Maarten Bos and Amy Cuddy, "A Counter-Intuitive Approach to Making Complex Decisions," *Harvard Business Review Blog*, May 14, 2011, available at: http://blogs.hbr.org/2011/05/a-counter -intuitive-approach-t/; Maarten Bos, Ap Dijksterhuis, and Rick B. Van Baaren, "The Benefits of 'Sleeping on Things': Unconscious Thought Leads to Automatic Weighting," *Journal of Consumer Psychology* 21, no. 1 (2011): 4–8; Maarten Bos, Ap Dijksterhuis, and Rick B. Van Baaren, "On the Goal-Dependency of Unconscious Thought," *Journal of Experimental Social Psychology* 44, no. 4 (2008): 1114–20; J. David Creswell, James Bursley, and Ajay Satpute, "Neural Reactivation Links Unconscious Thought to Decision-Making Performance," *Social Cognitive and Affective*

Neuroscience 8, no. 8 (2013): 863–69; Ap Dijksterhuis, "On Making the Right Choice: The Deliberation-Without-Attention Effect," *Science* 311, no. 5763 (2006): 1005–7; Ap Dijksterhuis and Teun Meurs, "Where Creativity Resides: The Generative Power of Unconscious Thought," *Consciousness and Cognition* 15, no. 1 (2006): 135–46; Simone M. Ritter, Rick B. Van Baaren, and Ap Dijksterhuis, "Creativity: The Role of Unconscious Processes in Idea Generation and Idea Selection," *Thinking Skills and Creativity* 7, no. 1 (2012): 21–27; Chen-Bo Zhong, Ap Dijksterhuis, and Adam D. Galinsky, "The Merits of Unconscious Thought in Creativity," *Psychological Science* 19, no. 9 (2008): 912–18.

54 **The rituals of Einstein, Beethoven, and Allen:** See Mason Currey, *Daily Rituals: How Artists Work* (New York: Knopf, 2013); Brian Foster, "Einstein and His Love of Music," *Physics World* (January 2005): 34; Walter Isaacson, *Einstein: His Life and Universe* (New York: Simon & Schuster, 2007).

58 **Problem solvers are like artists:** A portion of this text first appeared in Ron Friedman, "Where You Spend the Most Creative Minutes of Your Day," *Fast Company*, July 11, 2012, available at: www.fastcompany.com/1842441/where-you-spend -most-creative-minutes-your-day.

58 **Scheduling play into the workday:** See Kaomi Goetz, "How 3M Gave Everyone Days Off and Created an Innovation Dynamo," *Fast Company*, February 1, 2011, available at: www.fastcodesign.com/1663137/how-3m-gave-everyone-days-off-and -created-an-innovation-dynamo; Bruce Nussbaum, "How Serious Play Leads to Breakthrough Innovation," *Fast Company*, March 4, 2013, available at: www.fast codesign.com/1671971/how-serious-play-leads-to-breakthrough-innovation; Rachel Rodriguez, "Goofing Off on Company Time? Go for It," CNN.com, March 29, 2013, available at: www.cnn.com/2013/03/29/living/play-at-work-irpt/.

58 **Childlike mind-set:** See Darya L. Zabelina and Michael D. Robinson, "Child's Play: Facilitating the Originality of Creative Output by a Priming Manipulation," *Psychology of Aesthetics, Creativity, and the Arts* 4, no. 1 (2010): 57–65.

59 **Play . . . is a mind-set:** See Laurie Tarkan, "Work Hard, Play Harder: Fun at Work Boosts Creativity, Productivity," Fox News, September 15, 2012, available at: www.foxnews.com/health/2012/09/13/work-hard-play-harder-fun-at-work-boosts -creativity-productivity/; Stuart Brown, *Play: How It Shapes the Brain, Opens the Imagination, and Invigorates the Soul* (New York: Avery, 2009).

61 **The cognitive benefits of exercise:** See Aderbal S. Aguiar et al., "Short Bouts of Mild-Intensity Physical Exercise Improve Spatial Learning and Memory in Aging Rats: Involvement of Hippocampal Plasticity via AKT, CREB and BDNF Signaling," *Mechanisms of Ageing and Development* 132, no. 11–12 (2011): 560–67; David M. Blanchette, Stephen P. Ramocki, John N. O'del, and Michael S. Casey, "Aerobic Exercise and Cognitive Creativity: Immediate and Residual Effects," *Creativity Research Journal* 17 (2005): 257–64; Stanley Colcombe and Arthur F. Kramer, "Fitness Effects

on the Cognitive Function of Older Adults: A Meta-Analytic Study," *Psychological Science* 14, no. 2 (2003): 125–30; Candice L. Hogan, Jutta Mata, and Laura L. Carstensen, "Exercise Holds Immediate Benefits for Affect and Cognition in Younger and Older Adults," *Psychology and Aging* 28, no. 2 (2013): 587–94; John J. Ratey and Eric Hagerman, *Spark: The Revolutionary New Science of Exercise and the Brain* (New York: Little, Brown, 2008); Robert M. Sapolsky, *Why Zebras Don't Get Ulcers: A Guide to Stress, Stress-Related Diseases, and Coping* (New York: W. H. Freeman, 1994); Shannon Stapleton, "How Exercise Fuels the Brain," *New York Times*, February 22, 2012, available at: http://well.blogs.nytimes.com/2012/02/22/how-exercise-fuels-the-brain.

62 Salo: See Eric V. Copage, "Don't Just Sit There, Work Out at Your Desk," *New York Times*, December 3, 2011, available at: www.nytimes.com/2011/12/04/jobs/working-out-inside-the-office.html.

62 Meeting room filled with stationary bikes: See Rachael King, "Jumping on a Bike or Treadmill to Meet with the Boss," *Wall Street Journal*, April 25, 2013, available at: http://blogs.wsj.com/cio/2013/04/25/jumping-on-a-bike-or-treadmill -to-meet-with-the-boss/.

62 John Osborn, CEO of BBDO: See Parekh Rupal, "Would You Try a Treadmill Desk, Like BBDO's New York CEO?" *Advertising Age*, August 28, 2012, available at: http://adage.com/article/adages/a-treadmill-desk-bbdo-s-york-ceo/236902/; Jen Wieczner, "Falling Down on the Job?" *Wall Street Journal*, January 29, 2013, available at: http://online.wsj.com/news/articles/SB10001424127887324539304578263 650060635048.

63 A 2009 University of Tennessee study: Dinesh John also included several other performance measures in his study but results for the two groups did not differ significantly. His study is reported in Dinesh John, Dixie L. Thompson, Hollie Raynor, et al., "Effects of Treadmill Workstations as a Worksite Physical Activity Intervention in Overweight and Obese Office Workers," *Medicine and Science in Sports and Exercise* 42 (2010): 1034–43.

63 Treadmill walkers can adapt: See Avner Ben-Ner, Darla J. Hamann, Gabriel Koepp, et al., "Treadmill Workstations: The Effects of Walking While Working on Physical Activity and Work Performance," *PLoS ONE* 9, no. 2 (2014): e88620.

63 A 2004 Leeds Metropolitan University study: See Jim McKenna and Jo Coulson, "How Does Exercising at Work Influence Work Productivity? A Randomized Cross-Over Trial," *Medicine and Science in Sports and Exercise* 37 (2005): S323. See also Jo C. Coulson, Jim McKenna, and Matthew Field, "Exercising at Work and Self-Reported Work Performance," *International Journal of Workplace Health Management* 1, no. 3 (2008): 176–197.

64 Atlassian: See Thomas Owens, "Inside Atlassian: This Is Where They Make the Software That Software Makers Use," *Business Insider*, July 19, 2012, available at: www.businessinsider.com/atlassian-san-francisco-office-tour-2012-7?op=1.

64 **Radio Flyer encourages employees:** See "The 25 Best Small Companies to Work for: Radio Flyer," CNNMoney.com, October 25, 2012, available at: http://money.cnn.com/gallery/news/companies/2012/10/25/best-small-companies.for tune/11.html.

64 **Physical arousal begets liking:** See Craig Foster, Betty Witcher, Keith Campbell, and Jeffery Green, "Arousal and Attraction: Evidence for Automatic and Controlled Processes," *Journal of Personality and Social Psychology* 74, no. 1 (1998): 86–101.

65 **A diet of diverse mental stimulation:** See Steven Johnson, *Where Good Ideas Come From: The Natural History of Innovation* (New York: Riverhead Books, 2010); Simone M. Ritter, Rodica Ioana Damian, Dean Keith Simonton, et al., "Diversifying Experiences Enhance Cognitive Flexibility," *Journal of Experimental Social Psychology* 48, no. 4 (2012): 961–64; Dean Keith Simonton, "The Science of Genius," *Scientific American Mind* 23, no. 5 (2012): 34–41, available at: www.scientific american.com/article/the-science-of-genius/.

66 **"Creativity is just connecting things":** See Gary Wolf, "Steve Jobs: The Next Insanely Great Thing," *Wired* (February 1996), available at: http://archive.wired .com/wired/archive/4.02/jobs_pr.html.

66 **"If you want to regularly generate brilliant ideas":** See Todd Henry, *The Accidental Creative: How to Be Brilliant at a Moment's Notice* (New York: Portfolio/Penguin, 2011).

67 **20 percent time:** See John Battelle, "The 70 Percent Solution," CNNMoney.com, December 1, 2005, available at: http://money.cnn.com/magazines/business2/busi ness2_archive/2005/12/01/8364616/; Goetz Kaomi, "How 3M Gave Everyone Days Off and Created an Innovation Dynamo," *Fast Company*, February 1, 2011, available   at: www.fastcodesign.com/1663137/how-3m-gave-everyone-days-off -and-created-an-innovation-dynamo; Bharat Mediratta, "The Google Way: Give Engineers Room," *New York Times*, October 20, 2007, available at: www.nytimes .com/2007/10/21/jobs/21pre.html; Ryan Tate, "Google Couldn't Kill 20 Percent Time Even If It Wanted," *Wired*, August 19, 2013, available at: www.wired.com/ 2013/08/20-percent-time-will-never-die/; "100 Best Companies to Work For: Qualcomm," CNNMoney.com, February 4, 2013, available at: http://money.cnn .com/magazines/fortune/best-companies/2013/snapshots/11.html.

68 **The benefits of napping:** See Cotton Delo, "Why Companies Are Cozying Up to Napping at Work," CNNMoney.com, August 18, 2011, available at: http://manage ment.fortune.cnn.com/2011/08/18/why-companies-are-cozying-up-to-napping -at-work/; Amie Gordon and Serena Chen, "The Role of Sleep in Interpersonal Conflict: Do Sleepless Nights Mean Worse Fights?" *Social Psychological and Personality Science* 5, no. 2 (2014): 168–75; Angela Haupt, "Why Power Naps at Work Are Catching On," *U.S. News & World Report,* November 15, 2010, available at: http://health.usnews

.com/health-news/family-health/sleep/articles/2010/11/15/why-power-naps-at-work
-are-catching-on; Phyllis Korkki, "To Stay on Schedule, Take a Break," *New York
Times*, June 16, 2012, available at: www.nytimes.com/2012/06/17/jobs/take-breaks
-regularly-to-stay-on-schedule-workstation.html?_r=0; Rebecca Mead, "Benefits Dept.:
Lights-out," *New Yorker*, June 25, 2007, available at: www.newyorker.com/talk/2007/06/
25/070625ta_talk_mead; Sara C. Mednick, *Take a Nap!: Change Your Life* (New York:
Workman, 2006); Tony Schwartz, *Be Excellent at Anything: The Four Keys to Transforming the Way We Work and Live* (New York: Free Press, 2011); Tony Schwartz, "Relax!
You'll Be More Productive," *New York Times*, February 9, 2013, available at: www
.nytimes.com/2013/02/10/opinion/sunday/relax-youll-be-more-productive.html?page
wanted=all; Zak Stone, "Tired at Work? Sleep on It, in This Space-Age Nap Pod," *Fast
Company*, November 11, 2012, available at: www.fastcoexist.com/1680864/tired-at-work
-sleep-on-it-in-this-space-age-nap-pod.

71 **A 2010 study published in the *Journal of Applied Psychology*:** See Sabine Son-
   nentag, Carmen Binnewies, and Eva J. Mojza, "Staying Well and Engaged When
   Demands Are High: The Role of Psychological Detachment," *Journal of Applied
   Psychology* 95, no. 5 (2010): 965–76.

71 **Jim Loehr:** See Christopher Clarey, "Strange Habits of Successful Tennis Players,"
   New York Times, June 20, 2008, available at: www.nytimes.com/2008/06/21/
   sports/tennis/21tennis.html?pagewanted=all; James E. Loehr, *The New Toughness
   Training for Sports: Mental, Emotional, and Physical Conditioning from One of the
   World's Premier Sports Psychologists* (New York: Dutton, 1994); James E. Loehr and
   Tony Schwartz, *The Power of Full Engagement: Managing Energy, Not Time, Is the Key
   to High Performance and Personal Renewal* (New York: Free Press, 2003).

72 **Limiting employee access to work:** See Blaire Briody, "The New Workplace
   Trend: Goof Off to Get Ahead," *Fiscal Times*, April 25, 2012, available at: www
   .thefiscaltimes.com/Articles/2012/04/25/The-New-Workplace-Trend-Goof
   -Off-to-Get-Ahead; Craig Kanalley, "FullContact Pays Its Employees $7,500 to Go
   on Vacation," *Huffington Post*, July 12, 2012, available at: www.huffingtonpost.com/
   2012/07/12/fullcontact-employees-vacation_n_1669668.html; Bart Lorang, "Paid
   Vacation? Not Cool. You Know What's Cool? Paid, PAID Vacation," FullContact
   .com, July 10, 2012, available at: www.fullcontact.com/blog/paid-paid-vacation/;
   Tanya Mohn, "Silencing the Smartphone," *New York Times*, December 31, 2012,
   available at: www.nytimes.com/2013/01/01/business/some-companies-seek-to-wean
   -employees-from-their-smartphones.html; Gary M. Stern, "Put the Smartphone
   Down: It'll Be Okay," CNNMoney.com, June 21, 2012, available at: http://manage
   ment.fortune.cnn.com/2012/06/21/smartphones-work-life-balance/; Alina Tugend,
   "The Workplace Benefits of Being out of Touch," *New York Times*, July 13, 2012,
   available at: www.nytimes.com/2012/07/14/your-money/companies-see-benefit-of
   -time-away-from-mobile-devices.html; "100 Best Companies to Work For: The

Boston Consulting Group," CNNMoney.com, February 4, 2013, available at: http://
money.cnn.com/magazines/fortune/best-companies/2013/snapshots/4.html.

73 **Obama's Decision, Part Two:** See George E. Condon Jr., "Obama Reveals New
Details on Bin Laden Raid," *National Journal* (2012), available at: www.national
journal.com/whitehouse/obama-reveals-new-details-on-bin-laden-raid-20120502;
Jennifer Hopper, Subrata De, and Tim Uehlinger, "President Obama: Bin Laden
Raid Is 'Most Important Single Day of My Presidency,'" NBC News, May 2, 2012,
available at: http://rockcenter.nbcnews.com/_news/2012/05/02/11493919-president
-obama-bin-laden-raid-is-most-important-single-day-of-my-presidency?lite.

76 *Vanity Fair*'s **Michael Lewis:** See Michael Lewis, "Obama's Way," *Vanity Fair*
(October 2012), available at: www.vanityfair.com/politics/2012/10/michael-lewis
-profile-barack-obama.

76 **New York Times columnist Thomas Friedman:** See Thomas L. Friedman, "Do
You Want the Good News First?" *New York Times*, May 18, 2012, available at:
www.nytimes.com/2012/05/20/opinion/sunday/friedman-do-you-want-the-good
-news-first.html. For additional research-based tips leaders can use to foster
greater organizational creativity, also see Teresa M. Amabile and Mukti Khaire,
"Creativity and the Role of Leaders," *Harvard Business Review* 86, no. 10 (October
2008): 100–109.

77 **The Mercedes-Benz "You Don't Have to Read the Book" club:** See "Top Ten
People Practices from the 2012 Best Small & Medium Workplaces List," Great
Place to Work Institute, accessed May 23, 2014, available at: www.greatplaceto
work.com/storage/documents/publications/top-ten-people-practices.pdf.

Chapter 4: What Happy Workplaces Can Learn from a Casino

81 **What casino operators know:** See Henry W. Chase and Luke Clark, "Gambling
Severity Predicts Midbrain Response to Near-Miss Outcomes," *Journal of Neuroscience* 30, no. 18 (2010): 6180–87; Kaylia Cornett, "The Psychology Behind Casino Design," *Time Out New York*, August 24, 2011, available at: www.timeout
.com/chicago/things-to-do/the-psychology-behind-casino-design; Karl J. Mayer
and Lesley Johnson, "A Customer-Based Assessment of Casino Atmospherics,"
UNLV Gaming Research and Review Journal 7, no. 1 (2003): 21–32; Linda Rodriguez McRobbie, "Time Stands Still: The Psychology of Casinos," *Mental Floss*,
January 23, 2009, available at: http://mentalfloss.com/article/20697/time-stands
-still-psychology-casinos; Catharine A. Winstanley, Paul J. Cocker, and Robert D.
Rogers, "Dopamine Modulates Reward Expectancy During Performance of a Slot
Machine Task in Rats: Evidence for a 'Near-Miss' Effect," *Neuropsychopharmacology*
36, no. 5 (2011): 913–25.

82 **Happy people tend to be more effective:** See Julia K. Boehm and Sonja Lyubomirsky, "Does Happiness Promote Career Success?" *Journal of Career Assessment,*

16, no. 1 (2008): 101–16; Ed Diener, "New Findings and Future Directions for Subjective Well-Being Research," *American Psychologist* 67, no. 8 (2012): 590–97; Claudia M. Haase, Michael J. Poulin, and Jutta Heckhausen, "Happiness as a Motivator: Positive Affect Predicts Primary Control Striving for Career and Educational Goals," *Personality and Psychology Bulletin* 38, no. 8 (2012): 1093–104; James K. Harter, Frank L. Schmidt, and Corey L. Keyes, "Well-Being in the Workplace and Its Relationship to Business Outcomes: A Review of the Gallup Studies," in *Flourishing: The Positive Person and the Good Life*, eds. Corey. L. Keyes and Jonathan Haidt (Washington, DC: American Psychological Association, 2002), 205–24.

83 **Our inclination to adapt:** See Philip Brickman, Dan Coates, and Ronnie Janoff-Bulman, "Lottery Winners and Accident Victims: Is Happiness Relative?" *Journal of Personality and Social Psychology* 36, no. 8 (1978): 917–27; Daniel Gilbert, *Stumbling on Happiness* (New York: Knopf, 2006); Daniel T. Gilbert, Elizabeth C. Pinel, Timothy D. Wilson, et al., "Immune Neglect: A Source of Durability Bias in Affective Forecasting," *Journal of Personality and Social Psychology* 75, no. 3 (1998): 617–38; Daniel Kahneman, Ed Diener, and Norbert Schwarz, *Well-Being: The Foundations of Hedonic Psychology* (New York: Russell Sage Foundation, 1999).

84 **Frequency is more important than size:** See Elizabeth W. Dunn, Daniel T. Gilbert, and Timothy D. Wilson, "If Money Doesn't Make You Happy, Then You Probably Aren't Spending It Right," *Journal of Consumer Psychology* 21, no. 2 (2011): 115–25; Jordi Quoidbach, Elizabeth W. Dunn, K. V. Petrides, and Moïra Mikolajczak, "Money Giveth, Money Taketh Away: The Dual Effect of Wealth on Happiness," *Psychological Science* 21, no. 6 (2010): 759–63.

85 **On the-job rewards:** See Sebastian Kube, Michel André Maréchal, and Clemens Puppe, "The Currency of Reciprocity—Gift Exchange in the Workplace," *American Economic Review* 102, no. 4 (2012): 1644–62.

85 **Executives at Pictometry:** This story was told to me by a high-level Pictometry executive.

86 **Variety Prevents Adaptation:** See Sonja Lyubomirsky, "New Love: A Short Shelf Life," *New York Times*, December 1, 2012, www.nytimes.com/2012/12/02/opinion/sunday/new-love-a-short-shelf-life.html?pagewanted=all&_r=0; Sonja Lyubomirsky, *The How of Happiness* (New York: Penguin Press, 2008); Acacia C. Parks, Matthew D. Della Porta, et al., "Pursuing Happiness in Everyday Life: A Naturalistic Investigation of Online Happiness Seekers," *Emotion* 12, no. 6 (2012): 1222–34; Kennon M. Sheldon and Sonja Lyubomirsky, "Change Your Actions, Not Your Circumstances: An Experimental Test of the Sustainable Happiness Model," *Journal of Happiness Studies* 7, no. 1 (2006): 55–86; Kennon Sheldon, Julia Boehm, and Sonja Lyubomirsky, "Variety Is the Spice of Happiness: The Hedonic Adaptation Prevention Model," in *Oxford Handbook of Happiness*, eds. Ilona Boniwell, Susan A. David, and Amanda Conley Ayers (Oxford: Oxford University Press, 2013).

87 **Breaks in the warm months:** See Colleen Leahey, "Best Companies to Work For Perks," CNNMoney.com, January 18, 2013, http://money.cnn.com/gallery/news/companies/2013/01/17/best-companies-perks.fortune/6.html.

87 **An annual Dog Day:** Ibid.

87 **Ministry of Fun:** See Will Smale, "The Boss Who Wants Staff to Have Fun," BBC News, April 13, 2014, available at: www.bbc.com/news/business-26873125.

88 **Unexpected Pleasures Deliver a Bigger Thrill:** See Sonja Lyubomirsky, *The Myths of Happiness* (New York: Penguin Press, 2013); Timothy D. Wilson, David B. Centerbar, Deborah A. Kermer, and Daniel T. Gilbert, "The Pleasures of Uncertainty: Prolonging Positive Moods in Ways People Do Not Anticipate," *Journal of Personality and Social Psychology* 88, no. 1 (2005): 5–21.

89 **The emerging science of smarter spending:** See Peter A. Caprariello and Harry T. Reis, "To Do, to Have, or to Share? Valuing Experiences over Material Possessions Depends on the Involvement of Others," *Journal of Personality and Social Psychology* 104, no. 2 (2013): 199–215; Leaf Van Boven and Thomas Gilovich, "To Do or to Have? That Is the Question," *Journal of Personality and Social Psychology* 85, no. 6, 2003: 1193–202; Elizabeth W. Dunn, Daniel T. Gilbert, and Timothy D. Wilson, "If Money Doesn't Make You Happy, Then You Probably Aren't Spending It Right," *Journal of Consumer Psychology* 21, no. 2 (2011): 115–25; Elizabeth Dunn and Michael Norton, *Happy Money: The Science of Smarter Spending* (New York: Simon & Schuster, 2013).

90 **Our environment often has a powerful impact:** See Adam Alter, *Drunk Tank Pink* (New York: Penguin Press, 2013); Leonard Mlodinow, *Subliminal: How Your Unconscious Mind Rules Your Behavior* (New York: Pantheon Books, 2012).

91 **We rarely pay attention to . . . scent:** See Alan R. Hirsch, "Effects of Ambient Odors on Slot-Machine Usage in a Las Vegas Casino," *Psychology and Marketing* 12, no. 7 (1995): 585–94; Rob Holland, Merel Hendriks, and Henk Aarts, "Smells Like Clean Spirit: Nonconscious Effects of Scent on Cognition and Behavior," *Psychological Science* 16 (2005): 689–93; Aradhna Krishna, "An Integrative Review of Sensory Marketing: Engaging the Senses to Affect Perception, Judgment and Behavior," *Journal of Consumer Psychology* 22, no. 3 (2012): 332–51; Katie Liljenquist, Chen-Bo Zhong, and Adam D. Galinsky, "The Smell of Virtue: Clean Scents Promote Reciprocity and Charity," *Psychological Science* 21, no. 3 (2010): 381–83; Eric R. Spangenberg, Ayn E. Crowley, and Pamela W. Henderson, "Improving the Store Environment: Do Olfactory Cues Affect Evaluations and Behaviors?" *Journal of Marketing* 60, no. 2 (1996): 67–80.

91 **Music can also lift our mood unconsciously:** See Francine Garlin and Katherine Owen, "Setting the Tone with the Tune: A Meta-Analytic Review of the Effects of Background Music in Retail Settings," *Journal of Business Research* 59 (2006): 755–64; Celine Jacob, "Styles of Background Music and Consumption in

a Bar: An Empirical Evaluation," *Hospitality Management* 25, no. 4 (2006): 710–20; Aradhna Krishna, "An Integrative Review of Sensory Marketing: Engaging the Senses to Affect Perception, Judgment and Behavior," *Journal of Consumer Psychology* 22, no. 3 (2012): 332–51; Michael Morrison, Sarah Gan, Chris Dubelaar, and Harmen Oppewal, "In-Store Music and Aroma Influences on Shopper Behavior and Satisfaction," *Journal of Business Research* 64, no. 6 (2011): 558–64.

92 **Train ourselves to be grateful:** See Robert Emmons, "Why Gratitude Is Good," Greater Good Science Center at the University of California, Berkeley, November 16, 2010, available at: http://greatergood.berkeley.edu/article/item/why_gratitude_is_good; Robert Emmons, *Thanks!: How the New Science of Gratitude Can Make You Happier* (Boston: Houghton Mifflin, 2007); Adam M. Grant and Francesca Gino, "A Little Thanks Goes a Long Way: Explaining Why Gratitude Expressions Motivate Prosocial Behavior," *Journal of Personality and Social Psychology* 98, no. 6 (2010): 946–55; Linda J. Levine and Martin A. Safer, "Sources of Bias in Memory for Emotions," *Current Directions in Psychological Science* 11, no. 5 (2002): 169–73.

94 **The Progress Principle:** See Teresa Amabile and Steven Kramer, *The Progress Principle: Using Small Wins to Ignite Joy, Engagement, and Creativity at Work* (Boston: Harvard Business Review Press, 2011).

94 **The Dark Side of Happiness:** See Roy F. Baumeister, Ellen Bratslavsky, Catrin Finkenauer, and Kathleen D. Vohs, "Bad Is Stronger Than Good," *Review of General Psychology* 5, no. 4 (2001): 323–70; Jeremy Dean, "4 Dark Sides to the Pursuit of Happiness," *PSYBlog*, accessed May 23, 2014, available at: www.spring.org.uk/2013/08/4-dark-sides-to-the-pursuit-of-happiness.php; Joseph P. Forgas, "Don't Worry, Be Sad! On the Cognitive, Motivational, and Interpersonal Benefits of Negative Mood," *Current Directions in Psychological Sciences* 22, no. 3 (2013): 225–32; Adam Grant and Barry Schwartz, "Too Much of a Good Thing: The Challenge and Opportunity of the Inverted U," *Perspectives on Psychological Science* 6, no. 1 (2011): 61–76; June Gruber, Iris B. Mauss, and Maya Tamir, "A Dark Side of Happiness? How, When, and Why Happiness Is Not Always Good," *Perspectives on Psychological Science* 6, no. 3 (2011): 222–33; Shigehiro Oishi, Ed Diener, and Richard Lucas, "The Optimum Level of Well-Being: Can People Be Too Happy?" *Perspectives on Psychological Science* 2, no. 4 (2007): 346–60; Justin Storbeck and Gerald L. Clore, "With Sadness Comes Accuracy; With Happiness, False Memory," *Psychological Science* 16, no. 10 (2005): 785–90.

99 **Incentivizing employees to live near work:** See David Zax, "By Paying Employees to Live Near the Office, Imo Cuts Commutes, Ups Happiness," *Fast Company*, March 25, 2013, available at: www.fastcompany.com/3007365/creative-conversations/paying-employees-live-near-office-imo-cuts-commutes-ups-happiness.

Chapter 5: How to Turn a Group of Strangers into a Community

101 **Donald Clifton:** See James K. Harter, Frank L. Schmidt, Emily A. Killham, and James W. Asplund, "Q^{12} Meta-Analysis," Gallup, available at: http://strengths.gal lup.com/private/resources/q12meta-analysis_flyer_gen_08%2008_bp.pdf; Todd Purdum, "Nebraska Concern Buys Gallup Organization," *New York Times*, September 18, 1988, available at: www.nytimes.com/1988/09/18/us/nebraska-concern -buys-gallup-organization.html; "Don Clifton and the Gallup Organization's Work on Strengths," Strengths Foundation, accessed May 23, 2014, available at: www.thestrengthsfoundation.org/don-clifton-and-the-gallup-organizations -work-on-strengths.

102 **Do you have a best friend at work?:** See Marcus Buckingham and Curt Coffman, *First, Break All the Rules* (New York: Simon & Schuster, 1999); Steve Crabtree, "Getting Personal in the Workplace," *Gallup Business Journal*, June 10, 2004, available at: http://businessjournal.gallup.com/content/11956/getting-personal-in-the -workplace.aspx; James K. Harter, Frank L. Schmidt, Sangeeta Agrawal, and Stephanie K. Plowman, "The Relationship Between Engagement at Work and Organizational Outcomes: 2012 Q^{12} Meta-Analysis," Gallup, available at: http:// employeeengagement.com/wp-content/uploads/2013/04/2012-Q12-Meta-Analysis -Research-Paper.pdf; Harter et al. "Q^{12} Meta-Analysis"; Tom Rath, *Vital Friends* (New York: Gallup Press, 2006); Jennifer Robison, "The Business of Good Friends," *Gallup Business Journal*, December 21, 2011, available at http://businessjournal.gal lup.com/content/151499/business-good-friends.aspx; Rodd Wagner and Jim Har ter, "The Tenth Element of Great Managing," *Gallup Business Journal*, February 14, 2008, available at: http://businessjournal.gallup.com/content/104197/tenth-element -great-managing.aspx; Rodd Wagner and James K. Harter, *12: The Elements of Great Managing* (New York: Gallup Press, 2006); "Item 10: I Have a Best Friend at Work," *Gallup Business Journal*, May 26, 1999, available at: http://businessjournal.gallup.com/ content/511/item-10-best-friend-work.aspx.

102 **A joint study by management professors at the University of Pennsylvania and University of Minnesota:** See Karen A. Jehn and Priti Pradhan Shah, "Interpersonal Relationships and Task Performance: An Examination of Mediating Processes in Friendship and Acquaintance Groups," *Journal of Personality and Social Psychology* 72, no. 4 (1997): 775–90.

103 **More on the line:** For related research, see Adam M. Grant and Amy Wrzesniewski, "I Won't Let You Down . . . or Will I? Core Self-Evaluations, Other-Orientation, Anticipated Guilt and Gratitude, and Job Performance," *Journal of Applied Psychology* 95, no. 1 (2010): 108–21; Hsiao-Yen Mao, An-Tien Hsieh, and Chien-Yu Chen, "The Relationship Between Workplace Friendship and Perceived Job Significance," *Journal of Management and Organization* 18, no. 2 (2012): 247–62.

103 **Employees with better friendships tend to stay on . . . longer:** See Rachel L. Morrison, "Informal Relationships in the Workplace: Associations with Job Satisfaction, Organisational Commitment and Turnover Decisions," *New Zealand Psychological Society* 33, no. 3 (2004): 114–28; Rath, *Vital Friends.*

104 **Process loss:** See Ivan D. Steiner, *Group Processes and Productivity* (New York: Academic Press, 1972).

105 **The cost of loneliness:** See Stephanie Cacioppo and John T. Cacioppo, "Social Relationships and Health: The Toxic Effects of Perceived Social Isolation," *Social and Personality Psychology Compass* 8, no. 2 (2014): 58–72; Louise Hawkley and John T. Cacioppo, "Loneliness and Health," in *Encyclopedia of Behavioral Medicine,* eds. Marc Gellman and J. Rick Turner (New York: Springer, 2013); Phyllis Korkki, "Building a Bridge to a Lonely Colleague," *New York Times,* January 28, 2012, available at: www.nytimes.com/2012/01/29/jobs/building-a-bridge-to-a-lonely -colleague-workstation.html; Mark Leary and Geoff MacDonald, "Why Does Social Exclusion Hurt? The Relationship Between Social and Physical Pain," *Psychological Bulletin* 131, no. 2 (2005): 202–23; Hakan Ozcelik and Sigal Barsade, "Work Loneliness and Employee Performance," *Academy of Management Annual Meeting Proceedings* 8, no. 1 (2011): 1–6.

106 **Ingredients at the core of successful friendships:** See Ellen Berscheid and Harry Reis, "Attraction and Close Relationships," in *The Handbook of Social Psychology,* 4th edition, eds. Daniel T. Gilbert, Susan T. Fiske, and Gardner Lindzey (New York: McGraw-Hill, 1998), 193–281; Peter A. Caprariello, Shannon M. Smith, Harry T. Reis, and Susan K. Sprecher, "Acquaintance Process," in *The Encyclopedia of Human Relationships,* eds. Harry Reis and Susan K. Sprecher (Thousand Oaks, CA: Sage Publications, 2009): 22–26; Peter A. Caprariello, Shannon M. Smith, Harry T. Reis, and Susan K. Sprecher, "Liking," in *The Encyclopedia of Human Relationships,* eds. Harry Reis and Susan K. Sprecher (Thousand Oaks, CA: Sage Publications, 2009), 978–89; Hilla Dotan and Ramat Aviv, "Workplace Friendships: Origins and Consequences for Managerial Effectiveness," *Academy of Management Annual Meeting Proceedings* 8, no. 1 (2009): 1–6; Rowland Miller, *Intimate Relationships* (New York: McGraw-Hill, 2002); Richard Moreland and Scott Beach, "Exposure Effects in the Classroom: The Development of Affinity Among Students," *Journal of Experimental Social Psychology* 28 (1992): 255–76; Harry T. Reis, Michael Maniaci, Peter Caprariello, et al., "Familiarity Does Indeed Promote Attraction in Live Interaction," *Journal of Personality and Social Psychology* 101, no. 3 (2011): 557–70; Mady W. Segal, "Alphabet and Attraction: An Unobtrusive Measure of the Effect of Propinquity in a Field Setting," *Journal of Personality and Social Psychology* 30 (1974): 654–57.

108 **"Friendship is born":** C. S. Lewis, *The Four Loves* (New York: Harcourt, Brace, 1960).

108 A study of best friends: See Andrew M. Ledbetter, E. M. Griffin, and Glenn G. Sparks, "Forecasting 'Friends Forever': A Longitudinal Investigation of Sustained Closeness Between Best Friends," *Personal Relationships* 14, no. 2 (2007): 343–50. Also see William W. Hartup and Nan Stevens, "Friendships and Adaptation in the Life Course," *Psychological Bulletin* 121, no. 3 (1997): 355–70.

108 similarity beats differences: Familiarity can, on relatively few occasions, also breed contempt. If your initial impression of another person is negative, chances are future interactions will only make it worse. Repeated contact tends to reinforce our initial response because of our tendency to seek out confirmatory information. We see what we want to see. For more, see Michael I. Norton and Jeana H. Frost, "Does Familiarity Breed Contempt or Liking? Comment on Reis, Maniaci, Caprariello, Eastwick, and Finkel (2011)," *Journal of Personality and Social Psychology* 101, no. 3 (2011): 571–74; Harry T. Reis et al., "Familiarity Does Indeed Promote Attraction in Live Interaction," *Journal of Personality and Social Psychology* 101, no. 3 (2011): 557–70.

108 Relationship expert Art Aron was facing a problem: See Arthur Aron, Edward Melinat, Elaine N. Aron, et al., "The Experimental Generation of Interpersonal Closeness: A Procedure and Some Preliminary Findings," *Personality and Social Psychology Bulletin* 23, no. 4 (1997): 363–77; Nancy Collins and Carol Miller, "Self-Disclosure and Liking: A Meta-Analytical Review," *Psychological Bulletin* 116, no. 3 (1994): 457–75.

110 Sharing emotionally sensitive information with coworkers: See Patricia M. Sias, *Organizing Relationships: Traditional and Emerging Perspectives on Workplace Relationships* (Los Angeles: Sage Publications, 2009); Patricia Sias and Daniel Cahill, "From Coworkers to Friends: The Development of Peer Friendships in the Workplace," *Western Journal of Communication* 62, no. 3 (Summer 1998): 273–99; Patricia M. Sias and Erin Gallagher, "Developing, Maintaining and Disengaging from Workplace Relationships," in *Friends and Enemies in Organizations: A Work Psychology Perspective*, eds. Sarah Wright and Rachel Morrison (Houndmills, Basingstoke, Hampshire: Palgrave Macmillan, 2009).

115 Snagger Confessions: See Jason Fell, "Beyond the Free Snacks: Spotlighting the Best Small Workplace Practices," *Entrepreneur*, October 17, 2011, available at: www.entrepreneur.com/article/220512.

117 Rush of adrenaline: See Arthur Aron et al., "Couples' Shared Participation in Novel and Arousing Activities and Experienced Relationship Quality," *Journal of Personality and Social Psychology* 78, no. 2 (2000): 273–84; Craig Foster, Betty Witcher, Keith Campbell, and Jeffery Green, "Arousal and Attraction: Evidence for Automatic and Controlled Processes," *Journal of Personality and Social Psychology* 74, no. 1 (1998): 86–101.

117   **Muzafer Sherif's 1954 experiment:** See Muzafer Sherif, O. J. Harvey, B. Jack
      White, et al., *Intergroup Conflict and Cooperation: The Robbers Cave Experiment* (Nor-
      man, OK: University Book Exchange, 1961).

120   **Innovation expert Tom Kelley:** See Tom Kelley with Jonathan Littman, *The Art
      of Innovation* (New York: Currency/Doubleday, 2001).

120   **a Day of Osmosis:** See Michael Burchell and Jennifer Robin, "Canada's Best
      Workplaces," *Globe and Mail*, April 19, 2012, available at: http://v1.theglobeand
      mail.com/partners/free/sr/gptw_apr_19_2012/Great%20Places%20to%20Work%
      20April%2019.pdf.

120   **A department rotation program:** See Jen Wetherow, "Canada's Best Work-
      places," *Globe and Mail*, April 12, 2011.

121   **A check for $100,000:** See Jack Stack, "Hilcorp Energy Shares the Wealth," *New
      York Times Blog*, July 6, 2010, available at: http://boss.blogs.nytimes.com/2010/07/
      06/hilcorp-energy-shares-the-wealth/; "100 Best Companies to Work For: Hilcorp
      Energy Company," CNNMoney.com, February 4, 2013, available at: http://money
      .cnn.com/magazines/fortune/best-companies/2013/snapshots/7.html.

121   **Psychologist Sheldon Cohen:** See Sheldon Cohen et al., "Social Ties and Suscep-
      tibility to the Common Cold—Reply," *JAMA: The Journal of the American Med-
      ical Association* 278, no. 15 (1997): 1232; Susan Gilbert, "Social Ties Reduce Risk
      of a Cold," *New York Times*, June 24, 1997, available at: www.nytimes.com/1997/
      06/25/us/social-ties-reduce-risk-of-a-cold.html?scp=49&sq=sheldon+cohen
      &st=nyt.

122   **The way we perceive our social network is vital to our mental health:** See
      Roy F. Baumeister and Mark R. Leary, "The Need to Belong: Desire for Interper-
      sonal Attachments as a Fundamental Human Motivation," *Psychological Bulletin*
      117, no. 3 (1995): 497–529; Joseph Cesario and Carlos Navarrete, "Perceptual Bias
      in Threat Distance: The Critical Roles of In-Group Support and Target Evalua-
      tions in Defensive Threat Regulation," *Social Psychological and Personality Science* 5,
      no. 1 (2014): 12–17; Shelley E. Taylor, "Fostering a Supportive Environment at
      Work," *Psychologist-Manager Journal* 11 (2008): 265–83; Shelley E. Taylor and
      Annette Stanton, "Coping Resources, Coping Processes, and Mental Health," *An-
      nual Review of Clinical Psychology* 3, no. 1 (2007): 129–53.

122   **Sharing positive and negative events:** See Jennifer K. Bosson, Amber B. John-
      son, Kate Niederhoffer, and William B. Swann, "Interpersonal Chemistry
      Through Negativity: Bonding by Sharing Negative Attitudes About Others," *Per-
      sonal Relationships* 13, no. 2 (2006): 135–50; Diane E. Macready et al., "Can Public
      versus Private Disclosure Cause Greater Psychological Symptom Reduction?"
      Journal of Social and Clinical Psychology 30, no. 10 (2011): 1015–104; Harry T. Reis
      et al., "Are You Happy for Me? How Sharing Positive Events with Others Provides

Personal and Interpersonal Benefits," *Journal of Personality and Social Psychology* 99, no. 2 (2010): 311–29.

123 **Caring Unites Partners (or CUP):** To see the actual application Starbucks employees are asked to fill out in order to receive financial support, visit: http://lifeat.sbux.com/NR/rdonlyres/2D1714B2-9D39-4A4D-8800-0CCECDFE96D0/0/USCUPFundapplicationJune2007.pdf.

123 **The benefits of altruism:** See C. Daniel Batson, *Altruism in Humans* (Oxford: Oxford University Press, 2011); Barbara L. Fredrickson et al., "What Good Are Positive Emotions in Crisis? A Prospective Study of Resilience and Emotions Following the Terrorist Attacks on the United States on September 11th, 2001," *Journal of Personality and Social Psychology* 84, no. 2 (2003): 365–76.

124 **The psychology of gossip:** See Roy F. Baumeister, Liqing Zhang, and Kathleen D. Vohs, "Gossip as Cultural Learning," *Review of General Psychology* 8, no. 2 (2004): 111–21; Bianca Beersma and Gerben A. Van Kleef, "Why People Gossip: An Empirical Analysis of Social Motives, Antecedents, and Consequences," *Journal of Applied Social Psychology* 42, no. 11 (2012): 2640–70; Robin Dunbar, *Grooming, Gossip, and the Evolution of Language* (Cambridge, MA: Harvard University Press, 1998); Tanushree Mitra and Eric Gilbert, "Have You Heard?: How Gossip Flows Through Workplace E-mail," Association for the Advancement of Artificial Intelligence, accessed May 23, 2014, available at: http://ts-si.org/files/ICWSM12GossipMitraAAAI.pdf; Sally Farley, "Is Gossip Power? The Inverse Relationships Between Gossip, Power, and Likability," *European Journal of Social Psychology* 41, no. 5 (2011): 574–79; Matthew Feinberg et al., "The Virtues of Gossip: Reputational Information Sharing as Prosocial Behavior," *Journal of Personality and Social Psychology* 102, no. 5 (2012): 1015–30; Sarah R. Wert and Peter Salovey, "A Social Comparison Account of Gossip," *Review of General Psychology* 8, no. 2 (2004): 122–37.

Chapter 6: The Leadership Paradox

133 **The story of Charles Henry:** See Debra Lau, "Forbes Faces: Charles (Jerry) Henry," *Forbes*, December 12, 2000, available at: www.forbes.com/2000/12/12/1212faces.html; Carol J. Loomis, "The Value Machine," *Fortune*, February 2001; Tom McGhee, "Buffett to Buy Johns Manville," *Denver Post*, December 21, 2000, available at: http://extras.denverpost.com/business/biz1221.htm; Tom McGhee, "Manville: Buffett Sought Buyout," *Denver Post*, December 22, 2000, available at: http://extras.denverpost.com/business/biz1222a.htm; Gil Rudawsky, "Old Job, New Mission: 'Gentleman from Omaha' Stalled Johns Manville CEO's Retirement Plans," *Rocky Mountain News*, March 4, 2001, available at: www.highbeam.com/doc/IGI-72101824.html.

134 **Background on Warren Buffett:** See Mary Buffett and David Clark, *Buffettol-ogy* (New York: Scriber, 1999); Mac Greer, "Interview with Alice Schroeder: Buf-fett's Biggest Weakness," *Motley Fool*, November 9, 2009, available at: www.fool.com/investing/general/2009/11/09/interview-with-alice-schroeder-buffetts-biggest-we.aspx; Carol J. Loomis, *Tap Dancing to Work: Warren Buffett on Practic-ally Everything, 1966–2012* (New York: Portfolio Trade, 2012); Roger Lowenstein, *Buffett, Making of an American Capitalist* (New York: Random House, 1995); Alice Schroeder, *The Snowball: Warren Buffett and the Business of Life* (New York: Bantam Books, 2008); Andrew Ross Sorkin,"Warren Buffett, Delegator in Chief," *New York Times*, April 23, 2011, available at: www.nytimes.com/2011/04/24/weekinre-view/24buffett.html; Gary M. Stern, "Why Warren Buffett's Laissez-Faire Man-agement Style Works," *Investor's Business Daily*, May 28, 2010, available at: http://news.investors.com/management-managing-for-success/052810-535754-why-warren-buffetts-laissez-faire-management-style-works.htm.

136 **Frederick Winslow Taylor:** See Sudhir Kakar, *Frederick Taylor: A Study in Per-sonality and Innovation* (Cambridge, MA: MIT Press, 1970); Robert Kanigel, "Fred-erick Taylor's Apprenticeship," *Wilson Quarterly* 20, no. 3 (Summer 1996): 44–51; Robert Kanigel, "Taylor-Made," *Sciences* 37, no. 3 (May–June 1997): 18–23; Robert Kanigel, *The One Best Way: Frederick Winslow Taylor and the Enigma of Efficiency* (New York: Viking, 1997); Jill Lepore, "The History of Management Consulting," *New Yorker*, October 12, 2009, available at: www.newyorker.com/arts/critics/atlarge/2009/10/12/091012crat_atlarge_lepore?currentPage=all.

140 **Duke behavioral economist Dan Ariely:** See Dan Ariely, Uri Gneezy, George Loewenstein, and Nina Mazar, "Large Stakes and Big Mistakes," *Review of Economic Studies* 76 (2009): 451–69. For related research, see Uri Gneezy, Stephan Meier, and Pedro Rey-Biel, "When and Why Incentives (Don't) Work to Modify Behav-ior," *Journal of Economic Perspectives*, no. 4 (2011): 191–210; Dan Ariely, *The Upside of Irrationality: The Unexpected Benefits of Defying Logic at Work and at Home* (New York: Harper, 2010).

141 **The psychology of choking under pressure:** For more on this topic, see Sian Beilock, *Choke: What the Secrets of the Brain Reveal About Getting It Right When You Have To* (New York: Free Press, 2010).

142 **How do you get employees intrinsically motivated:** See Teresa Amabile, "Cre-ativity and Innovation in Organizations," Harvard Business School Background Note (1996): 9-396-239; Teresa M. Amabile, *Creativity in Context* (Boulder, CO: Westview, 1996); Edward L. Deci and Richard M. Ryan, *Intrinsic Motivation and Self-Determination in Human Behavior* (New York: Plenum, 1985); Edward L. Deci and Richard Flaste, *Why We Do What We Do: Understanding Self-Motivation* (New York: Penguin, 1996); Edward L. Deci and Richard M. Ryan, *Handbook of*

Self-Determination Research (Rochester, NY: University of Rochester Press, 2002); Bruno S. Frey, *Not Just for the Money: An Economic Theory of Personal Motivation* (Cheltenham, UK: Edward Elgar, 1997); Margit Osterloh and Bruno S. Frey, "Does Pay for Performance Really Motivate Employees?" *Business Performance Measurement* (2002): 107–22; Daniel H. Pink, *Drive: The Surprising Truth About What Motivates Us* (New York: Riverhead Books, 2009); Johnmarshall Reeve, *Understanding Motivation and Emotion* (Fort Worth: Harcourt Brace Jovanovich College Publishers, 1992).

144 **A note on the Romeo and Juliet effect:** Because we can't experimentally assign romantic couples to approving and disapproving parents, we can't be fully certain that parental criticism *causes* partners to love each other more. The article's authors do, however, present this as one explanation for the correlation. More data are obviously needed for this interpretation to be conclusive.

144 **Reactance:** See Mary M. Bischoff and Terence J. G. Tracey, "Client Resistance as Predicted by Therapist Behavior: A Study of Sequential Dependence," *Journal of Counseling Psychology* 42, no. 4 (1995): 487–95; Sharon S. Brehm and Jack Williams Brehm, *Psychological Reactance: A Theory of Freedom and Control* (New York: Academic Press, 1981); Jack Williams Brehm, *A Theory of Psychological Reactance* (San Diego: Academic Press, 1966); Richard Driscoll, Keith Davis, and Milton Lipetz, "Parental Interference and Romantic Love: The Romeo & Juliet Effect," *Journal of Personality and Social Psychology* 24 (1972): 1–10; David M. Erceg-Hurn and Lyndall G. Steed, "Does Exposure to Cigarette Health Warnings Elicit Psychological Reactance in Smokers?" *Journal of Applied Social Psychology* 41, no. 1 (2011): 219–37.

145 **Autonomy and turnover intention:** See Anders Dysvik and Bard Kuvaas, "Exploring the Relative and Combined Influence of Mastery-Approach Goals and Work Intrinsic Motivation on Employee Turnover Intention," *Personnel Review* 39, no. 5 (2010): 622–38; Maura Galletta, Igor Portoghese, and Adalgisa Battistelli, "Intrinsic Motivation, Job Autonomy and Turnover Intention in the Italian Healthcare: The Mediating Role of Affective Commitment," *Journal of Management Research* 3, no. 2 (2011): 1–19; Sylvie Richer, Cealine Blanchard, and Robert Vallerand, "A Motivational Model of Work Turnover," *Journal of Applied Social Psychology* 32 (2002): 2089–113; Jason Thatcher, Yongmei Liu, Lee Stepina, et al., "IT Worker Turnover: An Empirical Examination of Intrinsic Motivation," *Database for Advances in Information Systems* 37, no. 2–3 (2006): 133–46.

145 **The art of fostering autonomy:** See Deci and Flaste, *Why We Do What We Do*; Marylene Gagne, Richard Koestner, and Miron Zuckerman, "Facilitating Acceptance of Organizational Change: The Importance of Self-Determination," *Journal of Applied Social Psychology* 30, no. 9 (2000): 1843–52; Dan Stone, Edward Deci, and Richard Ryan, "Beyond Talk: Creating Autonomous Motivation Through Self-Determination Theory," *Journal of General Management* 34, no. 3 (2008): 75–91.

150 **Contribution fluctuates with the time of day:** See Ana Adan, "Influence of Morningness-Eveningness Preference in the Relationship Between Body Temperature and Performance: A Diurnal Study," *Personality and Individual Differences* 12, no. 11 (1991): 1159–69; Lynn Hasher, Cindy Lustig, and Rose Zacks, "Inhibitory Mechanisms and the Control of Attention," in *Variation in Working Memory*, eds. Andrew R. A. Conway, Christopher Jarrold, Michael Kane, et al. (Oxford: Oxford University Press, 2007), 227–49; Cynthia May, Lynn Hasher, and Ellen Stoltzfus, "Optimal Time of Day and the Magnitude of Age Differences in Memory," *Psychological Science* 4, no. 5 (1993): 326–30; Christina Schmidt, Fabienne Collette, Christian Cajochen, and Philippe Peigneux, "A Time to Think: Circadian Rhythms in Human Cognition," *Cognitive Neuropsychology* 24, no. 7 (2007): 755-89; Sue Shellenbarger, "The Peak Time for Everything," *Wall Street Journal*, September 26, 2012, available at: http://online.wsj.com/news/articles/SB10000872396390444 18000457801829405707 0544; Mareike B. Wieth and Rose T. Zacks, "Time of Day Effects on Problem Solving: When the Nonoptimal Is Optimal," *Thinking and Reasoning* 17, no. 4 (2011): 387–401.

151 **Research conducted by Stanford's economics department:** See Nicholas Bloom, James Liang, John Roberts, and Jenny Ying, "Does Working from Home Work? Evidence from a Chinese Experiment," under review at the *Quarterly Journal of Economics*, available at: www.stanford.edu/~nbloom/WFH.pdf; Nicholas Bloom, "To Raise Productivity, Let More Employees Work from Home," *Harvard Business Review* (January–February 2014), available at: http://hbr.org/2014/01/to-raise-productivity-let-more-employees-work-from-home/ar/1.

151 **A note on telecommuting:** Needless to say, call centers are not representative of every industry. And clearly not all jobs are well suited for employees working on their own for the majority of the week. Yet the fact that even tasks as repetitious as fielding customer calls can be improved by providing employees with flexibility over their schedules suggests that workplace oversight counts for less than we often think.

153 **Autonomy is a consistently better predictor:** See Ronald Fischer and Diana Boer, "What Is More Important for National Well-Being: Money or Autonomy? A Meta-Analysis of Well-Being, Burnout and Anxiety Across 63 Societies," *Journal of Personality and Social Psychology* 10, no. 1 (2011): 164–84.

Chapter 7: Better Than Money

155 **Dance Dance Revolution:** See Snorre Bryne, "Ready for European Cup in Machine Dancing," Dagbladet.no, March 15, 2005, available at: www.positivegaming.com/assets/downloads/press_archive/2005_xx_xx_pg_ec2005_dagbladet.pdf; David Liu, "A Case History in the Success of Dance Dance Revolution in the United States," accessed May 21, 2014, available at: www.stanford.edu/group/htgg/

sts145papers/dliu_2002_1.pdf; Seth Schiesel, "P.E. Classes Turn to Video Game That Works Legs, Not Thumbs," *New York Times*, April 29, 2007, available at: www.nytimes.com/2007/04/30/health/30exer.html?_r=0.

157 **Real impact of salary on job satisfaction:** See Timothy A. Judge, Ronald F. Piccolo, Nathan P. Podsakoff, et al., "The Relationship Between Pay and Job Satisfaction: A Meta-Analysis of the Literature," *Journal of Vocational Behavior* 77, no. 2 (2010): 157–67.

157 **"Level of pay had little relation":** To be clear, Judge *did* find a statistically significant correlation between salary and job satisfaction, but it was so small (0.15) that it can hardly be considered a major predictor of happiness at work.

157 **Around $75,000 a year:** See Daniel Kahneman and Angus Deaton, "High Income Improves Evaluation of Life but Not Emotional Well-Being," *Proceedings of the National Academy of Sciences* 107, no. 38 (2010): 16489–93.

158 **One answer . . . is status:** See Cameron Anderson, Michael Kraus, Adam Galinsky, and Dacher Keltner, "The Local-Ladder Effect: Social Status and Subjective Well-Being," *Psychological Science* 23 (2012): 764–71.

159 **We never quite get used to feeling respected:** See Roy F. Baumeister and Mark R. Leary, "The Need to Belong: Desire for Interpersonal Attachments as a Fundamental Human Motivation," *Psychological Bulletin* 117, no. 3 (1995): 497–529; David J. Becker, Kenneth Chay, and Shailender Swaminathan, "Mortality and the Baseball Hall of Fame: An Investigation into the Role of Status in Life Expectancy," paper given at iHEA 2007 6th World Congress: Explorations in Health Economics, available at: http://ssrn.com/abstract=995034; Donald A. Redelmeier and Sheldon M. Singh, "Survival in Academy Award–Winning Actors and Actresses," *Annals of Internal Medicine* 134, no. 10 (2001): 955–62.

159 **Competence is inherently motivating:** See Andrew J. Elliot and Carol S. Dweck, *Handbook of Competence and Motivation* (New York: Guilford Press, 2005).

159 **Your choice of career:** For more on this topic, see Cal Newport, "Follow a Career Passion? Let It Follow You," *New York Times*, September 29, 2012, available at: www.nytimes.com/2012/09/30/jobs/follow-a-career-passion-let-it-follow-you .html, and Amy Wrzesniewski, Clark McCauley, Paul Rozin, and Barry Schwartz, "Jobs, Careers, and Callings: People's Relations to Their Work," *Journal of Research in Personality* 31 (1997): 21–33.

160 **Jon Stewart:** See Paul Harris, "The Oscar for Best Satirist Goes to . . . ," *Guardian*, February 26, 2006, available at: www.theguardian.com/media/2006/ feb/26/broadcasting.oscars2006; Susan Howard, "Nighttime Talk, MTV Style," *Record* (1994), available at: http://jon.happyjoyfun.net/tran/1990/94_0000record .html.

160 **Recognition increases the perceived value of work:** See Jane Dutton, Gelaye Debebe, and Amy Wrzesniewski, "Being Valued and Devalued at Work: A Social Valuing Perspective," *Qualitative Organizational Research: Best Papers from the Davis Conference on Qualitative Research* 3 (2012): 1–57.

162 **"He who praises everybody praises nobody":** Quoted in James Boswell, *The Life of Samuel Johnson* (New York: Penguin Classics, 2008).

163 **The science of praise:** See Roy F. Baumeister, *Public Self and Private Self* (New York: Springer-Verlag, 1986); Roy F. Baumeister and Edward E. Jones, "When Self-Presentation Is Constrained by the Target's Knowledge: Consistency and Compensation," *Journal of Personality and Social Psychology* 36, no. 6 (1978): 608–18; Ayelet Fishbach, Tal Eyal, and Stacey R. Finkelstein, "How Positive and Negative Feedback Motivate Goal Pursuit," *Social and Personality Psychology Compass* 4, no. 8 (2010): 517–30; John Hattie and Helen Timperley, "The Power of Feedback," *Review of Educational Research* 77, no. 1 (2007): 81–112; Melissa L. Kamins and Carol S. Dweck, "Person Versus Process Praise and Criticism: Implications for Contingent Self-Worth and Coping," *Developmental Psychology* 35, no. 3 (1999): 835–47; Alan E. Kazdin, *Behavior Modification in Applied Settings* (Homewood, IL: Waveland Press, 2001).

164 **The CEO buys everyone ice cream:** See "The 25 Best Small Companies to Work For: Akraya, Inc.," CNNMoney.com, October 25, 2012, available at: http://money.cnn.com/gallery/news/companies/2012/10/25/best-small-companies.fortune/14.html.

165 **Peer-to-peer recognition:** See Austin Carr, "Can a Corporate Culture Be Built with Digital Tools?" *Fast Company*, August 24, 2012, available at: www.fastcompany.com/3000552/can-corporate-culture-be-built-digital-tools; Lydia Dishman, "Secrets of America's Happiest Companies," *Fast Company*, January 10, 2013, available at: www.fastcompany.com/3004595/secrets-americas-happiest-companies; Carmen Nobel, "The Most Powerful Workplace Motivator," *HBS Working Knowledge*, October 31, 2011, available at: http://hbswk.hbs.edu/item/6792.html.

167 **Unlike the craftsmen and laborers of the past:** This point was first made in Alain de Botton, *The Pleasures and Sorrows of Work* (New York: Pantheon Books, 2009).

167 **We are happier pursuing long-term:** See Elliot and Dweck, *Handbook of Competence and Motivation* Peter Schmuck and Kennon M. Sheldon, *Life Goals and Well-Being: Towards a Positive Psychology of Human Striving* (Seattle: Hogrefe & Huber, 2001).

167 **Our work as meaningful:** See Simon L. Albrecht, "Work Engagement and the Positive Power of Meaningful Work," in *Advances in Positive Organizational Psychology*, ed. Arnold B. Bakker (Bingley, UK: Emerald Group Publishing, 2013), 237–60; Roy F. Baumeister, *Meanings of Life* (New York: Guilford Press, 1991);

Viktor E. Frankl, *Man's Search for Meaning* (Boston: Beacon Press, 2006); Dan P. McAdams and Kate C. McLean, "Narrative Identity," *Current Directions in Psychological Science* 22, no. 3 (2013): 233–38.

167 **We feel better when our goals center on benefiting others:** See Melanie Rudd, Jennifer Aaker, and Michael I. Norton, "Getting the Most Out of Giving: Concretely Framing a Prosocial Goal Maximizes Happiness," forthcoming in *Journal of Experimental Social Psychology*, and available here: http://faculty-gsb.stanford.edu/aaker/documents/GettingMostOutGiving.pdf.

167 **Wharton business professor Adam Grant:** See Adam M. Grant, Elizabeth M. Campbell, Grace Chen, Keenan Cottone, David Lapedis, and Karen Lee, "Impact and the Art of Motivation Maintenance: The Effects of Contact with Beneficiaries on Persistence Behavior," *Organizational Behavior and Human Decision Processes* 103 (2007): 53–67. Also see Adam M. Grant, "The Significance of Task Significance: Job Performance Effects, Relational Mechanisms, and Boundary Conditions," *Journal of Applied Psychology* 93, no. 1 (2008): 108–24.

169 **Flow and progressive difficulty:** See Mihaly Csikszentmihalyi, *Flow: The Psychology of Optimal Experience* (New York: Harper Perennial Modern Classics, 2008); Johnmarshall Reeve, *Understanding Motivation and Emotion* (Fort Worth: Harcourt Brace Jovanovich College Publishers, 1992).

170 **Acquiring new information increases our production of dopamine:** See Nico Bunzeck and Emrah Düzel, "Absolute Coding of Stimulus Novelty in the Human Substantia Nigra/VTA," *Neuron* 51, no. 3 (2006): 369–79; John Tierney, "What's New? Exuberance for Novelty Has Benefits," *New York Times*, February 13, 2012, available at: www.nytimes.com/2012/02/14/science/novelty-seeking-neophilia-can-be-a-predictor-of-well-being.html.

171 **peer-to-peer coaching:** See Stew Friedman, "How to Cultivate a Peer Coaching Network," *Harvard Business Review Blog*, February 5, 2010, http://blogs.hbr.org/2010/02/cultivate-your-coaching-networ-2/; Robert Hargrove, *Masterful Coaching* (San Francisco: Jossey-Bass, 2008); Andrew Thorn, Marilyn McLeod, and Marshall Goldsmith, "Peer Coaching Overview," MarshallGoldsmith.com, available at: www.marshallgoldsmithlibrary.com/docs/articles/Peer-Coaching-Overview.pdf; Amy Wrzesniewski and Jane E. Dutton, "Crafting a Job: Revisioning Employees as Active Crafters of Their Work," *Academy of Management Review* 26, no. 2 (2001): 179–201.

174 **Flow has less to do with the person than the nature of the task:** See Mihaly Csikszentmihalyi, *Creativity: Flow and the Psychology of Discovery and Invention* (New York: Harper Collins Publishers, 1996).

174 **Learn from video games:** For more on the relationship between games and engagement, see Jane McGonigal, *Reality Is Broken: Why Games Make Us Better and How They Can Change the World* (New York: Penguin Press, 2011).

175 **Use positive feedback strategically:** For more on the strategic use of positive feedback, see Amy Sutherland, "What Shamu Taught Me About a Happy Marriage," *New York Times*, June 24, 2006, available at: www.nytimes.com/2006/06/25/fashion/25love.html?pagewanted=all.

Chapter 8: How Thinking Like a Hostage Negotiator Can Make You More Persuasive, Influential, and Motivating

177 **The Lindhurst High School Shooting:** See Laurie L. Charles, "Disarming People with Words: Strategies of Interactional Communication That Crisis (Hostage) Negotiators Share with Systemic Clinicians," *Journal of Marital and Family Therapy* 33, no. 1 (2007): 51–68; Laurie L. Charles, *When the Shooting Stopped: Crisis Negotiation at Jefferson High School* (Lanham, MD: Rowman & Littlefield, 2008); Mark Gladstone and Carl Ingram, "Man Surrenders After Terrorizing School," *Los Angeles Times*, May 2, 1992, available at: http://articles.latimes.com/1992-05-02/news/mn-1318_1_high-school-diploma; Robert B. Gunnison and Ken Hover, "School Gunman Surrenders—4 Killed in 10-Hour Ordeal," *San Francisco Chronicle*, May 2, 1992; Kathy Lachenauer, "Jury Urges Death for Houston," *Sacramento Bee*, August 17, 1993; Dan Morain and Carl Ingram, "School Dropout Questioned as Town Agonizes," *Los Angeles Times*, May 3, 1992, available at: http://articles.latimes.com/1992-05-03/news/mn-1981_1_high-school-teacher. First person accounts from survivors of the Lindhurst High School shooting are posted on the "Angels of Columbine" website, available here: www.columbine-angels.com/lindhurst_story.htm.

180 **Why do patients sue their doctors?:** See Howard B. Beckman, Kathryn M. Markakis, Anthony Suchman, and Richard Frankel, "The Doctor-Patient Relationship and Malpractice," *Archives of Internal Medicine* 154, no. 12 (1994): 1365–70.

181 **The quandary faced by car salesmen:** See Bonnie Kavoussi, "Car Salesmen Trusted Even Less Than Congressmen: Gallup," *Huffington Post*, December 3, 2012, available at: www.huffingtonpost.com/2012/12/03/car-salesmen_n_2231760.html.

181 **Customers at a Florida Ford dealership:** See Rosemary P. Ramsey and Ravipreet S. Sohi, "Listening to Your Customers: The Impact of Perceived Salesperson Listening Behavior on Relationship Outcomes," *Academy of Marketing Science* 25, no. 2 (1997): 127–37. A related article on this topic, well worth reading, is Adam M. Grant, "Rethinking the Extraverted Sales Ideal: The Ambivert Advantage," *Psychological Science* 24, no. 6 (2013): 1024–30.

182 **A 2008 study of financial advisers:** See Jasmin Bergeron and Michael Laroche, "The Effects of Perceived Salesperson Listening Effectiveness in the Financial Industry," *Journal of Financial Services Marketing* 14, no. 1 (2008): 6–25.

183 **Professors at Columbia University's Business School conducted a study to find out:** The actual measure is a bit longer; I've shortened it here for the sake of

simplicity. For the complete questionnaire and details on the study, see Daniel Ames, Lily Maissen, and Joel Brockner, "The Role of Listening in Interpersonal Influence," *Journal of Research in Personality* 46, no. 3 (2012): 345–49.

184 **Gallup research on the employee-manager relationship:** See Marcus Buckingham and Curt Coffman, *First, Break All the Rules* (New York: Simon & Schuster, 1999); Rodd Wagner and James K. Harter, *12: The Elements of Great Managing* (New York: Gallup Press, 2006).

185 **The client-therapist bond:** See David Orlinsky, Michael Ronnestad, and Ulrike Willutski, "Fifty Years of Psychotherapy Process-Outcome Research: Continuity and Change," in *Handbook of Psychotherapy and Behaviour Change*, ed. Allen E. Bergin, Sol L. Garfield, and Michael J. Lambert (New York: John Wiley & Sons, 2004); JoEllen Patterson, Lee Williams, Todd M. Edwards, et al., *Essential Skills in Family Therapy: From the First Interview to Termination* (New York: Guilford Press, 1998).

188 **Anthony Suchman:** I interviewed Dr. Suchman on December 3, 2012. For more information about his research, see Anthony L. Suchman, David J. Sluyter, and Penelope R. Williamson, *Leading Change in Healthcare: Transforming Organizations Using Complexity, Positive Psychology, and Relationship-centered Care* (London: Radcliffe Publishing, 2011), or visit www.rchcweb.com.

188 **Activation of a fear response:** For more on the way fight-or-flight responses can undermine interpersonal relationships, see Daniel Goleman, *Emotional Intelligence* (New York: Bantam Books, 1995).

189 **PEARLS:** The idea of using PEARLS to improve communication quality was originally introduced by William Clark, Mariana Hewson, Mary Fry, and Jan Shorey, *Communication Skills Reference Card* (St. Louis: American Academy on Communication in Healthcare, 1998).

190 **Laurie Charles:** To protect the anonymity of her interviewees, Charles used pseudonyms in her publications. During our interview on July 8, 2013, she maintained that anonymity and spoke only about the methodology she used to conduct her research. Her findings appear in Charles, "Disarming People with Words," and in Charles, *When the Shooting Stopped*.

192 **Hearing Houston out gave Tracy:** For more on the psychology behind Taylor's approach, see Janet B. Bavelas, Linda Coates, and Trudy Johnson, "Listeners as Co-Narrators," *Journal of Personality and Social Psychology* 79, no. 6 (2000): 941–52; Geoffrey L. Cohen, Joshua Aronson, and Claude M. Steele, "When Beliefs Yield to Evidence: Reducing Biased Evaluation by Affirming the Self," *Society for Personality and Social Psychology* 26, no. 9 (2000): 1151–64; Laurence Miller, "Hostage Negotiation: Psychological Principles and Practices," *International Journal of Emergency Mental Health* 7, no. 4 (2005): 277–98; Patterson et al., *Essential Skills in Family Therapy*.

196 **Research on successful marriages:** See Tara Parker-Pope, *For Better: The Science of a Good Marriage* (New York: Dutton, 2010).

197 **the shift response:** See Charles Derber, *The Pursuit of Attention: Power and Ego in Everyday Life* (Oxford: Oxford University Press, 2000).

Chapter 9: Why the Best Managers Focus on Themselves

199 **Monica Seles at the French Open:** See Robin Finn, "Tennis; Seles Stuns Graf to Capture French Open Title," *New York Times*, June 10, 1990, available at: www .nytimes.com/1990/06/10/sports/tennis-seles-stuns-graf-to-capture-french-open-title.html; Monica Seles, *Getting a Grip: On My Body, My Mind, My Self* (New York: Avery, 2009). As of this writing, Seles's first-set comeback could be viewed on YouTube (complete with 1990s commercials), here: https://www.youtube.com/ watch?v=CRtEm1Qybik.

201 **Grunting over the course of tennis history:** See Tom Geoghegan, "What a Racket," BBC News, June 22, 2009, available at: http://news.bbc.co.uk/1/hi/ magazine/8110998.stm; Richard Hinds, "Women's Tennis Grunting—A Historical Guide," *Sydney Morning Herald*, January 25, 2012, available at: www.stuff.co .nz/sport/tennis/6309163/Womens-tennis-grunting-a-historical-guide; Josh Levin, "Tennis: An Aural History," *Slate*, September 14, 2011, available at: www.slate .com/articles/sports/sports_nut/2011/09/tennis_an_aural_history.html; Jessica Testa, "The Unsettled Science of Tennis Grunting," *Buzzfeed*, September 4, 2012, available at: www.buzzfeed.com/jtes/the-unsettled-science-of-tennis-grunting.

202 **Consistent grunters:** Author analysis using match footage and the frequency of news stories describing the player's grunting in a Google search.

203 **Guidelines issued:** A comprehensive listing of OSHA's guidelines is available here: https://www.osha.gov/pls/oshaweb/owadisp.show_document?p_table=STAN DARDS&p_id=9735&p_text_version=FALSE.

205 **Behavior and emotions are contagious:** See Shawn Achor, *The Happiness Advantage: The Seven Principles of Positive Psychology That Fuel Success and Performance at Work* (New York: Broadway Books, 2010); Sigal G. Barsade, "The Ripple Effect: Emotional Contagion and Its Influence on Group Behavior," *Administrative Science Quarterly* 47, no. 4 (2002): 644–75; Nicholas A. Christakis and James H. Fowler, *Connected: The Surprising Power of Our Social Networks and How They Shape Our Lives* (New York: Little, Brown, 2011); Ap Dijksterhuis and John Bargh, "The Perception-Behavior Expressway: Automatic Effects of Social Perception and Social Behavior," *Advances in Experimental Social Psychology* 33 (2001): 1–40; Elaine Hatfield, John T. Cacioppo, and Richard L. Rapson, *Emotional Contagion* (Cambridge: Cambridge University Press, 1994); Peter C. Herman and Janet Polivy, "Normative Influences on Food Intake," *Physiological Behavior* 86, no. 5 (2005): 873–86; C. J. Roel Hermans, Anna Lichtwarck-Aschoff, et al., "Mimicry of Food Intake:

The Dynamic Interplay Between Eating Companions," *PLoS ONE* 7, no. 2 (2012): e31027; Brian Wansink, *Mindless Eating: Why We Eat More Than We Think* (New York: Bantam Books, 2006); Robert B. Zajonc, Pamela K. Adelmann, Sheila T. Murphy, and Paula M. Niedenthal, "Convergence in the Physical Appearance of Spouses," *Motivation and Emotion* 11, no. 4 (1987): 335–46.

205 **link between movement and mental state:** See Lawrence W. Barsalou, Paula M. Niedenthal, Aron K. Barbey, and Jennifer A. Ruppert, "Social Embodiment," *Personality and Social Psychology Review* 9, no. 3 (2003): 43–92; John H. Riskind and Carolyn Gotay, "Physical Posture: Could It Have Regulatory or Feedback Effects Upon Motivation and Emotion?" *Motivation and Emotion* 6, no. 3 (1982): 273–96; Fritz Strack, Leonard Martin, and Sabine Strepper, "Inhibiting and Facilitating Conditions of the Human Smile: A Nonobtrusive Test of the Facial Feedback Hypothesis," *Journal of Personality and Social Psychology* 54, no. 5 (1988): 768–77.

205 **Research I conducted with motivational experts at the University of Rochester:** See Ron Friedman, Edward L. Deci, Andrew J. Elliot, et al., "Motivational Synchronicity: Priming Motivational Orientations with Observations of Others' Behaviors," *Motivation and Emotion* 34, no. 1 (2009): 34–38.

205 **We arranged for participants to "accidentally" overhear either a highly motivated or highly unmotivated participant:** Within research circles, the motivation expressed by our actors is referred to as intrinsic and extrinsic motivation, respectively.

207 **To understand the value of mimicry:** See Benedict Carey, "You Remind Me of Me," *New York Times*, February 11, 2008, available at: www.nytimes.com/2008/02/12/health/12mimic.html?pagewanted=all&_r=0; Marco Iacoboni, *Mirroring People: The New Science of How We Connect with Others* (New York: Farrar, Straus and Giroux, 2008); Jessica Lakin, Valerie Jefferis, Clara Cheng, and Tanya Chartrand, "The Chameleon Effect as Social Glue: Evidence for the Evolutionary Significance of Nonconscious Mimicry," *Journal of Nonverbal Behavior* 27, no. 3 (2003): 145–62.

208 **Development of emotion [likely] preceded . . . language:** See Daniel Goleman, *Emotional Intelligence* (New York: Bantam Books, 1995).

208 **Mirror neurons:** See Sandra Blakeslee, "Cells That Read Minds," *New York Times*, January, 10, 2006, available at: www.nytimes.com/2006/01/10/science/10mirr.html?pagewanted=all; Vittorio Gallese, "The Roots of Empathy: The Shared Manifold Hypothesis and the Neural Basis of Intersubjectivity," *Psychopathology* 36, no. 4 (2003): 171–80; Iacoboni, *Mirroring People*.

209 **Social norms:** See Michael Hechter and Karl-Dieter Opp, *Social Norms* (New York: Russell Sage Foundation, 2001); Muzafer Sherif, *The Psychology of Social Norms* (New York: Harper, 1936); John W. Thibaut and Harold H. Kelley, *The*

Social Psychology of Groups (New York: Wiley, 1959); Edna Ullmann-Margalit, *The Emergence of Norms* (Oxford: Clarendon Press, 1977).

209 **Some group members are more influential than others:** See Cameron Anderson, Dacher Keltner, and Oliver P. John, "Emotional Convergence Between People over Time," *Journal of Personality and Social Psychology* 84, no. 5 (2003): 1054–68; Thomas Sy, Richard Saavedra, and Stephane Cote, "The Contagious Leader: Impact of the Leader's Mood on the Mood of Group Members, Group Affective Tone, and Group Process," *Journal of Applied Psychology* 90, no. 2 (2005): 295–305.

210 **MIT management professor Edgar Schein:** See Edgar H. Schein, *Organizational Culture and Leadership* (San Francisco: Jossey-Bass, 1985). For more along this line of thinking, see Charles A. O'Reilly and Jennifer A. Chatman, "Culture as Social Control: Corporations, Cults, and Commitment," *Research in Organizational Behavior* 18 (1996): 157–200.

212 **CEO's level of narcissism:** See Arijit Chatterjee and Donald C. Hambrick, "It's All About Me: Narcissistic Chief Executive Officers and Their Effects on Company Strategy and Performance," *Administrative Science Quarterly* 52, no. 3 (2007): 351–86. For more on narcissistic CEOs, see Antoinette Rijsenbilt and Harry Commandeur, "Narcissus Enters the Courtroom: CEO Narcissism and Fraud," *Journal of Business Ethics* 117, no. 2 (2013): 413–29, and Charles O'Reilly, Bernadette Doerr, David Caldwell, and Jennifer Chatman, "Narcissistic CEOs and Executive Compensation," *Leadership Quarterly* 25, no. 2 (2014): 218–31.

214 **Other features of a CEO's personality:** It's worth noting that neither of these studies provides enough data to definitively expose the process by which CEOs influence members of an organization. And given that most corporate leaders are unwilling to subject their companies to ongoing observation, it's possible that we'll never have sufficient evidence to unpack the full picture. What these studies do reveal, however, is that in a notable number of cases, *how a CEO thinks* has dramatic implications for *how an organization acts*.

214 **A research team led by London Business School's Randall Peterson:** See Randall S. Peterson, Paul V. Martorana, D. Brent Smith, and Pamela D. Owens, "The Impact of Chief Executive Officer Personality on Top Management Team Dynamics: One Mechanism by Which Leadership Affects Organizational Performance," *Journal of Applied Psychology* 88, no. 5 (2003): 795–808. For more on how CEO personality affects their firms' performances, see Charles A. O'Reilly III, David F. Caldwell, Jennifer A. Chatman, and Bernadette Doerr, "The Promise and Problems of Organizational Culture: CEO Personality, Culture, and Firm Performance," *HAAS School of Business*, available at: www.stybelpeabody.com/newsite/pdf/ceopersonalitycultureandfinancialperformance.pdf.

215 **Christakis and Fowler:** See Nicholas A. Christakis and James H. Fowler, "The Spread of Obesity in a Large Social Network over 32 Years," *New England Journal*

of Medicine 357, no. 4 (2007): 370–79; Nicholas A. Christakis and James H. Fowler, *Connected: The Surprising Power of Our Social Networks and How They Shape Our Lives* (New York: Little, Brown, 2011); James H. Fowler and Nicholas A. Christakis, "Dynamic Spread of Happiness in a Large Social Network: Longitudinal Analysis over 20 Years in the Framingham Heart Study," *British Medical Journal* 337, no. 1 (2008): 1–9.

215 **Similar dynamic in the spread of violence:** See Elizabeth Austin, "Treating Violence as a Contagious Disease," Robert Wood Johnson Foundation, June 16, 2003, available at: www.rwjf.org/en/about-rwjf/newsroom/newsroom-content/2003/06/treating-violence-as-a-contagious-disease.html; Alex Kotlowitz, "Blocking the Transmission of Violence, *New York Times*, May 4, 2008, available at: www.nytimes.com/2008/05/04/magazine/04health-t.html?pagewanted=all.

Chapter 10: Seeing What Others Don't

221 **Classical violinist Megan Prokes:** I interviewed Megan Prokes on April 17, 2013, after reading her story in Mary Kunz Goldman, "Like Father, Like Daughter," *Buffalo News*, June 17, 2012.

223 **Blind auditions:** See Jutta Allmendinger and J. Richard Hackman, "The More, the Better? A Four-Nation Study of the Inclusion of Women in Symphony Orchestras," *Social Forces* 74, no. 2 (1995): 423–60; Carol Neuls-Bates, *Women in Music*, 2nd edition (Boston: Northeastern University Press, 1996); Geoff Edgers, "6 Minutes to Shine," *Boston Globe*, September 4, 2005, available at: www.boston.com/news/globe/magazine/articles/2005/09/04/6_minutes_to_shine/; Malcolm Gladwell, *Blink: The Power of Thinking Without Thinking* (New York: Little, Brown, 2005); Claudia Goldin and Cecilia Rouse, "Orchestrating Impartiality: The Impact of 'Blind' Auditions on Female Musicians," *American Economic Review* 90, no. 4 (2000): 715–41; Amy Louise Phelps, "Beyond Auditions: Gender Discrimination in America's Top Orchestras," University of Iowa dissertation, available at: http://ir.uiowa.edu/etd/874.

224 **In a classic experiment conducted in the late 1970s:** See Mark Synder and Elizabeth Decker Tanke, "Social Perception and Interpersonal Behavior: On the Self-Fulfilling Nature of Social Stereotypes," *Journal of Personality and Social Psychology* 35, no. 9 (1977): 656–66.

225 **Our initial expectations lead us:** See Noah Eisenkraft, "Accurate by Way of Aggregation," *Journal of Experimental Social Psychology* 49, no. 2 (2013): 277–79; Malcolm Gladwell, "The New-Boy Network," *New Yorker*, May 29, 2000: 68–86, available at: http://gladwell.com/the-new-boy-network/; Monica J. Harris and Christopher P. Garris, "You Never Get a Second Chance to Make a First Impression," in *First Impressions*, ed. Nalini Ambady (New York: Guilford Press, 2008), 147–67; Christopher Y. Olivola and Alexander Todorov, "Fooled by First Impres-

sions? Reexamining the Diagnostic Value of Appearance-based Inferences," *Journal of Experimental Social Psychology* 46, no. 2 (2010): 315–24; Janine Willis and Alexander Todorov, "First Impressions: Making Up Your Mind After 100-Ms Exposure to a Face," *Psychological Science* 17, no. 7 (2006): 592–98.

226 **Cognitive anchor:** See Daniel Kahneman, *Thinking, Fast and Slow* (New York: Farrar, Straus and Giroux, 2011); Amos Tversky and Daniel Kahneman, "Judgment Under Uncertainty: Heuristics and Biases," *Science* 185, no. 4157 (1974): 1124–31.

226 **Preference for beauty:** See Melissa Commisso and Lisa Finkelstein, "Physical Attractiveness Bias in Employee Termination," *Journal of Applied Social Psychology* 42, no. 12 (2012): 2968–87; Karen Dion, Ellen Berscheid, and Elaine Walster, "What Is Beautiful Is Good," *Journal of Personality and Social Psychology* 24, no. 3 (1972): 285–90; Nancy Etcoff, *Survival of the Prettiest: The Science of Beauty* (New York: Doubleday, 1999); Daniel S. Hamermesh, *Beauty Pays* (Princeton, NJ: Princeton University Press, 2010); Brent Scott and Timothy Judge, "Beauty, Personality, and Affect as Antecedents of Counterproductive Work Behavior Receipt," *Human Performance* 26, no. 2 (2013): 93–113; Enbar Toledano, "May the Best (Looking) Man Win: The Unconscious Role of Attractiveness in Employment Decisions," *Cornell HR Review*, February 14, 2013, available at: http://digitalcom mons.ilr.cornell.edu/cgi/viewcontent.cgi?article=1045&context=chrr.

226 **Halo effect:** See Solomon Asch, "Forming Impressions of Personality," *Journal of Abnormal and Social Psychology* 41, no. 3 (1946): 258–90; Richard E. Nisbett and Timothy Wilson, "The Halo Effect: Evidence for Unconscious Alteration of Judgments," *Journal of Personality and Social Psychology* 35, no. 4 (1977): 250–56.

227 **Despite not being objectively better at any of these things:** One noteworthy exception to this conclusion is the position of sales. There is some evidence to suggest that better-looking salespeople bring in more business. Why this occurs is subject to some debate. One possible explanation: Attractive people are perceived as more trustworthy, which makes them more persuasive. Another is that customers unconsciously seek to maximize their time in the company of good-looking people and that the most obvious way of achieving this objective, at least when an attractive person is attempting to make a sale, is to purchase their product or service.

227 **Height and workplace success:** See Nancy M. Blaker, Irene Rompa, Inge H. Dessing, et al., "The Height Leadership Advantage in Men and Women: Testing Evolutionary Psychology Predictions About the Perceptions of Tall Leaders," *Group Processes and Intergroup Relations* 16, no. 1 (2013): 17–27; Timothy A. Judge and Daniel M. Cable, "The Effect of Physical Height on Workplace Success and Income: Preliminary Test of a Theoretical Model," *Journal of Applied Psychology* 16, no. 3 (2004): 428–41.

228 **Voice quality:** See Rindy C. Anderson and Casey A. Klofstad, "Preference for Leaders with Masculine Voices Holds in the Case of Feminine Leadership Roles," *PLoS ONE* 7, no. 12 (2012): e51216; Casey Klofstad, Rindy Anderson, and Susan Peters, "Sounds Like a Winner: Voice Pitch Influences Perception of Leadership Capacity in Both Men and Women," *Proceedings of the Royal Society B: Biological Sciences* 279, no. 1738 (2012): 2698–704.

228 **Their voices convey an audible cue of their size:** The same effect also holds for women. The reason? Researchers point out that the female voice tends to descend with age, which signals that a speaker with a deeper voice also possesses a fair amount of knowledge and experience.

229 **We can't help but favor those who remind us of ourselves:** See Lauren A. Rivera, "Hiring as Cultural Matching: The Case of Elite Professional Service Firms," *American Sociological Review* 77, no. 6 (2012): 999–1022.

229 **The order in which we meet the candidates:** See Uri Simonsohn and Francesca Gino, "Daily Horizons: Evidence of Narrow Bracketing in Judgment from 10 Years of M.B.A. Admission Interviews," *Psychological Science* 24, no. 2 (2013): 219–24.

230 **First warmth, and then competence:** See Amy J. C. Cuddy, "Just Because I'm Nice, Don't Assume I'm Dumb," Breakthrough Ideas of 2009, *Harvard Business Review* 87, no. 2 (February 2009), available at: http://hbr.org/web/2009/hbr-list/because-i-am-nice-dont-assume-i-am-dumb; Amy J. C. Cuddy, Matthew Kohut, and John Neffinger, "Connect, Then Lead," *Harvard Business Review* 91, nos. 7–8 (July–August 2013), available at: http://hbr.org/2013/07/connect-then-lead/ar/1; Amy J. C. Cuddy, Peter Glick, and Anna Beninger, "The Dynamics of Warmth and Competence Judgments, and Their Outcomes in Organizations," *Research in Organizational Behavior* 31, no. 1 (2011): 73–98; Susan T. Fiske, Amy J. C. Cuddy, and Peter Glick, "Universal Dimensions of Social Cognition: Warmth and Competence," *Trends in Cognitive Sciences* 11, no. 2 (2006): 77–83; Deborah Son Holoien and Susan T. Fiske, "Downplaying Positive Impressions: Compensation Between Warmth and Competence in Impression Management," *Journal of Experimental Social Psychology* 49, no. 1 (2013): 33–41.

231 **Often turns . . . candidates into outright liars:** See John Delery and Michele Kacmar, "The Influence of Applicant and Interviewer Characteristics on the Use of Impression Management," *Journal of Applied Social Psychology* 28, no. 18 (1998): 1649–69; Michele Kacmar, John Delery, and Gerald Ferris, "Differential Effectiveness of Applicant Impression Management Tactics on Employment Interview Decisions," *Journal of Applied Social Psychology* 22, no. 16 (1992): 1250–72; Deborah Kashy and Bella DePaulo, "Who Lies?" *Journal of Personality and Social Psychology* 70, no. 5 (1996): 1037–51; Cynthia Stevens and Amy Kristof, "Making the Right Impression: A Field Study of Applicant Impression Management During Job Interviews," *Journal of Applied Psychology* 80, no. 5 (1995): 587–606; Brent Weiss

and Robert S. Feldman, "Looking Good and Lying to Do It: Deception as an Impression Management Strategy in Job Interviews," *Journal of Applied Social Psychology* 36, no. 4 (2006): 1070–86.

232 **We're rarely effective at picking out dishonesty:** See Paul Ekman, *Telling Lies: Clues to Deceit in the Marketplace, Politics, and Marriage* (New York: Norton, 2009); Maria Hartwig and Charles Bond Jr., "Why Do Lie-Catchers Fail? A Lens Model Meta-Analysis of Human Lie Judgments," *Psychological Bulletin* 137, no. 4 (2011): 643–59; Marc-Andre Reinhard, Martin Scharmach, and Patrick Muller, "It's Not What You Are, It's What You Know: Experience, Beliefs, and the Detection of Deception in Employment Interviews," *Journal of Applied Social Psychology* 43, no. 3 (2013): 467–79.

233 **Google's 2004 recruitment campaign:** See Peter Howe and D. C. Denison, "Cracking the Formula for a Google Job," *Sydney Morning Herald*, September 10, 2004, available at: www.smh.com.au/articles/2004/09/09/1094530769493.html? from=storylhs; "Google Entices Job-Searchers with Math Puzzle," National Public Radio (NPR), September 14, 2004, available at: www.npr.org/templates/story/story .php?storyId=3916173.

235 **Comparing accountants:** See Nelson D. Schwartz, "In Hiring, a Friend in Need Is a Prospect, Indeed," *New York Times*, January 27, 2013, available at: www .nytimes.com/2013/01/28/business/employers-increasingly-rely-on-internal -referrals-in-hiring.html. See also Stephen Burks, Bo Cowgill, Mitchell Hoffman, and Michael Housman, "The Value of Hiring Through Referrals," Working Paper (Bonn Institute for the Study of Labor, 2013), available here: http://ftp.iza.org/ dp7382.pdf.

235 **Incentivizes employees with prizes:** Schwartz, "In Hiring, a Friend in Need Is a Prospect, Indeed."

235 **Offers its physicians a . . . bonus:** See "100 Best Companies to Work For: The Everett Clinic," CNNMoney.com, February 4, 2013, available at: http://money.cnn .com/magazines/fortune/best-companies/2013/snapshots/58.html.

236 **Referred candidates:** See John Sullivan, "The Complete List of Employee Referral Program Best Practices," ERE.net, August 22, 2011, available at: www.ere .net/2011/08/22/the-complete-list-of-employee-referral-program-best-practices -part-2-of-2/.

236 **Allows referrers to monitor:** Ibid.

236 **Announcing job openings internally first:** See Jen Wetherow, "Canada's Best Workplaces," *Globe and Mail*, April 12, 2011, available at: www.theglobeandmail .com/partners/advgreatplacestowork0413/.

237 **When we make a personal sacrifice to get something we want:** See Leon Festinger, "The Psychological Effects of Insufficient Rewards," *American Psychologist* 16, no. 1 (1961): 1–11.

239 Evaluates applicants . . . over a cooking class: See Michael Burchell and Jennifer Robin, "Canada's Best Workplaces," *Globe and Mail*, April 19, 2012, available at: http://v1.theglobeandmail.com/partners/free/sr/gptw_apr_19_2012/Great% 20Places%20to%20Work%20April%2019.pdf.

241 Candidates who have had positive workplace experiences in the past are likely to continue to have positive experiences in the future: See Wendy Boswell, Abbie Shipp, Stephanie Payne, and Satoris Culbertson, "Changes in Newcomer Job Satisfaction Over Time: Examining the Pattern of Honeymoons and Hangovers," *Journal of Applied Psychology* 94, no. 4 (2009): 844–58.

241 Teach me something I don't know: See Douglass Edwards, "The Beginning," *Wall Street Journal*, July 16, 2011, available at: http://online.wsj.com/news/articles/ SB10001424052702304911104576444363668512764?mg=reno64-wsj&url= http%3A%2F%2Fonline.wsj.com%2Farticle%2FSB10001424052702304911104576 444363668512764.html.

242 Candidate's use of humor: See Rod A. Martin, *The Psychology of Humor: An Integrative Approach* (Amsterdam: Elsevier Academic Press, 2007); Andrea C. Samson and James J. Gross, "Humor as Emotion Regulation: The Differential Consequences of Negative versus Positive Humor," *Cognition and Emotion* 26, no. 2 (2012): 375–84; James A. Thorson, F. C. Powell, Ivan Sarmany-Schuller, and William P. Hampes, "Psychological Health and Sense of Humor," *Journal of Clinical Psychology* 53, no. 6 (1997): 605–19.

243 Hiring for cultural fit: See Nigel Bassett-Jones, "The Paradox of Diversity Management, Creativity and Innovation," *Creativity and Innovation Management* 14, no. 2 (2005): 169–75; Katherine Phillips, Sun Young Kim-Jun, and So-Hyeon Shim, "The Value of Diversity in Organizations: A Social Psychological Perspective," in *Social Psychology and Organizations*, eds. David De Cremer, Rolf van Dick, and J. Keith Murnighan (New York: Routledge Press, 2012), 253–72; Katherine W. Phillips, Katie A. Liljenquist, and Margaret A. Neale, "Is the Pain Worth the Gain? The Advantages and Liabilities of Agreeing with Socially Distinct Newcomers," *Personality and Social Psychology Bulletin* 35, no. 3 (2009): 336–50.

Chapter 11: What Sports, Politics, and Religion Teach Us About Fostering Pride

249 pride is associated with: See Matthias H. J. Gouthier and Miriam Rhein, "Organizational Pride and Its Positive Effects on Employee Behavior," *Journal of Service Management* 22, no. 5 (2011): 633–49; Randy Hodson, "Pride in Task Completion and Organizational Citizenship Behavior: Evidence From the Ethnographic Literature," *Work & Stress* 12, no. 4 (1998): 307–21; Tobias Kraemer and Matthias H. J. Gouthier, "How Organizational Pride and Emotional Exhaustion Explain Turnover Intentions in Call Centers: A Multi-Group Analysis with Gender and Organizational Tenure,"

Journal of Service Management 25, no. 1 (2014): 125–48; Willem Verbeke, Frank Belschak, and Richard P. Bagozzi, "The Adaptive Consequences of Pride in Personal Selling," *Journal of the Academy of Marketing Science* 32, no. 4 (2004): 386–402; Lisa A. Williams and David DeSteno, "Pride and Perseverance: The Motivational Role of Pride," *Journal of Personality and Social Psychology* 94, no. 6 (2008): 1007–17.

250 **The impact of *making* people feel proud:** See Jeanna Bryner, "Hubristic Group Pride May Indicate Insecurity," NBCNews.com, October 28, 2008, available at: www.nbcnews.com/id/27425462/ns/health-behavior/t/hubristic-group-pride-may -indicate-insecurity/; Joey T. Cheng, Jessica L. Tracy, and Joseph Henrich, "Pride, Personality, and the Evolutionary Foundations of Human Social Status," *Evolution and Human Behavior* 31, no. 5 (2010): 334–47; Paul Gilbert, "Evolution and Social Anxiety," *Psychiatric Clinics of North America* 24, no. 4 (2001): 723–51; Paul Gilbert, "The Relationships of Shame, Social Anxiety and Depression: The Role of the Evaluation of Social Rank," *Clinical Psychology and Psychotherapy* 7, no. 3 (2000): 174–89; Simon M. Laham, *The Science of Sin: The Psychology of the Seven Deadlies (and Why They Are So Good for You)* (New York: Three Rivers Press, 2012); Christopher Oveis, E. J. Jorberg, and Dacher Keltner, "Compassion, Pride, and Social Intuitions of Self-Other Similarity," *Journal of Personality and Social Psychology* 98, no. 4 (2010): 618–30; Jessica L. Tracy and Richard W. Robins, "The Psychological Structure of Pride: A Tale of Two Facets," *Journal of Personality and Social Psychology* 92, no. 3 (2007): 506–25; Jessica L. Tracy, Richard W. Robbins, and June Price Tangney, *The Self-Conscious Emotions* (New York: Guilford Press, 2007); Jessica L. Tracy, Azim F. Shariff, and Joey T. Cheng, "A Naturalist's View of Pride," *Emotion Review* 2, no. 2 (2010): 163–77; Jessica L. Tracy, Aaron C. Weidman, Joey T. Cheng, and Jason P. Martens, "Pride: The Fundamental Emotion of Success, Power, and Status," in *Handbook of Positive Emotions,* eds. Michele M. Tugade, Michelle N. Shiota, and Leslie D. Kirby (New York: Guilford Press, 2014); Lisa A. Williams and David DeSteno, "Adaptive Social Emotion or Seventh Sin?" *Psychological Science* 20, no. 3 (2009): 284–88.

251 **Signaling our affiliations:** See Robert Cialdini, Richard Borden, Avril Thorne, et al., "Basking in Reflected Glory: Three (Football) Field Studies," *Journal of Personality and Social Psychology* 34, no. 3 (1976): 366–75; Chris B. Miller, "Yes We Did! Basking in Reflected Glory and Cutting Off Reflected Failure in the 2008 Presidential Election," *Analyses of Social Issues and Public Policy* 9, no. 1 (2009): 283–96; Charles Snyder, MaryAnne Lassegard, and Carol Ford, "Distancing After Group Success and Failure: Basking in Reflected Glory and Cutting Off Reflected Failure," *Journal of Personality and Social Psychology* 51 (1986): 382–88.

253 **"Big hairy audacious goal":** See James C. Collins and Jerry I. Porras, *Built to Last: Successful Habits of Visionary Companies* (New York: HarperBusiness, 1994); for an important qualifier on the usage of Big Hairy Audacious Goals, see Teresa

Amabile and Steven Kramer, "How Leaders Kill Meaning at Work," The McKinsey Quarterly 1 (2012): 124-131.

253 **Envisioning our future selves as a motivator:** See Martin E. P. Seligman, Peter Railton, Roy F. Baumeister, and Chandra Sripada. "Navigating Into the Future or Driven by the Past," *Perspectives on Psychological Science* 8, no. 2 (2013): 119–41.

256 **We're also hardwired to collaborate and act selflessly in certain circumstances:** See David M. Buss, *The Handbook of Evolutionary Psychology* (Hoboken, NJ: Wiley, 2005); Adam M. Grant, *Give and Take: A Revolutionary Approach to Success* (New York: Viking, 2013); Roberts Wright, *The Moral Animal: The New Science of Evolutionary Psychology* (New York: Pantheon Books, 1994).

256 **Inviting employees to nominate nonprofits:** See "Employee Votes Direct $100,000 in Contributions to Nonprofits," Reuters, March 10, 2014, available at: www.reuters.com/article/2014/03/10/mn-allianz-life-idUSnBw105945a%2B100%2BBSW20140310.

256 **Match employees' personal contributions:** See "Employee Matching Gifts," CharlesSchwab.com, accessed May 23, 2014, available at: www.aboutschwab.com/community/corporate_giving/employee_matching_gifts.

256 **It organizes a series of internships:** See "Patagonia Employee Internship Program," Patagonia.com, accessed May 23, 2014, available at: www.patagonia.com/us/patagonia.go?assetid=80524.

256 **Dollars for doers program:** See Ryan Scott, "The Best Gift You Can Give Your Employees," *Forbes* (2012), available at: www.forbes.com/sites/causeintegration/2012/06/26/the-best-gift-you-can-give-your-employees/. See also Akhtar Badshah, "Time, Talent and Treasure—An Essence of Successful Corporate Philanthropy," *Microsoft Citizenship Blog*, February 28, 2011, available at: http://blogs.technet.com/b/microsoftupblog/archive/2011/02/28/time-talent-and-treasure-an-essence-of-successful-corporate-philanthropy.aspx.

258 **Sending flowers or cookies:** See "2011 Great Place to Work Rankings: Best Small and Medium Workplaces," Great Place to Work Institute, accessed May 23, 2014, available at: http://createyours.greatplacetowork.com/rs/greatplacetowork/images/GPTW-SME-2011_booklet.pdf.

258 **Letter to the new hire's spouse:** See "2011 Great Place to Work Rankings: Best Small and Medium Workplaces," Great Place to Work Institute, accessed May 23, 2014, available at: http://createyours.greatplacetowork.com/rs/greatplacetowork/images/GPTW-SME-2011_booklet.pdf.

258 **Inviting family members for a tour:** See Omar Akhtar, "The 25 Best Small Companies to Work For: Talent Plus," CNNMoney.com, October 25, 2012, available at: http://money.cnn.com/gallery/news/companies/2012/10/25/best-small-companies.fortune/6.html.

258 **Gift baskets to loved ones:** See "100 Best Companies to Work For: Kimpton Hotels & Restaurants," CNNMoney.com, February 4, 2013, available at: http://money.cnn.com/magazines/fortune/best-companies/2013/snapshots/28.html.

258 **A weekend getaway:** See "100 Best Companies to Work For: DPR Construction," CNNMoney.com, February 4, 2013, available at: http://money.cnn.com/magazines/fortune/best-companies/2013/snapshots/15.html.

258 **Gift . . . to spouses:** See Omar Akhtar, "The 25 Best Medium-size Companies to Work For: Ehrhardt Keefe Steiner & Hottman PC," CNNMoney.com, October 29, 2012, available at: http://money.cnn.com/gallery/news/companies/2012/10/25/best-medium-companies.fortune/10.html.

258 **Additional week off and $5,000:** See Omar Akhtar, "The 25 Best Medium-size Companies to Work For: Akraya, Inc," CNNMoney.com, October 29, 2012, available at: http://money.cnn.com/gallery/news/companies/2012/10/25/best-small-companies.fortune/14.html.

258 **Chef-prepared meals:** See Omar Akhtar, "The 25 Best Medium-size Companies to Work For: Snagajob," CNNMoney.com, October 29, 2012, available at: http://money.cnn.com/gallery/news/companies/2012/10/25/best-medium-companies.fortune/12.html.

258 **Teddy bears:** See "Best Medium Businesses to Work for 2011: #3—Holder Construction Company," *Entrepreneur*, accessed May 23, 2014, available at: www.entrepreneur.com/gptw/78.

258 **"Babycash":** See Julianne Pepitone, "Marissa Mayer Extends Yahoo's Maternity Leave," CNNMoney.com, April 30, 2013, available at: http://money.cnn.com/2013/04/30/technology/yahoo-maternity-leave/index.html.

259 **New car seat:** See Omar Akhtar, "The 25 Best Medium-size Companies to Work For: Integrated Project Management," CNNMoney.com, October 29, 2012, available at: http://money.cnn.com/gallery/news/companies/2012/10/25/best-small-companies.fortune/22.html.

259 **Bonus to parents whose child is adopted:** See "The Top 20 Job Perks that Make Jobs Better," *Good Magazine*, October 12, 2010, available at: http://magazine.good.is/slideshows/the-top-20-perks-that-make-jobs-better/9.

259 **Gift certificate on . . . child's birthday:** See Omar Akhtar, "The 25 Best Medium-size Companies to Work For: Struder Group," CNNMoney.com, October 29, 2012, available at: http://money.cnn.com/gallery/news/companies/2012/10/25/best-small-companies.fortune/4.html.

259 **Time off for children's school events:** See Omar Akhtar, "The 25 Best Medium-Size Companies to Work For: Spokane Teachers Credit Union," CNNMoney.com, October 29, 2012, available at: http://money.cnn.com/gallery/news/companies/2012/10/25/best-medium-companies.fortune/16.html.

259 **Wall [for] artwork of employees' children:** See "100 Best Companies to Work For: Alston & Bird LLP," CNNMoney.com, February 4, 2013, available at: http://money.cnn.com/magazines/fortune/best-companies/2013/snapshots/23.html.

259 **Annual scholarship:** See Omar Akhtar, "The 25 Best Medium-Size Companies to Work For: Badger Mining," CNNMoney.com, October 29, 2012, available at: http://money.cnn.com/gallery/news/companies/2012/10/25/best-small-companies.fortune/3.html.

259 **Children [design] company holiday card:** See Omar Akhtar, "The 25 Best Medium-size Companies to Work For: Integrity Applications Incorporated," CNNMoney.com, October 29, 2012, http://money.cnn.com/gallery/news/compa nies/2012/10/25/best-medium-companies.fortune/2.html.

260 **Inflated and creative job titles:** See Christine Canabou, "Chief Detonator," *Fast Company*, June 30, 2000, available at: www.fastcompany.com/40913/chief -detonator; Diane Jermyn, "Why You Should Give Fancy Job Titles the Cold Shoulder," *Globe and Mail*, June 30, 2013, available at: www.theglobeandmail .com/report-on-business/small-business/sb-managing/human-resources/why-you -should-give-fancy-job-titles-the-cold-shoulder/article6583366/; Jerald Greenberg and Suzyn Ornstein, "High Status Job Title as Compensation for Underpayment: A Test of Equity Theory," *Journal of Applied Psychology* 68, no. 2 (1983): 285–97; Arthur D. Martinz, Mary Dana Laird, John A. Martin, and Gerald R. Ferris, "Job Title Inflation," *Human Resource Management* 18, no. 1 (2008): 19–27, Richard Mowday, "Equity Theory Predictions of Behavior in Organizations," in *Motivation and Work Behavior, 4th edition*, eds. Richard M. Steers and Lyman W. Porter (New York: McGraw-Hill, 1987), pp. 89–110; Erica Swallow, "Should Your Job Title Be More Creative?" *Mashable*, December 10, 2011, available at: http://mashable.com/ 2011/12/10/creative-job-titles/; William Taylor, "Does Your Job Title Get the Job Done?" *Fast Company*, July 20, 2010, available at: www.fastcompany.com/1672474/ does-your-job-title-get-job-done; Brad Tuttle, "What's It's Really Like to Have a Quirky Job Title? The 'Ambassador of Buzz' Has His Say," *Time*, February 25, 2013, available at: http://business.time.com/2013/02/25/whats-its-really-like-to-have -a-quirky-job-title-the-ambassador-of-buzz-has-his-say/.

262 **Authentic and hubristic pride:** See Jeanna Bryner, "Hubristic Group Pride May Indicate Insecurity"; Cheng, Tracy, and Henrich, "Pride, Personality, and the Evolutionary Foundations of Human Social Status"; Tom Jacobs, "Group Members' Insecurity Can Foster Being a Jerk," *Pacific Standard*, October 26, 2008, available at: www .psmag.com/navigation/books-and-culture/group-members-insecurity-can-foster -being-a-jerk-4152; Laham, *The Science of Sin*; Tracy et al., "Pride: The Fundamental Emotion of Success, Power, and Status"; Tracy and Robins, "The Psychological Struc ture of Pride"; Tracy, Shariff, Cheng, "A Naturalist's View of Pride"; Williams and DeSteno, "Adaptive Social Emotion or Seventh Sin?"

Conclusion: Three Keys to Creating an Extraordinary Workplace

267 **70 percent of employees are disengaged:** See Gretchen Gavett, "Ten Charts That Show We've All Got a Case of the Mondays," *Harvard Business Review Blog*, June 14, 2013, available at: http://blogs.hbr.org/2013/06/ten-charts-that-show-weve-all-got -a-case-of-the-mondays/; "State of the American Workplace," Gallup, available at: www.gallup.com/strategicconsulting/163007/state-american-workplace.aspx.

267 **internationally 84 percent of employees:** See "The State of the Global Workplace," Gallup, available at: www.gallup.com/strategicconsulting/157196/state -global-workplace.aspx.

269 **"There is a gap between knowing about engagement":** See Ricardo Lopez, "Most Workers Hate Their Jobs or Have 'Checked Out,' Gallup Says," *Los Angeles Times*, June 17, 2013, available at: www.latimes.com/business/la-fi-mo-employee -engagement-gallup-poll-20130617-story.html.

272 **"work-life balance":** For more on "work-life integration" have a look at these articles, where I first encountered the phrase: Craig Chappelow, "Strive for Work-Life Integration, Not Balance," *Fast Company*, March 16, 2012, available at: www.fast company.com/1825042/strive-work-life-integration-not-balance; Ty Kiisel, "'Work Life Balance' Should Be 'Work Life Integration,'" *Forbes*, July 16, 2013, available at: www.forbes.com/sites/tykiisel/2013/07/16/work-life-balance-maybe-we-should -recognize-its-really-work-life-integration. Also worth reading is Jeffrey Pfeffer, "Building Sustainable Organizations: The Human Factor," *Academy of Management Perspectives* 24, no. 1 (2011): 34–45.

INDEX

Ron Friedman, PhD, is an award-winning psychologist and founder of ignite80, a consulting firm that helps smart leaders build extraordinary workplaces.

An expert on human motivation, Friedman has served on the faculty of the University of Rochester, Nazareth College, and Hobart and William Smith Colleges. Popular accounts of his research have appeared on NPR and in major newspapers, including the *New York Times*, the *Washington Post*, the *Boston Globe*, *Vancouver Post*, the *Globe and Mail*, the *Guardian*, as well as magazines such as *Men's Health*, *Shape*, and *Allure*.

He contributes to the blogs of *Harvard Business Review*, *Fast Company*, *Forbes*, *99u*, and *Psychology Today*. To learn more about his work, visit ignite80.com and connect with him on Twitter @RonFriedman.

25